ISBN 978-0-331-09346-9
PIBN 11013432

Heath's Modern Language Series

Die Harzreise

von

Heinrich Heine

EDITED WITH INTRODUCTION, NOTES, AND
VOCABULARY

BY

B. J. VOS

PROFESSOR OF GERMAN IN INDIANA UNIVERSITY

BOSTON, U. S. A.

D. C. HEATH & CO., PUBLISHERS

1911

19

PREFACE

The text of the present edition of the *Harzreise* follows that of Elster in the third volume of Heine's *Sämtliche Werke*, which is itself based on the second edition of the *Reisebilder*, *Erster Teil*, Hamburg, 1830. The somewhat radical pruning to which the text has been subjected is justified, it would seem, in a work in which there need be no fear of destroying an organic unity. The Introduction seeks to give as complete a sketch of Heine's career as the limits imposed would allow. Both for it and for the Notes, Elster's edition has been freely drawn upon. Other direct indebtedness has been acknowledged in the place where it is incurred. Some of the points in which the commentary differs from the hitherto accepted view will be found expounded more fully in the Modern Language Notes for January and February, 1908. In the preparation of the Vocabulary I have had the assistance of my colleague, Dr. W. Kurrelmeyer.

B. J. V.

Johns Hopkins University
    October, 1907

iii

INTRODUCTION

Heinrich Heine — or rather Harry Heine[1] — was born[2] December 13, 1797, at Düsseldorf on the Rhine, of Jewish parents. His father, Samson Heine, was a merchant in moderate circumstances, dealing in English velveteens. Salomon Heine, a younger brother of his father, had in early youth settled in Hamburg, where as a banker he gradually amassed an enormous fortune. On his mother's side, Heine's immediate parentage was of a more intellectual cast: Peira, or Betty, van Geldern was the daughter of a Jewish physician, Gottschalk van Geldern, whose oldest son Joseph likewise early achieved a reputation as physician. A second son, Simon, with whom Betty lived at the time of her marriage, and who was not without a share in Harry's early training, made some pretension to literary attainments. Betty herself was a woman of great mental alertness and considerable education, who followed the careers of her three sons with an intelligent interest. As his numerous letters to her testify, Heine throughout life felt a deep love and tenderness for his mother. The father before his marriage had served as quartermaster in the campaigns in Flanders, and qualities of the typical military man are evident in his make-up. Handsome, fond of dress and the showy side of life, of horses, of gaming and of women, he developed little energy or ability in

[1] The name Harry, given in honor of a Mr. Harry, an English business friend, was formally changed to Heinrich at the time of baptism. On the title-pages of his published works the poet sought to avoid both names by writing merely the initial H.

[2] As between 1797 and 1799 there has been a prolonged controversy, but opinion now distinctly favors the earlier date.

the pursuit of business. The mother was of another, stronger if not finer, mould. Capable and discerning, efficient in devising means whenever the future of her children was at stake, she was, with all her appreciation of literature and music, an intensely practical nature. Temperamentally at least, the son's heritage clearly descended from the father.

Düsseldorf was the capital of the duchy of Berg and with the latter fell into the hands of Napoleon in March, 1806, remaining under French control until November, 1813. French rule was not without its blessings to the people, and more particularly the Jews, of Düsseldorf. Serfdom and feudal tenure of land were abolished, laws emphasizing class distinctions revoked, the *Code Napoléon* made the law of the land. Furthermore, in 1808, the disabilities of the Jews were wholly removed, and Jew and Gentile became peers in every sphere of activity. It is doubtless here that the first germ of that extravagant admiration of Napoleon,[1] so characteristic of Heine, is to be sought: in origin it is racial; in its growth, the natural outcome of a temperament which, in its antagonism to all the little and commonplace, developed a marked tendency towards hero-worship.

In the period of French occupation falls also the founding of the Düsseldorf Lycée in the buildings of the old Franciscan school.[2] Heine seems to have entered the institution about 1808. Most of his teachers were Catholic priests, a circumstance that did not, however, imply religious conviction. Thus the rector Schallmayer, an especial friend of the family, was a pronounced freethinker.

Heine's mother had destined him for an official post in the state service under Napoleon. With the latter's downfall and the reaction against the Jews that immediately set in, these plans underwent a revision. Harry was now launched upon a commercial career and in 1815 set out for Frankfurt to serve an apprenticeship in a banking house. Frankfurt had a large

---

[1] Cf. the footnote on page 98.　　[2] Cf. *Harzreise*, p. 17, l. 11.

Jewish population and was a centre of the anti-Semitic movement, a fact to which some bitter lines of the *Harzreise*[1] allude.
The Frankfurt venture proved a miserable failure, and Harry
was, in the summer of 1816, sent to Hamburg in the hope that
under his uncle's eyes he might show greater eagerness to emu-
late the latter's career. In 1818 his uncle even furnished him
with funds to establish a business of his own under the legend
Harry Heine u. Komp., but the firm was short-lived, being
forced into liquidation the very next year. Harry had meanwhile promptly fallen in love with his beautiful cousin Amalie,[2]
but his love-affair also suffered shipwreck: Amalie turned a deaf
ear to his suit and in 1821 accepted the hand of another.

It was now agreed, with the aid of the uncle, to send Heine
to the university to study law, and in December, 1819, he managed,
not without difficulty, to matriculate at the University of Bonn.
In both the faculties of law and philosophy this young and vigor-
ous university had a number of notable men, among whom Ernst
Moritz Arndt[3] and August Wilhelm von Schlegel demand special
mention. At Bonn, Heine, whose bent toward literature had
even some years earlier found lyric expression, availed himself
of the opportunity of following, aside from his legal studies,
lectures on German literature and history. From Schlegel
especially he received helpful and encouraging criticism, and it
was at Bonn that he first felt himself poet and began his tragedy
Almansor.[4]

In accordance with German custom the young *studiosus juris*
migrated to the University of Göttingen in the autumn of 1820.
The change did not prove a happy one. In comparison with
Bonn, Göttingen seemed dreary, the university narrow and
pedantic, and the Hanoverian squires, who set the tone, unbear-
able in their class pride and ignorance. German literature and
history continued to exert their fascination upon Heine; the

---

[1] Cf. p. 71, l. 18.   [2] Cf. *Harzreise*, p. 88, l. 21.
[3] *Harzreise*, p. 66, l. 17.   [4] *Harzreise*, p. 53, l. 7.

former as represented by Georg Friedrich Benecke — a scholar of note and worth, the latter by Georg Sartorius, to whom Heine pays a feeling tribute in the concluding portion of the *Harzreise*.[1]

The stay at Göttingen was presently brought to an abrupt end. For an infraction of the law against dueling — to avenge an insult he had challenged a fellow-student — Heine was, in January, 1821, suspended for a half-year. About the same time, for a cause that is not altogether clear, he was expelled from the Göttingen "Burschenschaft." Whatever sympathy Heine may originally have had with "Burschenschaft" ideas and ideals — he had joined the organization at Bonn — his opposition to its narrow views on "Deutschtum" and patriotism becomes marked from this time on and finds expression also in the *Harzreise*.[2]

From Göttingen Heine went to Berlin, then a new university but already taking rank with the foremost. Again he drew inspiration, not from the lectures on jurisprudence, but from the courses in literature and philosophy. He sat at the feet of Hegel and it was to his teaching that later in life, after returning to a deistic belief, he attributed his breaking loose from the moorings of religion. Socially also the new life was a revelation. In the brilliant salon of Rahel Varnhagen he met the celebrities and notabilities of the day, and it was at Berlin that he first won recognition as poet through the publication, in December, 1821, of a group of poems, *Gedichte von H. Heine*. This was followed, in April, 1823, by the *Tragödien nebst einem lyrischen Intermezzo*. At least two of Heine's finest poems, *Die Grenadiere* and *Die Wallfahrt nach Kevlaar*, belong to this early period. Of the two tragedies, *Ratcliff* and *Almansor*, neither is important.

Meanwhile Heine's parents had, in 1822, removed to Lüneburg, and in May, 1823, Heine paid them a brief visit. His health in Berlin had left much to be desired, and an appeal to the uncle in person resulted in the latter's furnishing the necessary funds for a six weeks' sojourn at Cuxhaven on the North Sea. Heine

---

[1] Page 84, ll. 8–24.   [2] Pages 65, l. 13ff.; 74, Note 1.

afterwards repeatedly visited the North Sea, and it was during these visits that the two cycles of *Nordseebilder* were written, among the most unique and beautiful, not only of the products of Heine's muse, but of sea poetry in general.

Returning to Hamburg in September, Heine spent some weeks with his uncle, and it was at this time that his love for Therese,[1] Amalie's sister, sprang into blossom, destined like his earlier passion not to come to fruition.

With promise of renewed financial support from his uncle, Heine returned, in January, 1824, to his legal studies at Göttingen. While poetry continued to engage his attention, preparation for the examination was taken somewhat more seriously. But Göttingen proved as dull as ever, and to vary the monotony of existence two trips were undertaken during this year, the first at Easter to Berlin, and the second in the autumn to the Hartz. It is of this latter that the *Harzreise* has left an imperishable record. This foot-tour led the poet through the entire Hartz region, the Lower as well as the Upper Hartz, although the *Harzreise* deals almost wholly with the latter. He also availed himself of the opportunity to visit Weimar, and paid his respects to Goethe. Of this meeting Heine has nowhere given a serious account, but it seems that owing in part to his own lack of tact the reception was not very cordial.

Before proceeding to his degree, Heine finally decided upon taking a step that he had for some time been contemplating, his reception by baptism into the Lutheran church. The ceremony was performed on June 28, 1825, at Heiligenstadt, in the neighborhood of Göttingen. Except for the fact that Heine no longer adhered to the tenets of the Jewish faith in which he had been reared, this apostasy was in no wise based on conviction, but wholly regarded as a question of expediency: without it the obtaining of an official appointment was out of question. Never a moral coward, Heine made no secret of his motive, and it thus

[1] *Harzreise*, p. 87, l. 13 and Note.

came about that he lost caste with both sides: a renegade to the Jew, he was to the Gentile a time-serving hypocrite, but still the Jew. Ultimately the figure of Christ becomes to Heine that of a liberating hero of humanity, one of a trinity with Prometheus and Napoleon.

The final tests for the degree took place in July, and while the result was by no means brilliant the degree was granted. Göttingen was bid farewell without a pang, and the ensuing months were spent recuperating at Norderney. Plans for qualifying as *privatdozent* at the University of Berlin and for settling as advocate in Hamburg, were considered for a time but soon abandoned. His suit for the hand of Therese, Heine was still hopeful of bringing to successful issue, but evil reports on his manner of life in Hamburg still further prejudiced him in his uncle's eyes.

In May, 1826, the first volume of the *Reisebilder* was issued in Hamburg, by the firm Hoffmann and Campe, who from this time on remained Heine's regular publishers. Aside from two groups of lyrics, including the first cycle of *Nordseebilder*, the volume contained the *Harzreise*. The latter had already, during January and February, 1826, been printed, in a somewhat mutilated form, in the *Gesellschafter*, a Berlin periodical. A second volume of the *Reisebilder* was issued April, 1827. It contained both prose and verse, the former represented more particularly[1] by Heine's apotheosis of Napoleon. The effect of this volume the author decided to await in England. The visit proved a bitter disappointment. As a liberal political thinker he found much to admire in English institutions and political life; as poet he exclaims: "Send a philosopher to London, but for heaven's sake not a poet!" What impressed him most was the mechanicalness, the materialism and the colorless monotony of British existence. It was the country of men-like machines, and machine-like men.

A single incident connected with this English visit is worth

[1] In *Nordsee, Dritte Abteilung*, and *Ideen, Das Buch Le Grand*.

noting in detail for the light it throws on the relations between uncle and nephew. Salomon had given him a draft on Rothschild for £400. This was not to be cashed but was to serve merely for Repräsentation, i.e. as an effective introduction. However, Heine on his arrival in London instantly presented his letter of credit and pocketed the entire amount. The larger part of the sum was spent during the five months of the trip, and some £120 were sent for safe-keeping to Varnhagen in Berlin, to serve a future emergency. When remonstrances were presently made, the nephew replied with great audacity and impudence, capping it all with the statement: „Weißt Du, Onkel, das Beste an Dir ist, daß Du meinen Namen trägst."

Returning to Germany by way of Holland, Heine, in October, 1827, received an offer from the famous publisher Cotta to become the editor of the Munich *Neue Allgemeine Politische Annalen*. The duties of this position he assumed January 1, 1828. On his journey to Munich he touched also at Frankfurt, spending several days with Börne, a visit of which he has given an amusing account in his essay on Börne.

In Munich Heine strove to establish influential connections with governmental circles, and for a time lived in hopes of obtaining a professorship at the University of Munich. Notwithstanding an evident willingness to trim his political sails to the prevailing wind, his past record as liberal and free-lance stood in his way and he failed of the prize, if such in this case it was. He had meanwhile given up the editorship of the *Annals* and crossed the Alps to Italy. The impressions of this visit are recorded in the third volume of the *Reisebilder*. As on his trip to England, ignorance of the vernacular greatly detracted from both the enjoyment and profit of the trip. The end of the year 1828 saw Heine back in Hamburg, distressed at the death of his father, news of which had reached him on his return journey.

The next year was largely spent in Berlin and its environs, working on the new volume of the *Reisebilder*. Platen's attack upon Heine and consorts in *Der Romantische Ödipus*, a comedy in the Aristophanic vein, appeared at this time. Platen's bludgeon was no match for Heine's rapier, and scurrilous though Heine's reply in *Reisebilder III* (*Die Bäder von Lucca*) was, his adversary was silenced.

The July revolution in Paris, in 1830, was destined to work a great change also in Heine's future. To German liberals Paris now became a Jerusalem, the Rhine the river Jordan across which beckoned the Land of Promise that the goddess of Liberty had prepared for the elect of all nations. Heine obeyed the call. The journey was made in May, 1831, and except for brief visits to Hamburg in the autumn of 1843 and 1844, this self-imposed exile was destined to be permanent.

From the outset Heine felt at home in Paris, — like a fish in the water, to use his own expression. The German colony, of considerable size, included also Ludwig Börne. The relations between these two were at first cordial, but soon became strained and at last openly hostile. In part this was a conflict between the radical and the liberal, but in the last analysis it is traceable to a difference in mental make-up: Heine's artistic temperament shrank from the ultimate consequences, social and political, of the radical program. Heine did not deign to reply to Börne's attacks during the latter's lifetime, but shortly after his death he issued, in 1840, his *Ludwig Börne: Eine Denkschrift*, which, while perhaps tolerably correct in its estimate of Börne as writer and political thinker, contained also a wholly uncalled-for and malicious attack upon the woman in the case, a Frau Strauss. These insinuations Heine himself subsequently felt impelled to retract. As it was, they drew from Herr Strauss a challenge to a duel, which was fought on September 7, 1841, without being attended with serious consequences to either contestant.

Financially Heine's situation in Paris was, or should have been, fairly satisfactory. His uncle made him an annual allowance of 4000 francs, which in 1838 was increased to 4800 francs. From 1836 or 1837 to 1848 he also enjoyed a pension of 4800 francs from the French government. This latter came from the secret fund, and when the revolution of 1848 led to the publication of the list of pensioners, a great hue and cry was raised among the German radicals, that one who in his correspondence from Paris had posed as an objective critic of the French government should actually have been the recipient of its bounty. Even now this fact is frequently urged by those who are inclined to condone the other shortcomings in Heine's moral character.

In October, 1834, Heine, who in Paris had not relaxed his pursuit of pleasure, was captivated by the charms of Crescentia Eugenie Mirat, a young milliner's apprentice. A liaison followed, and although there was a break in their relations the following year, the breach was soon healed, and from December, 1835, he looked upon their relationship as permanent and regarded Mathilde — this was the name he had adopted instead of the preposterous Crescentia — as his wife. A legal marriage was contracted some years later, on August 31, 1841, just previous to the duel with Herr Strauss, when Heine was anxious to assure Mathilde's future beyond peradventure. Heine was passionately devoted to this impulsive, irresponsible, affectionate, gay "child of nature." Although fond of amusement, not a good housekeeper, and quite as great a spendthrift as he himself, she on the whole made the poet, if not a good helpmate, at least a cheering and congenial companion and materially helped to lighten the sufferings of his later years.

In December, 1835, a resolution of the Federal Diet aimed at "Young Germany," as the group of writers to which Börne and Heine belonged came to be called, bound the German governments to prevent by all lawful means the circulation of the works of members of the group. Heine was the first among those named and the decree seems actually to have interfered with the dissemination of his literary output. At any rate, Heine subsequently pleaded this in justification of his acceptance, at approximately the same time, of the secret French pension, "the munificent alms that the French nation bestowed upon so many thousands of strangers who through their zeal for the cause of the Revolution have more or less gloriously compromised themselves in their native land."

In 1836 began Heine's quarrel with the Swabian School, which on his side culminated in the prose *Schwabenspiegel* (1838). Through all his later writings, however, daring and witty sallies against this group of poets abound.

A stay in the Pyrenees during the summer of 1841 is reflected in the brilliant satirical poem *Atta Troll*. Somewhat similarly, *Deutschland, ein Wintermärchen*, is the poetical precipitate of his return to Germany in October, 1843.

Meanwhile Heine's health, at no time good, had been rapidly failing. Always a neurasthenic, racked by nervous headaches, the more serious symptoms of spinal disease set in, in 1832, with a partial paralysis of the left hand. In 1837 his right eye became affected and his sight much impaired. The death of his uncle in December, 1844, gave rise to a controversy which, prolonged until May, 1846, greatly aggravated the poet's condition.[1] After the middle of 1848 walking became entirely impossible and he was reduced to the state of a complete paralytic. The month of May of that year of revolution saw him for the last time on the streets of his beloved Paris. He tells us how he took refuge in the Louvre from the crowd and the turmoil,

---

[1] The uncle had left him the beggarly sum of 8000 francs and had made no provision for the continuance of his annual allowance, whereas Heine insisted that he had had the verbal promise of his uncle that the pension should continue for life. The chief heir, his cousin Karl Heine, proposed a compromise that was wholly unacceptable. Heine threatened to seek redress in the courts, but saner counsel prevailed and the alarming aggravation of his malady finally induced Karl Heine to accede to the poet's wishes. Everything was satisfactorily arranged, Heine's pension being ultimately even increased and provision made for Mathilde in the event of his death.

and broke down and wept at the feet of the Venus of Milo, the
goddess of beauty — a striking pendant to the scene so vividly
described in the *Harzreise*.[1]

A man like Heine, with so keen a relish for life and the joys
of life, might well have been overwhelmed by such an affliction.
But here his spirit showed its true temper and would not be
broken. In the midst of this final phase of his malady, from
his mattress-grave (Matraṇengruft) as it has come to be called,
at a moment when his very existence had assumed mythical
aspects, he surprised the world by the publication, in 1853, of
his *Romanzero*, a group of lyrics that contain some of his truest
and greatest poems, striking notes deeper and stronger than any
that had yet come from Heine's lips, notes that in their in-
tensity grip the very soul of the reader.

The poet's attitude towards religion had also undergone a
gradual change. He had returned to the belief in a personal
god. His interminable illness brought him to a realization of
his own insignificance: he no longer felt himself as a Hegelian
„zweibeiniger Gott," a "divine biped," but as the „armer tod=
franfer Jube," that he was. This deistic faith at no time, however, assumed very definite form and did not greatly affect the
character of his later work.

Heine's death took place in the early morning of February 17,
1856. He lies buried in Paris, at Montmartre, where a simple
monument with the superscription *"Henri Heine"* marks his
resting-place.

We cannot here essay a final estimate of Heine as man
and poet ; the less so as the assizes of literature, whose compe-
tence alone Heine was ready to acknowledge, cannot as yet be
said to have agreed upon a verdict. Some of the obstacles that
have stood and still stand in the way of an objective evaluation
of his work may, however, be pointed out. Since Heine lived
and died, values in the political, and to a less extent in the

----

[1] Page 12, l. 10.

religious and moral worlds, have undergone a vast change. Cosmopolitanism and humanitarianism have, as German watchwords, yielded to nationalism and patriotism. Under the hegemony of that very Prussia which was Heine's abomination, a united Germany has entered upon a struggle for mastery with other great nations of the world, and it is hence small wonder that subjects once tolerant of treatment in a frivolous vein should now have assumed a wholly serious aspect. Outward moral standards, the moral amenities of life, have also, "Youngest Germany" to the contrary notwithstanding, undergone a decided change for the better.

The reproach of being un-German has often been flung at Heine. In a measure this charge is doubtless suggested by his Jewish descent. Whatever other justification it has lies in the sneering, scoffing attitude he so frequently assumes in dealing with what others hold sacred, an attitude that at times seems nothing short of fred). Germans, even German freethinkers, have, as Scherer remarks, never been scoffers. If his wit — Heine is undoubtedly one of the world's great wits — and his lucid style be un-German, that is a matter for comment in connection with German character rather than with Heine.

The charge of insincerity, of posing, that is frequently made against Heine, is in the main unwarranted. In his poems he doubtless gives us himself, possibly with an element of wilful exaggeration and over-statement, but still himself. The force of the criticism directed against Heine's personality is in fact derived very largely from this source. In one respect at least it would seem that this very sincerity, this fidelity to things as he saw them, led him beyond the bounds of true art. We refer to what is usually called Stimmungsbredjung in Heine. If historically this traces its origin to the "Irony" of the romanticists, the smile of superiority of the ego to its product, and is psychologically to be attributed to a dualism existing in the poet's own character, the fact should not be lost to sight that its artistic *raison d'être* is a realistic one — the existence of the sublime and the ridiculous, of the ideal and its travesty, side by side in nature. In this sense all creation resolves itself into the product of a grandiose "irony" on the part of the creator.

As a writer of prose Heine has for lucidity, grace, biting satire and sparkling wit, no equal among German men of letters. The *Harzreise*, though perhaps not in all respects attaining the height of some of his later work, is an excellent example of his prose style. In its whimsicality, its "sentimental" view of nature, its swift changes of mood, it is clearly reminiscent of Sterne, and Sterne, "the spoiled child of the Muses," Heine held to be the compeer of Shakespeare.

Die Harzreise

(1824)

Nichts ist dauernd, als der Wechsel; nichts beständig, als der Tod. Jeder Schlag des Herzens schlägt uns eine Wunde, und das Leben wäre ein ewiges Verbluten, wenn nicht die Dichtkunst wäre. Sie gewährt uns, was uns die Natur versagt: eine goldene Zeit, die nicht rostet, einen Frühling, der nicht abblüht, wolkenloses Glück und ewige Jugend.[1]   Börne.

Schwarze Röcke, seidne Strümpfe,
Weiße, höfliche Manschetten,
Sanfte Reden, Embrassieren[1] —
Ach, wenn sie nur Herzen hätten!

Herzen in der Brust, und Liebe,   5
Warme Liebe in dem Herzen —
Ach, mich tötet ihr Gesinge
Von erlognen Liebesschmerzen.

Auf die Berge will ich steigen,
Wo die frommen[2] Hütten stehen,   10
Wo die Brust sich frei erschließet,
Und die freien Lüfte wehen.

Auf die Berge will ich steigen,
Wo die dunkeln Tannen ragen,
Bäche rauschen, Vögel singen,   15
Und die stolzen Wolken jagen.

Lebet wohl, ihr glatten Säle,
Glatte Herren! Glatte Frauen!
Auf die Berge will ich steigen,
Lachend auf euch niederschauen.   20

Die Stadt Göttingen,[3] berühmt durch ihre Würste und
Universität, gehört dem Könige von Hannover[4] und ent=
hält 999 Feuerstellen,[5] diverse Kirchen, eine Sternwarte,
einen Karzer,[6] eine Bibliothek und einen Ratskeller,[7] wo
das Bier sehr gut ist. Der vorbeifließende Bach heißt   25
„die Leine" und dient des Sommers zum Baden; das
Wasser ist sehr kalt und an einigen Orten so breit, daß

3

Lüder[1] wirklich einen großen Anlauf nehmen mußte, als
er hinübersprang. Die Stadt selbst ist schön und gefällt
einem am besten, wenn man sie mit dem Rücken ansieht.
Sie muß schon sehr lange stehen; denn ich erinnere mich,
als ich vor fünf Jahren[2] dort immatrikuliert und bald
darauf konsiliiert wurde, hatte sie schon dasselbe graue,
altkluge Ansehen und war schon vollständig eingerichtet mit
Schnurren,[3] Pudeln,[4] Dissertationen, Thédansants, Wäsche-
rinnen, Kompendien, Taubenbraten, Guelfenorden,[5] Promotionskutschen,[6] Pfeifenköpfen, Hofräten, Justizräten, Relegationsräten,[7] Profaxen[8] und anderen Faxen. Einige
behaupten sogar, die Stadt sei zur Zeit der Völkerwanderung[9] erbaut worden, jeder deutsche Stamm habe damals ein ungebundenes[10] Exemplar seiner Mitglieder darin
zurückgelassen, und davon stammten all die Vandalen,[11]
Friesen, Schwaben, Teutonen, Sachsen, Thüringer u. s. w.,
die noch heutzutage in Göttingen, hordenweis und geschieden durch Farben[12] der Mützen und der Pfeifenquäste,
über die Weenderstraße[13] einherziehen, auf den blutigen
Wahlstätten der Rasenmühle,[14] des Ritschenkrugs und Bob-
dens sich ewig untereinander herumschlagen, in Sitten und
Gebräuchen noch immer wie zur Zeit der Völkerwanderung
dahinleben und teils durch ihre Duces,[15] welche Haupthähne heißen, teils durch ihr uraltes[16] Gesetzbuch, welches
Komment[17] heißt und in den legibus barbarorum[18] eine
Stelle verdient, regiert werden.

Im allgemeinen werden die Bewohner Göttingens eingeteilt in Studenten, Professoren, Philister[1] und Vieh, welche vier Stände doch nichts weniger als[2] streng geschieden sind. Der Viehstand ist der bedeutendste. Die Namen aller Studenten und aller ordentlichen und unordentlichen[3] Professoren hier herzuzählen, wäre zu weitläuftig;[4] auch sind mir in diesem Augenblick nicht alle Studentennamen im Gedächtnisse, und unter den Professoren sind manche, die noch gar keinen Namen haben.[5] Die Zahl der Göttinger Philister muß sehr groß sein, wie Sand, oder besser gesagt,[6] wie Kot[7] am Meer; wahrlich, wenn ich sie des Morgens, mit ihren schmutzigen Gesichtern und weißen Rechnungen,[8] vor den Pforten des akademischen Gerichtes aufgepflanzt sah, so mochte ich kaum begreifen, wie Gott nur[9] so viel Lumpenpack erschaffen konnte.

Ausführlicheres über die Stadt Göttingen läßt sich sehr bequem nachlesen in der Topographie[10] derselben von K. F. H. Marx. Obzwar ich gegen den Verfasser, der mein Arzt war und mir viel Liebes erzeigte, die heiligsten Verpflichtungen hege, so kann ich doch sein Werk nicht unbedingt empfehlen, und ich muß tadeln, daß er jener falschen Meinung, als hätten die Göttingerinnen allzu große Füße, nicht streng genug widerspricht.[11] Ja, ich habe mich sogar seit Jahr und Tag[12] mit einer ernsten Widerlegung dieser Meinung beschäftigt, ich habe deshalb vergleichende Anatomie gehört,[13] die seltensten Werke auf der Bibliothek exzerpiert, auf der Weenderstraße stundenlang die Füße der vorübergehenden Damen studiert, und in der

grundgelehrten Abhandlung, so[1] die Resultate dieser Stu-
dien enthalten wird, spreche ich 1) von den Füßen überhaupt, 2) von den Füßen bei den Alten, 3) von den
Füßen der Elefanten, 4) von den Füßen der Göttingerinnen, 5) stelle ich alles zusammen, was über diese Füße
auf Ullrichs Garten[2] schon gesagt worden, und endlich
6), wenn ich nur so großes Papier auftreiben kann, füge
ich noch hinzu einige Kupfertafeln mit dem Faksimile göt-
tingischer Damenfüße.

Es war noch sehr früh, als ich Göttingen verließ, und
der gelehrte**[3] lag gewiß noch im Bette und träumte wie
gewöhnlich: er wandle in einem schönen Garten, auf dessen
Beeten lauter weiße, mit Citaten beschriebene Papierchen
wachsen, die im Sonnenlichte lieblich glänzen, und von
denen er hier und da mehrere pflückt und mühsam in ein
neues Beet verpflanzt, während die Nachtigallen mit ihren
süßesten Tönen sein altes Herz erfreuen.

Vor dem Weender Tore begegneten mir zwei eingeborne
kleine Schulknaben, wovon der eine zum andern sagte:
„Mit dem Theodor will ich gar nicht mehr umgehen, er
ist ein Lumpenkerl, denn gestern wußte er nicht mal,[4] wie
der Genitiv von mensa[5] heißt." So unbedeutend diese
Worte klingen, so muß ich sie doch wieder erzählen, ja,
ich möchte sie als Stadtmotto gleich auf das Tor schreiben
lassen; denn die Jungen piepen, wie die Alten pfeifen,[6]
und jene Worte bezeichnen ganz den engen, trocknen
Notizenstolz der hochgelahrten[7] Georgia Augusta.

Auf der Chaussee wehte frische Morgenluft, und die
Vögel sangen gar freudig, und auch mir wurde allmählich
wieder frisch und freudig zu Mute. Eine solche Erquik=
kung tat not. Ich war die letzte Zeit[1] nicht aus dem
Pandektenstall[2] herausgekommen, römische Kasuisten hatten   5
mir den Geist wie mit einem grauen Spinnweb überzogen,
mein Herz war wie eingeklemmt zwischen den eisernen
Paragraphen selbstsüchtiger Rechtssysteme, beständig klang
es mir noch in den Ohren wie „Tribonian,[2] Justinian,
Hermogenian[3] und Dummerjahn,"[4] und ein zärtliches Liebes=   10
paar, das unter einem Baume saß, hielt ich gar für eine
Korpusjurisausgabe mit verschlungenen Händen. Auf der
Landstraße fing es an, lebendig zu werden. Milch=
mädchen zogen vorüber; auch Eseltreiber mit ihren grauen
Zöglingen. Hinter Weende begegneten mir der Schäfer   15
und Doris.[5] Dieses ist nicht das idyllische Paar, wovon
Geßner[5] singt, sondern es sind wohlbestallte[6] Universi=
tätspedelle, die wachsam aufpassen müssen, daß sich keine
Studenten in Bovden duellieren, und daß keine neuen
Ideen, die noch immer einige Dezennien vor Göttingen   20
Quarantäne halten müssen, von einem spekulierenden Pri=
vatdozenten[7] eingeschmuggelt werden. Schäfer grüßte mich
sehr kollegialisch; denn er ist ebenfalls Schriftsteller und
hat meiner in seinen halbjährigen Schriften[8] oft erwähnt;
wie er mich denn auch außerdem oft citiert[9] hat und,   25
wenn er mich nicht zu Hause fand, immer so gütig war,
die Citation mit Kreide auf meine Stubentür zu schreiben.

Dann und wann rollte auch ein Einspänner vorüber,
wohlbepackt mit Studenten, die für die Ferienzeit oder
auch für immer wegreisten. In solch einer Universitäts=
stadt ist ein beständiges Kommen und Abgehen, alle drei
5 Jahre findet man dort eine neue Studentengeneration,
das ist ein ewiger Menschenstrom, wo eine Semesterwelle[1]
die andere fortdrängt, und nur die alten Professoren
bleiben stehen in dieser allgemeinen Bewegung, unerschüt=
terlich fest, gleich den Pyramiden Ägyptens — nur daß in
10 diesen Universitätspyramiden keine Weisheit verborgen ist.

Hinter Nörten stand die Sonne hoch und glänzend am
Himmel. Sie meinte es recht ehrlich mit mir und er=
wärmte mein Haupt, daß alle unreife[2] Gedanken darin zur
Vollreife kamen. Die liebe Wirtshaussonne[3] in Northeim[4]
15 ist auch nicht zu verachten; ich kehrte hier ein und fand
das Mittagessen schon fertig. Alle Gerichte waren schmack=
haft zubereitet und wollten[5] mir besser behagen als die
abgeschmackten akademischen Gerichte,[6] die salzlosen, leder=
nen Stockfische mit ihrem alten[7] Kohl, die mir in Göt=
20 tingen vorgesetzt wurden. Nachdem ich meinen Magen
etwas beschwichtigt hatte, bemerkte ich in derselben Wirts=
stube einen Herrn mit zwei Damen, die im Begriff waren
abzureisen. Dieser Herr war ganz grün gekleidet, trug
sogar eine grüne Brille, die auf seine rote Kupfernase
25 einen Schein wie Grünspan warf, und sah aus, wie der
König Nebukadnezar in seinen spätern Jahren ausge=
sehen hat, als er, der Sage nach, gleich einem Tiere des

Waldes, nichts als Salat[1] aß. Der Grüne wünschte, daß ich ihm ein Hotel in Göttingen empfehlen möchte, und ich riet ihm, dort von dem ersten besten Studenten[2] das Hotel de Brühbach zu erfragen. Die eine Dame war die Frau[3] Gemahlin, eine gar große, weitläuftige Dame, ein 5 rotes Quadratmeilen=Gesicht mit Grübchen in den Wangen, und ein langfleischig herabhängendes Unterkinn, das eine schlechte Fortsetzung des Gesichtes zu sein schien. Die andere Dame, die Frau[3] Schwester, bildete ganz den Gegensatz der eben beschriebenen. Stammte jene von 10 Pharaos fetten Kühen, so stammte diese von den magern. Beide Damen fragten mich zu gleicher Zeit, ob im Hotel de Brühbach auch ordentliche Leute[4] logierten. Ich be= jahte es mit gutem Gewissen, und als das holde Klee= blatt abfuhr, grüßte ich nochmals zum Fenster hinaus. 15 Der Sonnenwirt lächelte gar schlau und mochte wohl wissen, daß der Karzer von den Studenten in Göttingen Hotel de Brühbach[5] genannt wird.

Hinter Northeim wird es schon gebirgig, und hier und da treten schöne Anhöhen hervor. Auf dem Wege traf 20 ich meistens Krämer, die nach der Braunschweiger Messe[6] zogen, auch einen Schwarm Frauenzimmer, deren jede ein großes, fast häuserhohes, mit weißem Leinen überzogenes Behältnis auf dem Rücken trug. Darin saßen allerlei eingefangene[7] Singvögel, die beständig piepsten und zwit= 25 scherten, während ihre Trägerinnen lustig dahinhüpften und schwatzten. Mir kam es gar närrisch vor, wie so ein Vogel den andern zu Markte trägt.

In pechdunkler Nacht kam ich an zu Osterode.[1] Es
fehlte mir der Appetit zum Essen, und ich legte mich gleich
zu Bette. Ich war müde wie ein Hund und schlief wie
ein Gott.[2] Im Traume kam ich wieder nach Göttingen
5 zurück, und zwar[3] nach der dortigen Bibliothek. Ich stand
in einer Ecke des juristischen Saals,[4] durchstöberte alte
Dissertationen, vertiefte mich im Lesen, und als ich auf=
hörte, bemerkte ich zu meiner Verwunderung, daß es Nacht
war und herabhängende Kristallleuchter den Saal erhellten.
10 Die nahe Kirchenglocke schlug eben zwölf, die Saaltüre
öffnete sich langsam, und herein trat eine stolze, gigantische
Frau, ehrfurchtsvoll begleitet von den Mitgliedern und
Anhängern der juristischen Fakultät. Das Riesenweib, ob=
gleich schon bejahrt, trug dennoch im Antlitz die Züge
15 einer strengen Schönheit, jeder ihrer Blicke verriet die
hohe Titanin,[5] die gewaltige Themis,[5] Schwert und Wage
hielt sie nachlässig zusammen in der einen Hand, in der
andern hielt sie eine Pergamentrolle, zwei junge Doctores
juris[6] trugen die Schleppe ihres grau verblichenen Ge=
20 wandes; an ihrer rechten Seite sprang windig hin und
her der dünne Hofrat Rusticus,[7] der Lykurg[8] Hannovers,
und deklamierte aus seinem neuen Gesetzentwurf; an ihrer
linken Seite humpelte, gar galant und wohlgelaunt, ihr
Cavaliere servente,[9] der geheime Justizrat Cujacius,[10]
25 und riß beständig juristische Witze, und lachte selbst darüber
so herzlich, daß sogar die ernste Göttin sich mehrmals
lächelnd zu ihm herabbeugte, mit der großen Pergament=

rolle ihm auf die Schulter klopfte, und freundlich flüsterte:
„Kleiner, loser Schalk, der die Bäume von oben herab
beschneidet!"[1] Jeder von den übrigen Herren trat jetzt
ebenfalls näher und hatte etwas hinzubemerken und hinzu=
lächeln, etwa ein neu ergrübeltes Systemchen, oder Hypothes= 5
chen, oder ähnliches Mißgebürtchen des eigenen Köpfchens.[2]
Durch die geöffnete Saaltüre traten auch noch mehrere
fremde Herren herein, die sich als die andern großen
Männer des illuſtren[3] Ordens kundgaben, meiſtens eckige,
lauernde Geſellen, die mit breiter Selbſtzufriedenheit gleich 10
drauf los definierten[4] und diſtinguierten und über jedes
Titelchen eines Pandektentitels disputierten. Und immer
kamen noch neue Geſtalten herein, alte Rechtsgelehrten,
in verſchollenen Trachten, mit weißen Allongeperücken und
längſt vergeſſenen Geſichtern, und ſehr erſtaunt, daß man 15
ſie, die Hochberühmten des verfloſſenen Jahrhunderts,
nicht ſonderlich regardierte; und dieſe ſtimmten nun ein,
auf ihre Weiſe, in das allgemeine Schwatzen und Schrillen
und Schreien, das, wie Meeresbrandung, immer ver=
wirrter und lauter, die hohe Göttin umrauſchte, bis dieſe 20
die Geduld verlor, und in einem Tone des entſetzlichſten
Rieſenſchmerzes plötzlich aufſchrie: „Schweigt! Schweigt!
Ich höre die Stimme des teuren Prometheus,[5] die höh=
nende Kraft und die ſtumme Gewalt ſchmieden den Schuld=
loſen an den Marterfelſen, und all euer Geſchwätz und 25
Gezänke kann nicht ſeine Wunden kühlen und ſeine Feſſeln
zerbrechen!" So rief die Göttin, und Tränenbäche ſtürz=

ten aus ihren Augen, die ganze Versammlung heulte wie
von Todesangst ergriffen, die Decke des Saales krachte,
die Bücher taumelten herab von ihren Brettern, vergebens
trat der alte Münchhausen[1] aus seinem Rahmen hervor,
5 um Ruhe zu gebieten, es tobte und kreischte immer wil=
der, — und fort aus diesem drängenden Tollhauslärm
rettete ich mich in den historischen Saal, nach jener
Gnadenstelle, wo die heiligen Bilder des belvederischen
Apolls und der mediceischen Venus nebeneinander stehen,
10 und ich stürzte zu den Füßen der Schönheitsgöttin, in
ihrem Anblick[2] vergaß ich all das wüste Treiben, dem ich
entronnen, meine Augen tranken entzückt das Ebenmaß
und die ewige Lieblichkeit ihres hochgebenedeiten[3] Leibes,
griechische Ruhe zog durch meine Seele, und über mein
15 Haupt, wie himmlischen Segen, goß seine süßesten Lyra=
klänge[4] Phöbus Apollo.

Erwachend hörte ich noch immer ein freundliches Klingen.
Die Herden zogen auf die Weide, und es läuteten ihre
Glöckchen.[5] Die liebe, goldene Sonne schien durch das
20 Fenster und beleuchtete die Schildereien an den Wänden
des Zimmers. Es waren Bilder aus dem Befreiungs=
kriege,[6] worauf treu dargestellt stand, wie wir alle Helden[6]
waren, dann auch Hinrichtungsscenen aus der Revolutions=
zeit, Ludwig XVI. auf der Guillotine und ähnliche
25 Kopfabschneidereien, die man gar nicht ansehen kann, ohne
Gott zu danken, daß man ruhig im Bette liegt und guten
Kaffee trinkt, und den Kopf noch so recht komfortabel auf
den Schultern sitzen hat.[7]

Nachdem ich Kaffee getrunken, mich angezogen, die Inschriften auf den Fensterscheiben gelesen, und alles im Wirtshause berichtigt hatte, verließ ich Osterode.

Diese Stadt hat so und so viel Häuser, verschiedene Einwohner, worunter auch mehrere Seelen, wie in Gott= 5 schalks „Taschenbuch für Harzreisende" genauer nachzulesen ist. Ehe ich die Landstraße einschlug, bestieg ich die Trümmer der uralten Osteroder Burg. Sie bestehen nur noch aus der Hälfte eines großen, dickmaurigen, wie von Krebsschäden angefressenen Turms. Der Weg nach Klaus= 10 tal führte mich wieder bergauf, und von einer der ersten Höhen schaute ich nochmals hinab in das Tal, wo Osterode mit seinen roten Dächern aus den grünen Tannenwäldern hervorguckt wie eine Moosrose. Die Sonne gab eine gar liebe, kindliche[1] Beleuchtung. Von[2] der erhaltenen Turm= 15 hälfte erblickt man hier die imponierende Rückseite.

Nachdem ich eine Strecke gewandert, traf ich zusammen mit einem reisenden Handwerksburschen,[3] der von Braun= schweig kam und mir als ein dortiges[4] Gerücht erzählte, der junge Herzog[5] sei auf dem Wege nach dem gelobten 20 Lande von den Türken gefangen worden und könne nur gegen ein großes Lösegeld frei kommen. Die große Reise des Herzogs mag diese Sage veranlaßt haben. Das Volk hat noch immer den traditionell fabelhaften Ideen= gang, der sich so lieblich ausspricht in seinem „Herzog 25 Ernst."[6] Der Erzähler jener Neuigkeit war ein Schnei= bergesell, ein niedlicher, kleiner junger Mensch, so dünn,

daß die Sterne durchschimmern konnten, wie durch Offians[1]
Nebelgeifter, und im ganzen eine volkstümlich barocke
Mischung von Laune und Wehmut. Dieses äußerte sich
besonders in der drollig rührenden Weise, womit er das
5 wunderbare Volkslied sang: „Ein Käfer auf dem Zaune
saß; summ, summ!"[2] Das ist schön bei uns Deutschen:
keiner ist so verrückt, daß er nicht einen noch Verrückteren
fände, der ihn versteht. Nur ein Deutscher kann jenes
Lied nachempfinden, und sich dabei totlachen und totweinen.
10 Wie tief das Goethesche[3] Wort ins Leben des Volks
gedrungen, bemerkte ich auch hier. Mein dünner Weg=
genosse trillerte ebenfalls zuweilen vor sich hin: „Leidvoll
und freudvoll, Gedanken sind frei!"[4] Solche Korruption
des Textes ist beim Volke etwas Gewöhnliches. Er sang
15 auch ein Lied, wo „Lottchen bei dem Grabe ihres
Werthers"[5] trauert. Der Schneider zerfloß vor Senti=
mentalität bei den Worten:

> „Einsam wein' ich an der Rosenstelle,
> Wo uns oft der späte Mond belauscht!
20 > Jammernd irr' ich an der Silberquelle,
> Die uns lieblich Wonne zugerauscht."

Aber bald darauf ging er in Mutwillen über und
erzählte mir: „Wir haben einen Preußen in der Herberge[6]
zu Kassel, der eben solche Lieder selbst macht; er kann
25 keinen seligen Stich nähen; hat er einen Groschen in der
Tasche, so hat er für zwei Groschen Durst, und wenn er
im Tran ist, hält er den Himmel für ein blaues Kamisol,
und weint wie eine Dachtraufe, und singt ein Lied mit der

doppelten Poesie!" Von letzterem Ausdruck wünschte ich
eine Erklärung, aber mein Schneiderlein, mit seinen Zie=
genhainer[1] Beinchen, hüpfte hin und her und rief beständ=
dig: „Die doppelte Poesie ist die doppelte Poesie!" Endlich
brachte ich es heraus, daß er doppelt gereimte Gedichte, 5
namentlich[2] Stanzen im Sinne hatte. — Unterdes, durch
die große Bewegung und durch den konträren Wind, war
der Ritter von der Nadel sehr müde geworden. Er
machte freilich noch einige große Anstalten zum Gehen und
bramarbasierte: „Jetzt will ich den Weg zwischen die 10
Beine nehmen!"[3] doch bald klagte er, daß er sich Blasen
unter die Füße gegangen, und die Welt viel zu weitläuftig
sei; und endlich, bei einem Baumstamme, ließ er sich sachte
niedersinken, bewegte sein zartes Häuptlein wie ein be=
trübtes Lämmerschwänzchen, und wehmütig lächelnd rief 15
er: „Da bin ich armes Schindluderchen schon wieder
marode!"[4]

Die Berge wurden hier noch steiler, die Tannenwälder
wogten unten wie ein grünes Meer, und am blauen
Himmel oben schifften die weißen Wolken. Die Wildheit 20
der Gegend war durch ihre Einheit und Einfachheit gleich=
sam gezähmt. Wie ein guter Dichter, liebt die Natur
keine schroffen Übergänge. Die Wolken, so bizarr gestaltet
sie auch zuweilen erscheinen, tragen ein weißes, oder doch
ein mildes, mit dem blauen Himmel und der grünen Erde 25
harmonisch korrespondierendes Kolorit, so daß alle Farben
einer Gegend wie leise Musik ineinander schmelzen, und

jeder Naturanblick krampfstillend und gemütberuhigend
wirkt. — Der selige Hoffmann[1] würde die Wolken bunt=
scheckig bemalt[2] haben. — Eben wie ein großer Dichter,
weiß die Natur auch mit den wenigsten Mitteln die größ=
5 ten Effekte hervorzubringen. Da sind nur eine Sonne,
Bäume, Blumen, Wasser und Liebe. Freilich, fehlt letztere
im Herzen des Beschauers, so mag das Ganze wohl einen
schlechten Anblick gewähren, und die Sonne hat dann bloß
so und so viel Meilen im Durchmesser, und die Bäume
10 sind gut zum Einheizen, und die Blumen werden nach
den Staubfäden klassifiziert, und das Wasser ist naß.

Ein kleiner Junge, der für seinen kranken Oheim im
Walde Reisig suchte, zeigte mir das Dorf Lerbach, dessen
kleine Hütten, mit grauen Dächern, sich über eine halbe
15 Stunde[3] durch das Tal hinziehen. „Dort," sagte er,
„wohnen dumme Kropfleute[4] und weiße Mohren", — mit
letzterem Namen werden die Albinos[5] vom Volke benannt.
Der kleine Junge stand mit den Bäumen in gar eigenem
Einverständnis; er grüßte sie wie gute Bekannte, und sie
20 schienen rauschend seinen Gruß zu erwidern. Er pfiff wie
ein Zeisig, ringsum antworteten zwitschernd die andern
Vögel, und ehe ich mich dessen versah, war er mit seinen
nackten Füßchen und seinem Bündel Reisig ins Wald=
dickicht fortgesprungen. Die Kinder, dacht' ich, sind jünger
25 als wir, können sich noch erinnern, wie sie ebenfalls
Bäume oder Vögel waren, und sind also noch im stande,
dieselben zu verstehen; unsereins aber ist schon alt und

hat zu viel Sorgen, Jurisprudenz und schlechte Verse[1] im
Kopf. Jene Zeit, wo es anders war, trat mir bei
meinem Eintritt in Klaustal wieder recht lebhaft ins
Gedächtnis. In dieses nette Bergstädtchen, welches man
nicht früher erblickt, als bis man davor steht, gelangte 5
ich, als eben die Glocke zwölf schlug und die Kinder
jubelnd aus der Schule kamen. Die lieben Knaben, fast
alle rotbäckig, blauäugig und flachshaarig,[2] sprangen und
jauchzten, und weckten in mir die wehmütig heitere Erinnerung, wie ich einst selbst, als ein kleines Bübchen, in 10
einer dumpfkatholischen Klosterschule[3] zu Düsseldorf den
ganzen lieben Vormittag[4] von der hölzernen Bank nicht
aufstehen durfte, und so viel Latein, Prügel und Geo-
graphie ausstehen mußte, und dann ebenfalls unmäßig
jauchzte und jubelte, wenn die alte Franziskanerglocke 15
endlich zwölf schlug.

In der „Krone"[5] zu Klaustal hielt ich Mittag. Ich
bekam frühlingsgrüne Petersiliensuppe, veilchenblauen Kohl,
einen Kalbsbraten, groß wie der Chimborasso in Miniatur,
sowie auch eine Art geräucherter Heringe, die Bückinge 20
heißen, nach dem Namen ihres Erfinders, Wilhelm Bücking,
der 1447 gestorben,[6] und um jener Erfindung willen von
Karl V. so verehrt wurde, daß derselbe anno 1556 von
Middelburg nach Biebliéd[7] in Zeeland reiste, bloß um
dort das Grab dieses großen Mannes zu sehen. Wie 25
herrlich schmeckt doch[8] solch ein Gericht, wenn man die
historischen Notizen dazu weiß und es selbst verzehrt! Nur

der Kaffee nach Tische wurde mir verleidet, indem sich ein
junger Mensch diskurfierend zu mir fetzte und fo entfetzlich
fchwabronierte, daß die Milch auf dem Tifche fauer wurde.
Es war ein junger Handlungsbefliffener[1] mit fünfund-
5 zwanzig bunten Weften und ebenfoviel goldenen Petfchaften,
Ringen, Bruftnadeln u. f. w. Er fah aus wie ein Affe,
der eine rote Jacke angezogen hat und nun zu fich felber
fagt: „Kleider machen Leute."[2] Eine ganze Menge Charaden
wußte er auswendig, fowie auch Anekdoten, die er immer
10 da anbrachte, wo fie am wenigften paßten. Er fragte mich,
was es in Göttingen Neues gäbe, und ich erzählte ihm,
daß vor meiner Abreife von dort ein Dekret des akademifchen
Senats erfchienen, worin bei[3] drei Taler Strafe verboten
wird, den Hunden die Schwänze abzufchneiden, indem die
15 tollen Hunde in den Hundstagen die Schwänze zwifchen
den Beinen tragen, und man fie dadurch von den nichttollen
unterfcheidet, was doch[4] nicht gefchehen könnte, wenn fie
gar keine Schwänze haben. — Nach Tifche machte ich mich
auf den Weg, die Gruben, die Silberhütten und die
20 Münze zu befuchen.

In den Silberhütten habe ich, wie oft im Leben, den
Silberblick[5] verfehlt. In der Münze traf ich es fchon
beffer und konnte zufehen, wie das Geld gemacht wird.
Freilich, weiter hab' ich es auch nie bringen können.[6] Ich
25 hatte bei folcher Gelegenheit immer das Zufehen,[7] und ich
glaube, wenn mal[8] die Taler vom Himmel herunterregneten,
fo bekäme ich davon nur Löcher in den Kopf, während die

Kinder Israel[1] die silberne Manna mit lustigem Mute einsammeln würden. Mit einem Gefühle, worin gar komisch Ehrfurcht und Rührung gemischt waren, betrachtete ich die neugebornen blanken Taler, nahm einen, der eben vom Prägstocke kam, in die Hand, und sprach zu ihm: „Junger Taler, welche Schicksale erwarten dich! Wie viel Gutes und wie viel Böses wirst du stiften! Wie wirst du das Laster beschützen und die Tugend[2] flicken! Wie wirst du geliebt und dann wieder verwünscht werden! Wie wirst du schwelgen, lügen und morden helfen! Wie wirst du rastlos umherirren, durch reine und schmutzige Hände, jahrhundertelang, bis du endlich, schuldbeladen und sündenmüd', versammelt wirst zu den Deinigen im Schoße Abrahams, der dich einschmelzt und läutert und umbildet zu einem neuen besseren Sein."

Das Befahren der zwei vorzüglichsten Klaustaler Gruben, der „Dorothea" und „Karolina," fand ich sehr interessant, und ich muß ausführlich davon erzählen.

Eine halbe Stunde vor der Stadt gelangt man zu zwei großen schwärzlichen Gebäuden. Dort wird man gleich von den Bergleuten in Empfang genommen. Diese tragen dunkle, gewöhnlich stahlblaue, weite, bis über den Bauch herabhängende Jacken, Hosen von ähnlicher Farbe, ein hinten aufgebundenes Schurzfell[3] und kleine grüne Filzhüte, ganz randlos, wie ein abgekappter Kegel. In eine solche Tracht, bloß ohne Hinterleder, wird der Besuchende ebenfalls eingekleidet, und ein Bergmann, ein Steiger, nachdem er

fein Grubenlicht angezündet, führt ihn nach einer dunkeln
Öffnung, die wie ein Kaminfegeloch¹ aussieht, steigt bis an
die Brust hinab, gibt Regeln, wie man sich an den Leitern
festzuhalten habe, und bittet angstlos zu folgen.   Die Sache
5 selbst ist nichts weniger² als gefährlich; aber man glaubt
es nicht im Anfang, wenn man gar nichts vom Berg=
werkswesen versteht.   Es gibt³ schon eine eigene Empfin=
dung, daß man sich ausziehen und die dunkle Delinquenten=
tracht anziehen muß.   Und nun soll man auf allen vieren
10 hinabklettern, und das dunkle Loch ist so dunkel, und Gott
weiß, wie lang die Leiter sein mag.   Aber bald merkt
man doch, daß es nicht eine einzige, in die schwarze
Ewigkeit hinablaufende Leiter ist, sondern daß es mehrere
von⁴ fünfzehn bis zwanzig Sprossen sind, deren jede auf
15 ein kleines Brett führt, worauf man stehen kann, und
worin wieder ein neues Loch nach einer neuen Leiter
hinableitet.   Ich war zuerst in die Karolina gestiegen.   Die
Leitersprossen sind kotig naß.⁵   Und von einer Leiter zur
andern geht's hinab, und der Steiger voran, und dieser
20 beteuert immer, es sei gar nicht gefährlich, nur müsse man
sich mit den Händen fest an den Sprossen halten, und nicht
nach den Füßen sehen, und nicht schwindlig werden, und
nur beileibe nicht auf das Seitenbrett treten, wo jetzt das
schnurrende Tonnenseil heraufgeht, und wo vor vierzehn
25 Tagen ein unvorsichtiger Mensch hinuntergestürzt und leider
den Hals gebrochen.   Da unten⁶ ist ein verworrenes
Rauschen und Summen, man stößt beständig an Balken und

Seile, die in Bewegung sind, um die Tonnen mit geklopften
Erzen oder das hervorgesinterte Wasser heraufzuwinden.
Zuweilen gelangt man auch in durchgehauene Gänge,
Stollen genannt, wo man das Erz wachsen sieht, und wo
der einsame Bergmann den ganzen Tag sitzt und mühsam 5
mit dem Hammer die Erzstücke aus der Wand herausklopft.
Bis in die unterste Tiefe, wo man, wie einige behaupten,
schon hören kann, wie die Leute in Amerika „Hurrah
Lafayette!"[1] schreien, bin ich nicht gekommen; unter uns
gesagt,[2] dort, bis wohin ich kam, schien es mir bereits tief 10
genug: — immerwährendes Brausen und Sausen, unheimliche
Maschinenbewegung, unterirdisches Quellengeriesel, von allen
Seiten herabtriefendes Wasser, qualmig aufsteigende Erd=
dünste, und das Grubenlicht immer bleicher hineinflimmernd
in die einsame Nacht. Wirklich, es war betäubend, das 15
Atmen wurde mir schwer, und mit Mühe hielt ich mich an
den glitschrigen Leitersprossen. Ich habe keinen Anflug von
sogenannter Angst empfunden, aber, seltsam genug, dort
unten in der Tiefe erinnerte ich mich, daß ich im vorigen
Jahre,[3] ungefähr um dieselbe Zeit, einen Sturm auf der 20
Nordsee erlebte, und ich meinte jetzt, es sei doch eigentlich
recht traulich angenehm, wenn das Schiff hin und her
schaukelt, die Winde ihre Trompeterstückchen losblasen,
zwischendrein der lustige Matrosenlärmen erschallt, und
alles frisch überschauert wird von Gottes lieber, freier Luft. 25
Ja, Luft! — Nach Luft schnappend stieg ich einige Dutzend
Leitern wieder in die Höhe, und mein Steiger führte mich

durch einen schmalen, sehr langen, in den Berg gehauenen
Gang nach der Grube Dorothea. Hier ist es luftiger und
frischer, und die Leitern sind reiner, aber auch länger und
steiler als in der Karolina. Hier wurde mir auch besser
5 zu Mute, besonders da ich wieder Spuren lebendiger
Menschen gewahrte. In der Tiefe zeigten sich nämlich
wandelnde Schimmer; Bergleute mit ihren Grubenlichtern
kamen allmählich in die Höhe mit dem Gruße „Glückauf!"[1]
und mit demselben Wiedergruße von unserer Seite stiegen
10 sie an uns vorüber; und wie eine befreundet ruhige, und
doch zugleich quälend rätselhafte Erinnerung, trafen mich,
mit ihren tiefsinnig klaren Blicken, die ernstfrommen, etwas
blassen und vom Grubenlicht geheimnisvoll beleuchteten
Gesichter dieser jungen und alten Männer, die in ihren
15 dunkeln, einsamen Bergschachten den ganzen Tag gearbeitet
hatten, und sich jetzt hinaufsehnten nach dem lieben Tageslicht,
und nach den Augen von Weib und Kind.

Mein Cicerone[2] selbst war eine kreuzehrliche, pudeldeutsche[3]
Natur. Mit innerer Freudigkeit zeigte er mir jene Stolle,
20 wo der Herzog von Cambridge,[4] als er die Grube befahren,
mit seinem ganzen Gefolge gespeist hat, und wo noch der
lange hölzerne Speisetisch steht, sowie auch der große Stuhl
von Erz, worauf der Herzog gesessen. Dieser bleibe[5] zum
ewigen Andenken stehen, sagte der gute Bergmann, und
25 mit Feuer erzählte er, wie viele Festlichkeiten damals
stattgefunden, wie der ganze Stollen mit Lichtern, Blumen
und Laubwerk verziert gewesen, wie ein Bergknappe die

Zither gespielt und gesungen, wie der vergnügte, liebe, dicke
Herzog sehr viele Gesundheiten ausgetrunken habe, und wie
viele Bergleute, und er selbst ganz besonders, sich gern
würden totschlagen lassen für den lieben, dicken Herzog und
das ganze Haus Hannover. — Innig rührt es mich jedesmal, 5
wenn ich sehe, wie sich dieses Gefühl der Untertanstreue in
seinen einfachen Naturlauten ausspricht. Es ist ein so schönes
Gefühl! Und es ist ein so wahrhaft deutsches Gefühl!
Andere Völker mögen gewandter sein, und witziger und
ergötzlicher, aber keines ist so treu wie das treue deutsche 10
Volk. Wüßte ich nicht, daß die Treue so alt ist wie die
Welt, so würde ich glauben, ein deutsches Herz habe sie
erfunden. Deutsche Treue! sie ist keine moderne Adressen=
floskel.¹ An euren Höfen, ihr deutschen Fürsten, sollte
man singen und wieder singen das Lied von dem getreuen 15
Eckart² und dem bösen Burgund, der ihm die lieben Kinder
töten lassen, und ihn alsdann doch noch immer treu befunden
hat. Ihr habt das treueste Volk, und ihr irrt, wenn ihr
glaubt,³ der alte, verständige, treue Hund sei plötzlich toll
geworden und schnappe nach euern geheiligten⁴ Waden.   20
      Wie die deutsche Treue, hatte uns jetzt das kleine
Grubenlicht, ohne viel Geflacker, still und sicher geleitet
durch das Labyrinth der Schachten und Stollen; wir
stiegen hervor aus der dumpfigen Bergnacht, das Sonnen=
licht strahlt — Glückauf!   25
      Die meisten Bergarbeiter wohnen in Klaustal und in
dem damit verbundenen Bergstädtchen Zellerfeld. Ich

besuchte mehrere dieser wackern Leute, betrachtete ihre
kleine häusliche Einrichtung, hörte einige ihrer Lieder, die
sie mit der Zither, ihrem Lieblingsinstrumente, gar hübsch
begleiten, ließ mir alte Bergmärchen von ihnen erzählen,
5 und auch die Gebete hersagen, die sie in Gemeinschaft zu
halten pflegen, ehe sie in den dunkeln Schacht hinunter-
steigen, und manches gute Gebet habe ich mitgebetet.
Ein alter Steiger meinte sogar, ich sollte bei ihnen bleiben und Bergmann werden; und als ich dennoch Abschied
10 nahm, gab er mir einen Auftrag an seinen Bruder, der
in der Nähe von Goslar wohnt, und viele Küsse für
seine liebe Nichte.

So stillstehend ruhig auch[1] das Leben dieser Leute
erscheint, so ist es dennoch ein wahrhaftes, lebendiges
15 Leben. Die steinalte, zitternde Frau, die, dem großen
Schranke gegenüber, hinterm Ofen saß, mag dort schon
ein Vierteljahrhundert lang gesessen haben, und ihr Denken
und Fühlen ist gewiß innig verwachsen mit allen Ecken
dieses Ofens und allen Schnitzeleien dieses Schrankes.
20 Und Schrank und Ofen leben, denn ein Mensch hat ihnen
einen Teil seiner Seele eingeflößt.

Nur durch solch tiefes Anschauungsleben, durch die
„Unmittelbarkeit" entstand die deutsche Märchenfabel;[2] deren
Eigentümlichkeit darin besteht, daß nicht nur die Tiere
25 und Pflanzen, sondern auch ganz leblos scheinende Gegenstände sprechen und handeln.[3] Sinnigem, harmlosen Volke,
in der stillen, umfriedeten Heimlichkeit seiner niedern Berg-

oder Waldhütten offenbarte sich das innere Leben solcher
Gegenstände, diese gewannen einen notwendigen, konsequen=
ten Charakter, eine süße Mischung von phantastischer Laune
und rein menschlicher Gesinnung; und so sehen wir im Mär=
chen, wunderbar und doch als wenn es sich von selbst 5
verstände: Nähnadel und Stecknadel[1] kommen von der
Schneiderherberge und verirren sich im Dunkeln; Strohhalm
und Kohle[1] wollen über den Bach setzen und verunglücken;
Schippe und Besen[1] stehen auf der Treppe und zanken und
schmeißen sich; der befragte Spiegel[1] zeigt das Bild der schön= 10
sten Frau; sogar die Blutstropfen[1] fangen an zu sprechen,
bange, dunkle Worte des besorglichsten Mitleids. — Aus dem=
selben Grunde[2] ist unser Leben in der Kindheit so unendlich
bedeutend, in jener Zeit ist uns alles gleich wichtig, wir hören
alles, wir sehen alles, bei allen Eindrücken ist Gleichmäßigkeit, 15
statt daß[3] wir späterhin absichtlicher werden, uns mit dem
Einzelnen ausschließlicher beschäftigen, das klare Gold der
Anschauung für das Papiergeld der Bücherdefinitionen
mühsam einwechseln und an Lebensbreite gewinnen, was
wir an Lebenstiefe verlieren. Jetzt sind wir ausgewachsene, 20
vornehme Leute; wir beziehen oft neue Wohnungen, die
Magd räumt täglich auf und verändert nach Gutdünken
die Stellung der Möbeln, die uns wenig interessieren, da
sie entweder neu sind, oder heute dem Hans, morgen dem
Isaak[4] gehören; selbst unsere Kleider bleiben uns fremd, 25
wir wissen kaum, wieviel Knöpfe an dem Rocke sitzen, den
wir eben jetzt auf dem Leibe tragen; wir wechseln ja so

oft als möglich mit Kleidungsstücken, keines derselben bleibt
im Zusammenhange mit unserer inneren und äußeren Ge=
schichte; — kaum vermögen wir uns zu erinnern, wie jene
braune Weste aussah, die uns einst so viel Gelächter zu=
5 gezogen hat, und auf deren breiten Streifen dennoch die
liebe Hand der Geliebten so lieblich ruhte![1]

Die alte Frau, dem großen Schrank gegenüber, hinterm
Ofen, trug einen geblümten Rock von verschollenem Zeuge,
das Brautkleid ihrer seligen Mutter. Ihr Urenkel, ein
10 als Bergmann gekleideter, blonder, blitzäugiger Knabe,
saß zu ihren Füßen und zählte die Blumen ihres Rockes,
und sie mag ihm von diesem Rocke wohl schon viele Ge=
schichtchen erzählt haben, viele ernsthafte, hübsche Geschichten,
die der Junge gewiß nicht so bald vergißt, die ihm noch
15 oft vorschweben werden, wenn er bald, als ein erwach=
sener Mann, in den nächtlichen Stollen der Karolina ein=
sam arbeitet, und die er vielleicht wieder erzählt,[2] wenn
die liebe Großmutter längst tot ist, und er selber, ein
silberhaariger, erloschener Greis, im Kreise seiner Enkel
20 sitzt, dem großen Schranke gegenüber, hinterm Ofen.[3]

Ich blieb die Nacht ebenfalls in der Krone, wo unter=
dessen auch der Hofrat B.[4] aus Göttingen angekommen
war. Ich hatte das Vergnügen, dem alten Herrn meine
Aufwartung zu machen. Als ich mich ins Fremdenbuch
25 einschrieb und im Monat Juli blätterte, fand ich auch den
vielteuern Namen Adalbert von Chamisso, den Biographen
des unsterblichen Schlemihl.[5] Der Wirt erzählte mir,

dieser Herr sei in einem unbeschreibbar schlechten Wetter
angekommen und in einem ebenso schlechten Wetter wieder
abgereist.

Den andern Morgen erleichterte ich meinen Ranzen,
das eingepackte Paar Stiefel warf ich über Bord, und ich 5
hob auf[1] meine Füße und ging nach Goslar. Ich kam
dahin, ohne zu wissen wie. Nur so viel kann ich mich
erinnern: ich schlenderte wieder bergauf, bergab; schaute
hinunter in manches hübsche Wiesental; silberne Wasser
brausten, süße Waldvögel zwitscherten, die Herdenglöckchen 10
läuteten, die mannigfaltig grünen Bäume wurden von der
lieben Sonne goldig angestrahlt, und oben war die blau=
seidene Decke des Himmels so durchsichtig, daß man tief
hineinschauen konnte, bis ins Allerheiligste, wo die Engel
zu den Füßen Gottes sitzen. Ich aber lebte noch in dem 15
Traum der vorigen Nacht, den ich nicht aus meiner Seele
verscheuchen konnte. Es war das alte Märchen,[2] wie ein
Ritter hinabsteigt in einen tiefen Brunnen, wo unten die
schönste Prinzessin zu einem starren Zauberschlafe ver=
wünscht ist. Ich selbst war der Ritter, und der Brunnen 20
die dunkle Klaustaler Grube, und plötzlich erschienen viele
Lichter, aus allen Seitenlöchern stürzten die wachsamen
Zwerglein, schnitten zornige Gesichter, hieben nach mir
mit ihren kurzen Schwertern, bliesen gellend ins Horn,
daß immer mehr und mehre[3] herzueilten, und es wackelten 25
entsetzlich ihre breiten Häupter.[4] Wie ich darauf[5] zu=
schlug, und das Blut herausfloß, merkte ich erst, daß es

die rotblühenden, langbärtigen Distelköpfe waren, die ich
den Tag vorher an der Landstraße mit dem Stocke abge=
schlagen hatte. Da waren sie auch gleich alle verscheucht,
und ich gelangte in einen hellen Prachtsaal; in der Mitte
5 stand, weiß verschleiert, und wie eine Bildsäule starr und
regungslos, die Herzgeliebte, und ich küßte ihren Mund,
und, beim lebendigen Gott! ich fühlte den beseligenden
Hauch ihrer Seele und das süße Beben der lieblichen
Lippen. Es war mir, als hörte ich, wie Gott rief: „Es
10 werde Licht!"¹ blendend schoß herab ein Strahl des
ewigen Lichts; aber in demselben Augenblick wurde es
wieder Nacht, und alles rann chaotisch zusammen in ein
wildes, wüstes Meer. Ein wildes, wüstes Meer! Über
das gärende Wasser jagten ängstlich die Gespenster der
15 Verstorbenen, ihre weißen Totenhembe flatterten im Winde,
hinter ihnen her, hetzend, mit klatschender Peitsche, lief
ein buntscheckiger Harlekin, und dieser war ich selbst —
und plötzlich aus den dunkeln Wellen reckten die Meer=
ungetüme ihre mißgestalteten Häupter und langten nach
20 mir mit ausgebreiteten Krallen, und vor Entsetzen er=
wacht' ich.

Wie doch² zuweilen die allerschönsten Märchen verdor=
ben werden! Eigentlich muß der Ritter, wenn er die
schlafende Prinzessin gefunden hat, ein Stück aus ihrem
25 kostbaren Schleier herausschneiden; und wenn durch seine
Kühnheit ihr Zauberschlaf gebrochen ist, und sie wieder in
ihrem Palast auf dem goldenen Stuhle sitzt, muß der Ritter

zu ihr treten und sprechen: „Meine allerschönste Prinzessin,
kennst du mich?" Und dann antwortet sie: „Mein aller=
tapferster Ritter, ich kenne dich nicht." Und dieser zeigt
ihr alsdann das aus ihrem Schleier herausgeschnittene
Stück, das just[1] in denselben wieder hineinpaßt, und beide 5
umarmen sich zärtlich, und die Trompeten blasen, und die
Hochzeit wird gefeiert.

Es ist wirklich ein eigenes[2] Mißgeschick, daß meine Lie=
besträume selten ein so schönes Ende nehmen.

Der Name Goslar[3] klingt so erfreulich, und es knüpfen 10
sich daran so viele uralte Kaisererinnerungen, daß ich eine
imposante, stattliche Stadt erwartete. Aber so geht es,
wenn man die Berühmten in der Nähe besieht! Ich fand
ein Nest mit meistens schmalen, labyrinthisch krummen
Straßen, allwo[4] mittendurch ein kleines Wasser, wahr= 15
scheinlich die Gose, fließt, verfallen und dumpfig, und ein
Pflaster, so holprig wie Berliner Hexameter.[5] Nur die
Altertümlichkeiten der Einfassung, nämlich Reste von
Mauern, Türmen und Zinnen, geben der Stadt etwas
Pikantes. Einer dieser Türme, der Zwinger genannt, 20
hat so dicke Mauern, daß ganze Gemächer darin aus=
gehauen sind. Der Platz vor der Stadt, wo der weitbe=
rühmte Schützenhof[6] gehalten wird, ist eine schöne große
Wiese, ringsum hohe Berge. Der Markt ist klein, in der
Mitte steht ein Springbrunnen, dessen Wasser sich in ein 25
großes Metallbecken ergießt. Bei Feuersbrünsten wird
einigemal daran geschlagen; es[7] gibt dann einen weit=

schallenden Ton. Man weiß nichts vom Ursprunge dieses
Beckens. Einige sagen, der Teufel habe es einst zur
Nachtzeit dort auf den Markt hingestellt. Damals waren
die Leute noch dumm, und der Teufel war auch dumm,
5 und sie machten sich wechselseitig Geschenke.

Das Rathaus[1] zu Goslar ist eine weiß angestrichene
Wachtstube. Das danebenstehende Gildenhaus[2] hat schon
ein besseres Ansehen. Ungefähr von der Erde und vom
Dach gleich weit entfernt stehen da die Standbilder deut=
10 scher Kaiser, räucherig schwarz und zum Teil vergoldet,
in der einen Hand das Scepter, in der andern die Welt=
kugel; sehen aus[3] wie gebratene[4] Universitätspedelle.
Einer dieser Kaiser hält ein Schwert, statt des Scepters.
Ich konnte nicht erraten, was dieser Unterschied sagen
15 soll;[5] und es hat doch gewiß seine Bedeutung, da die
Deutschen die merkwürdige Gewohnheit haben, daß sie
bei allem, was sie tun, sich auch etwas denken.

In Gottschalks „Handbuch“ hatte ich von dem uralten
Dom und von dem berühmten Kaiserstuhl zu Goslar viel
20 gelesen. Als ich aber beides besehen wollte, sagte man
mir: der Dom sei niedergerissen,[6] und der Kaiserstuhl[7]
nach Berlin gebracht worden. Wir leben in einer bedeu=
tungschweren Zeit: tausendjährige Dome werden abge=
brochen, und Kaiserstühle[8] in die Rumpelkammer geworfen.
25 Einige Merkwürdigkeiten des seligen[9] Doms sind jetzt
in der Stephanskirche aufgestellt. Glasmalereien, die
wunderschön sind, einige schlechte Gemälde, worunter auch

Goslar, Kaiserworth (Gildenhaus).

ein Lukas Cranach[1] sein soll, ferner ein hölzerner Christus
am Kreuz und ein heidnischer Opferaltar[2] aus unbekann=
tem Metall; er hat die Gestalt einer länglich viereckigen
Lade und wird von vier Karyatiden[3] getragen, die, in
gebuckter Stellung, die Hände stützend über dem Kopfe 5
halten und unerfreulich häßliche Gesichter schneiden. In=
dessen noch unerfreulicher ist das dabeistehende, schon
erwähnte große hölzerne Kruzifix. Dieser Christuskopf
mit natürlichen Haaren und Dornen und blutbeschmiertem
Gesichte zeigt freilich höchst meisterhaft das Hinsterben 10
eines Menschen, aber nicht eines gottgebornen Heilands.
Nur das materielle Leiden ist in dieses Gesicht hineinge=
schnitzelt, nicht die Poesie des Schmerzes. Solch Bild
gehört eher in einen anatomischen Lehrsaal als in ein
Gotteshaus. 15

Ich logierte in einem Gasthofe nahe dem Markte, wo
mir das Mittagessen noch besser geschmeckt haben würde,
hätte sich nur nicht der Herr Wirt mit seinem langen,
überflüssigen Gesichte und seinen langweiligen Fragen zu
mir hingesetzt; glücklicherweise ward ich bald erlöst durch 20
die Ankunft eines andern Reisenden, der dieselben Fragen
in derselben Ordnung aushalten mußte: quis?[4] quid? ubi?
quibus auxiliis? cur? quomodo? quando? Dieser Fremde
war ein alter, müder, abgetragener[5] Mann, der, wie aus
seinen Reden hervorging, die ganze Welt durchwandert, 25
besonders lang auf Batavia[6] gelebt, viel Geld erworben
und wieder alles verloren hatte, und jetzt, nach dreißig=

jähriger Abwesenheit, nach Quedlinburg, seiner Vaterstadt,
zurückkehrte, — „denn", setzte er hinzu, „unsere Familie
hat dort ihr Erbbegräbnis". Der Herr Wirt machte die
sehr aufgeklärte[1] Bemerkung, daß es doch für die Seele
5 gleichgültig sei, wo unser Leib begraben wird. „Haben
Sie es schriftlich?" antwortete der Fremde, und dabei
zogen sich unheimlich schlaue Ringe um seine kümmerlichen
Lippen und verblichenen Äugelein. „Aber," setzte er
ängstlich begütigend hinzu, „ich will[2] darum über fremde
10 Gräber doch nichts Böses gesagt haben; — die Türken
begraben ihre Toten noch weit schöner als wir, ihre
Kirchhöfe sind ordentlich[3] Gärten, und da sitzen sie auf
ihren weißen, beturbanten[4] Grabsteinen, unter dem Schat=
ten einer Cypresse, und streichen ihre ernsthaften Bärte
15 und rauchen ruhig ihren türkischen Tabak aus ihren langen
türkischen Pfeifen; — und bei den Chinesen gar[5] ist es
eine ordentliche Lust zuzusehen, wie sie auf den Ruhe=
stätten ihrer Toten manierlich herumtänzeln, und beten,
und Thee trinken, und die Geige spielen, und die geliebten
20 Gräber gar hübsch zu verzieren wissen mit allerlei ver=
goldetem Lattenwerk, Porzellanfigürchen, Fetzen von buntem
Seidenzeug, künstlichen Blumen und farbigen Laternchen —
alles sehr hübsch — wie weit hab' ich noch bis Quedlin=
burg?"

25 Der Kirchhof in Goslar hat mich nicht sehr ange=
sprochen. Desto mehr aber jenes wunderschöne Locken=
köpfchen, das bei meiner Ankunft in der Stadt aus einem

etwas hohen Parterrefenster lächelnd herausschaute. Nach
Tische suchte ich wieder das liebe Fenster; aber jetzt stand
dort nur ein Wasserglas mit weißen Glockenblümchen.
Ich kletterte hinauf, nahm die artigen Blümchen aus dem
Glase, steckte sie ruhig auf meine Mütze und kümmerte 5
mich wenig um die aufgesperrten Mäuler,[1] versteinerten
Nasen und Glotzaugen, womit die Leute auf der Straße,
besonders die alten Weiber, diesem qualifizierten Dieb=
stahle zusahen. Als ich eine Stunde später an demselben
Hause vorbeiging, stand die Holde am Fenster, und wie 10
sie die Glockenblümchen auf meiner Mütze gewahrte, wurde
sie blutrot und stürzte zurück. Ich hatte jetzt das schöne
Antlitz noch genauer gesehen; es war eine süße, durchsich=
tige Verkörperung von Sommerabendhauch, Mondschein,
Nachtigallenlaut und Rosenduft. — Später, als es ganz 15
dunkel geworden, trat sie vor die Türe. Ich kam — ich
näherte mich — sie zieht sich langsam zurück in den dunkeln
Hausflur — ich fasse sie bei der Hand und sage: „Ich bin
ein Liebhaber von schönen Blumen und Küssen, und was
man mir nicht freiwillig gibt, das stehle ich" — und ich 20
küßte sie rasch — und wie sie entfliehen will, flüstere
ich beschwichtigend: „Morgen reis' ich fort und komme
wohl nie wieder" — und ich fühle den geheimen Widerdruck
der lieblichen Lippen und der kleinen Hände — und lachend
eile ich von hinnen. Ja, ich muß lachen, wenn ich bedenke, 25
daß ich unbewußt jene Zauberformel ausgesprochen, wo=
durch unsere Rot= und Blauröcke,[2] öfter als durch ihre

schnurrbärtige Liebenswürdigkeit,¹ die Herzen der Frauen
bezwingen: „Ich reise morgen fort und komme wohl nie
wieder!"

Mein Logis² gewährte eine herrliche Aussicht nach dem
5 Rammelsberg.³ Es war ein schöner Abend. Die Nacht
jagte auf ihrem schwarzen Rosse, und die langen Mähnen
flatterten im Winde. Ich stand am Fenster und betrachtete
den Mond. Gibt es wirklich einen Mann im Monde?
Die Slaven sagen, er heiße Chlotar, und das Wachsen
10 des Mondes bewirke er durch Wasseraufgießen. Als ich
noch klein war, hatte ich gehört, der Mond sei eine
Frucht, die, wenn sie reif geworden, vom lieben Gott ab=
gepflückt und zu den übrigen Vollmonden in den großen
Schrank gelegt werde, der am Ende der Welt steht, wo
15 sie mit Brettern zugenagelt⁴ ist. Als ich größer wurde,
bemerkte ich, daß die Welt nicht so eng begrenzt ist, und
daß der menschliche Geist die hölzernen Schranken durch=
brochen und mit einem riesigen Petrischlüssel,⁵ mit der
Idee der Unsterblichkeit, alle sieben Himmel aufgeschlossen
20 hat. Unsterblichkeit! Schöner Gedanke! Wer hat dich
zuerst erdacht? War es ein Nürnberger Spießbürger,⁶
der, mit weißer Nachtmütze auf dem Kopfe und weißer
Tonpfeife im Maule,⁷ am lauen Sommerabend vor seiner
Haustüre saß und recht behaglich meinte, es wäre doch
25 hübsch, wenn er nun so immerfort, ohne daß sein Pfeif=
chen und sein Lebensatemchen ausgingen, in die liebe
Ewigkeit hineinvegetieren könnte! Oder war es ein junger

Liebender, der in den Armen seiner Geliebten jenen Un=
sterblichkeitsgedanken[1] dachte, und ihn dachte, weil er ihn
fühlte, und weil er nichts anders fühlen und denken
konnte! — Liebe! Unsterblichkeit! — in meiner Brust ward
es plötzlich so heiß, daß ich glaubte, die Geographen hätten
den Äquator verlegt, und er laufe jetzt gerade durch mein
Herz. Und aus meinem Herzen ergossen sich die Gefühle
der Liebe, ergossen sich sehnsüchtig in die weite Nacht.
Die Blumen im Garten unter meinem Fenster dufteten
stärker. Düfte sind die Gefühle der Blumen, und wie
das Menschenherz in der Nacht, wo es sich einsam und
unbelauscht glaubt, stärker fühlt,[2] so scheinen auch die
Blumen sinnig verschämt[3] erst die umhüllende Dunkelheit
zu erwarten, um sich gänzlich ihren Gefühlen hinzugeben
und sie auszuhauchen in süßen Düften. — Ergießt euch,
ihr Düfte meines Herzens! und sucht hinter jenen Bergen
die Geliebte meiner Träume! Sie liegt jetzt schon und
schläft; zu ihren Füßen knieen Engel, und wenn sie im
Schlafe lächelt, so ist es[4] ein Gebet, das die Engel nach=
beten; in ihrer Brust liegt der Himmel mit allen seinen
Seligkeiten, und wenn sie atmet, so bebt mein Herz in
der Ferne; hinter den seidnen Wimpern ihrer Augen ist
die Sonne untergegangen, und wenn sie die Augen wieder
aufschlägt, so ist es Tag, und die Vögel singen, und die
Herdenglöckchen läuten, und die Berge schimmern in ihren
smaragdenen Kleidern, und ich schnüre den Ranzen[5] und
wandre.

In jener Nacht, die ich in Goslar zubrachte, ist mir etwas höchst Seltsames begegnet. Noch immer kann ich nicht ohne Angst daran zurückdenken. Ich bin von Natur nicht ängstlich, aber vor Geistern fürchte ich mich fast so sehr wie der Östreichische Beobachter.[1] Was ist Furcht? Kommt sie aus dem Verstande oder aus dem Gemüt? Über diese Frage disputierte ich so oft mit dem Doktor Saul Ascher,[2] wenn wir zu Berlin, im Café Royal, wo ich lange Zeit meinen Mittagstisch hatte, zufällig zusammentrafen. Er behauptete immer, wir fürchten etwas, weil wir es durch Vernunftschlüsse für furchtbar erkennen. Nur die Vernunft sei eine Kraft, nicht das Gemüt. Während ich gut aß und gut trank, demonstrierte er mir fortwährend die Vorzüge der Vernunft. Gegen das Ende seiner Demonstration pflegte er nach seiner Uhr zu sehen, und immer schloß er damit: „Die Vernunft ist das höchste Prinzip!"[3] — Vernunft! Wenn ich jetzt dieses Wort höre, so sehe ich noch immer den Doktor Saul Ascher mit seinen abstrakten Beinen, mit seinem engen, transcendentalgrauen[4] Leibrock und mit seinem schroffen, frierend kalten Gesichte, das einem Lehrbuche der Geometrie als Kupfertafel dienen konnte. Dieser Mann, tief in den Fünfzigen, war eine personifizierte grade Linie. In seinem Streben nach dem Positiven hatte der arme Mann sich alles Herrliche aus dem Leben heraus= philosophiert, alle Sonnenstrahlen, allen Glauben und alle Blumen, und es blieb ihm nichts übrig als das kalte, positive Grab. Auf den Apoll von Belvedere und auf

das Christentum hatte er eine spezielle Malice. Gegen
letzteres schrieb er sogar eine Broschüre, worin er dessen
Unvernünftigkeit und Unhaltbarkeit bewies. Er hat über=
haupt[1] eine ganze Menge Bücher geschrieben, worin immer
die Vernunft[2] von ihrer eigenen Vortrefflichkeit renommiert, 5
und wobei es der arme Doktor gewiß ernsthaft genug meinte
und also in dieser Hinsicht alle Achtung verdiente. Darin
aber bestand ja eben der Hauptspaß, daß er ein so ernsthaft
närrisches Gesicht schnitt, wenn er dasjenige nicht begreifen
konnte, was jedes Kind begreift, eben weil es ein Kind ist. 10
Als ich ihn einst besuchen wollte, sagte mir sein Bedienter:
„Der Herr Doktor ist eben gestorben." Ich fühlte nicht
viel mehr dabei, als wenn er gesagt hätte: „Der Herr
Doktor ist ausgezogen."

Doch zurück nach Goslar. „Das höchste Prinzip ist die 15
Vernunft!" sagte ich beschwichtigend zu mir selbst, als ich
ins Bett stieg. - Indessen, es half nicht. Ich hatte eben in
Varnhagen von Enses[3] „Deutsche Erzählungen," die ich von
Klaustal mitgenommen hatte, jene entsetzliche Geschichte[4]
gelesen, wie der Sohn, den sein eigener Vater ermorden 20
wollte, in der Nacht von dem Geiste seiner toten Mutter
gewarnt wird. Die wunderbare Darstellung dieser Geschichte
bewirkte, daß mich während des Lesens ein inneres Grauen
durchfröstelte. Auch[5] erregen Gespenstererzählungen ein
noch schauerlicheres Gefühl, wenn man sie auf der Reise 25
liest, und zumal des Nachts,[6] in einer Stadt, in einem
Hause, in einem Zimmer, wo man noch nie gewesen.

Wie viel Gräßliches mag sich schon zugetragen haben auf
diesem Flecke, wo du eben liegst? so denkt man unwillkürlich.
Überdies schien jetzt der Mond so zweideutig ins Zimmer
herein, an der Wand bewegten sich allerlei unberufene
5 Schatten, und als ich mich im Bett aufrichtete, um hinzusehen,
erblickte ich —

Es gibt nichts Unheimlicheres, als wenn man bei Mond=
schein das eigene Gesicht zufällig im Spiegel sieht. In
demselben Augenblicke schlug eine schwerfällige, gähnende
10 Glocke, und zwar[1] so lang und langsam, daß ich nach dem
zwölften Glockenschlage sicher glaubte, es seien unterdessen
volle[2] zwölf Stunden verflossen, und es müßte wieder von
vorn anfangen, zwölf zu schlagen.   Zwischen dem vorletzten
und letzten Glockenschlage schlug noch eine andere Uhr, sehr
15 rasch, fast keifend gell, und vielleicht ärgerlich über die
Langsamkeit ihrer Frau Gevatterin.   Als beide eiserne
Zungen schwiegen, und tiefe Todesstille im ganzen Hause
herrschte, war es mir plötzlich, als hörte ich auf dem Kor=
ridor, vor meinem Zimmer, etwas schlottern und schlappen,
20 wie der unsichere Gang eines alten Mannes.   Endlich öffnete
sich meine Tür, und langsam trat herein der verstorbene
Doktor Saul Ascher.   Ein kaltes Fieber rieselte mir durch
Mark und Bein, ich zitterte wie Espenlaub, und kaum wagte
ich das Gespenst anzusehen.   Er sah aus wie sonst, derselbe
25 transcendentalgraue Leibrock, dieselben abstrakten Beine und
dasselbe mathematische Gesicht; nur war dieses etwas gelb=
licher als sonst, auch der Mund, der sonst zwei Winkel[3] von

22½ Grab bildete, war zusammengekniffen, und die Augen=
kreise hatten einen größern Radius. Schwankend und wie
sonst sich auf sein spanisches Röhrchen stützend, näherte er
sich mir, und in seinem gewöhnlichen mundfaulen Dialekte[1]
sprach er freundlich: „Fürchten Sie sich nicht, und glauben 5
Sie nicht, daß ich ein Gespenst sei. Es ist Täuschung Ihrer
Phantasie, wenn Sie mich als Gespenst zu sehen glauben.
Was ist ein Gespenst? Geben Sie mir eine Definition.
Deduzieren Sie mir die Bedingungen der Möglichkeit[2] eines
Gespenstes. In welchem vernünftigen Zusammenhange stände 10
eine solche Erscheinung mit der Vernunft? Die Vernunft,
ich sage die Vernunft —“ Und nun schritt das Gespenst
zu einer Analyse der Vernunft, citierte Kants „Kritik der
reinen Vernunft,“ 2. Teil, 1. Abschnitt, 2. Buch, 3. Haupt=
stück,[3] die Unterscheidung von Phänomena und Noumena,[3] 15
konstruierte alsdann den problematischen Gespensterglauben,
setzte einen Syllogismus auf den andern und schloß mit
dem logischen Beweise, daß es durchaus keine Gespenster
gibt. Mir unterdessen lief der kalte Schweiß über den
Rücken, meine Zähne klapperten wie Kastagnetten, und aus 20
Seelenangst nickte ich unbedingte Zustimmung bei jedem Satz,
womit der spukende Doktor die Absurdität aller Gespenster=
furcht bewies. „Die Vernunft ist das höchste —“ da schlug
die Glocke eins, und das Gespenst verschwand.

Von Goslar ging ich den andern Morgen weiter, halb 25
auf Geratewohl, halb in der Absicht, den Bruder des Klaus=
taler Bergmanns aufzusuchen. Wieder schönes, liebes Sonn=

tagswetter. Ich bestieg Hügel und Berge, betrachtete, wie
die Sonne den Nebel zu verscheuchen suchte, wanderte freudig
durch die schauernden Wälder, und um mein träumendes
Haupt klingelten die Glockenblümchen[1] von Goslar. In
5 ihren weißen Nachtmänteln standen die Berge, die Tannen
rüttelten sich den Schlaf aus den Gliedern, der frische
Morgenwind frisierte ihnen die herabhängenden, grünen
Haare, die Vöglein hielten Betstunde, das Wiesental blitzte
wie eine diamantenbesäete Golddecke, und der Hirt schritt
10 darüber hin mit seiner läutenden Herde. Ich mochte[2]
mich wohl eigentlich verirrt haben. Man schlägt immer
Seitenwege und Fußsteige ein und glaubt dadurch näher[3]
zum Ziele zu gelangen. Wie im Leben überhaupt,[4] geht's
uns auch auf dem Harze. Aber es gibt immer gute Seelen,
15 die uns wieder auf den rechten Weg bringen; sie tun es
gern und finden noch obendrein ein besonderes Vergnügen
daran, wenn sie uns mit selbstgefälliger Miene und wohl=
wollend[5] lauter Stimme bedeuten, welche große[6] Umwege
wir gemacht, in welche Abgründe und Sümpfe wir versinken
20 konnten, und welch ein Glück es sei, daß wir so wegkundige
Leute, wie sie sind, noch zeitig angetroffen. Einen solchen
Berichtiger fand ich unweit der Harzburg. Es war ein
wohlgenährter Bürger von Goslar, ein glänzend wampiges,
dummkluges Gesicht; er sah aus, als habe er die Viehseuche
25 erfunden. Wir gingen eine Strecke zusammen, und er er=
zählte mir allerlei Spukgeschichten, die hübsch klingen konnten,[7]
wenn sie nicht alle darauf hinausliefen, daß es doch kein

wirklicher Spuk gewesen, sondern daß die weiße Gestalt
ein Wilddieb war, und daß die wimmernden Stimmen[1]
von den eben geworfenen Jungen[2] einer Bache (wilden
Sau), und das Geräusch auf dem Boden von der Hauskatze
herrührte. Nur wenn der Mensch krank ist, setzte er hinzu, 5
glaubt er Gespenster zu sehen; was aber seine Wenigkeit
anbelange,[3] so sei er selten krank, nur zuweilen leide er an
Hautübeln, und dann kuriere er sich jedesmal mit nüchternem[4]
Speichel. Er machte mich auch aufmerksam auf die Zweckmäßigkeit und Nützlichkeit in der Natur.[5] Die Bäume sind 10
grün, weil Grün gut für die Augen ist. Ich gab ihm recht
und fügte hinzu, daß Gott das Rindvieh erschaffen, weil
Fleischsuppen den Menschen stärken, daß er die Esel erschaffen, damit sie den Menschen zu Vergleichungen dienen
können, und daß er den Menschen selbst erschaffen, damit 15
er Fleischsuppen essen und kein Esel sein soll. Mein Begleiter
war entzückt, einen Gleichgestimmten gefunden zu haben, sein
Antlitz erglänzte noch freudiger, und bei dem Abschiede
war er gerührt.

Solange er neben mir ging, war gleichsam die ganze 20
Natur entzaubert, sobald er aber fort war, fingen die Bäume
wieder an zu sprechen, und die Sonnenstrahlen erklangen
und die Wiesenblümchen tanzten, und der blaue Himmel
umarmte die grüne Erde. Ja, ich weiß es besser: Gott
hat den Menschen erschaffen, damit er die Herrlichkeit der 25
Welt bewundere. Jeder Autor, und sei er noch so groß,[6]
wünscht, daß sein Werk gelobt werde. Und in der Bibel,

den Memoiren Gottes, steht ausdrücklich, daß er die Menschen
erschaffen zu seinem Ruhm und Preis.

Nach einem langen Hin= und Herwandern gelangte ich
zu der Wohnung des Bruders meines Klaustaler Freundes,
5 übernachtete alldort und erlebte folgendes schöne Gedicht:

I

Auf dem Berge steht die Hütte,
Wo der alte Bergmann wohnt;
Dorten rauscht die grüne Tanne,
Und erglänzt der goldne Mond.

10 In der Hütte steht ein Lehnstuhl,
Reich geschnitzt und wunderlich,
Der darauf sitzt, der ist glücklich,
Und der Glückliche bin Ich!

Auf dem Schemel sitzt die Kleine,
15 Stützt den Arm auf meinen Schoß;
Äuglein wie zwei blaue Sterne,
Mündlein wie die Purpurros'.

Und die lieben, blauen Sterne
Schaun mich an so himmelgroß,
20 Und sie legt den Lilienfinger
Schalkhaft auf die Purpurros'.

Nein, es sieht uns nicht die Mutter,
Denn sie spinnt mit großem Fleiß,
Und der Vater spielt die Zither,
25 Und er singt die alte Weis'.[1]

Und die Kleine flüstert leise,
Leise, mit gedämpftem Laut;
Manches wichtige Geheimnis
Hat sie mir schon anvertraut.

„Aber seit die Muhme tot ist,
Können wir ja nicht mehr gehn
Nach dem Schützenhof[1] zu Goslar,
Und dort ist es gar zu schön.

„Hier dagegen ist es einsam,
Auf der kalten Bergeshöh',
Und des Winters sind wir gänzlich
Wie vergraben in dem Schnee.

„Und ich bin ein banges Mädchen,
Und ich fürcht' mich wie ein Kind   10
Vor den bösen Bergesgeistern,
Die des Nachts geschäftig sind."

Plötzlich schweigt die liebe Kleine,
Wie vom eignen Wort erschreckt,
Und sie hat mit beiden Händchen   15
Ihre Äugelein bedeckt.

Lauter rauscht die Tanne draußen,
Und das Spinnrad schnarrt und brummt,
Und die Zither klingt dazwischen,
Und die alte Weise summt: 20

„Fürcht' dich nicht, du liebes Kindchen,
Vor der bösen Geister Macht;
Tag und Nacht, du liebes Kindchen,
Halten Englein bei dir Wacht!"

II

Tannenbaum, mit grünen Fingern,   25
Pocht ans niedre Fensterlein,
Und der Mond, der gelbe Lauscher,
Wirft sein süßes Licht herein.

Vater, Mutter schnarchen leise
In dem nahen Schlafgemach,   30
Doch wir beide, selig schwatzend,
Halten uns einander[2] wach.

„Daß du gar[1] zu oft gebetet,
Das zu glauben wird mir schwer,
Jenes Zucken deiner Lippen
Kommt wohl nicht vom Beten her.

5 „Jenes böse, kalte Zucken,[2]
Das erschreckt mich jedesmal,
Doch die dunkle Angst beschwichtigt
Deiner Augen frommer Strahl.

„Auch bezweifl' ich, daß du glaubest,
10 Was so rechter Glauben heißt,[3]
Glaubst wohl nicht an Gott den Vater,
An den Sohn und heil'gen Geist?"

„Ach, mein Kindchen, schon als Knabe,
Als ich saß auf Mutters[4] Schoß,
15 Glaubte ich an Gott den Vater,
Der da waltet[5] gut und groß;

„Der die schöne Erd' erschaffen,
Und die schönen Menschen drauf,
Der den Sonnen, Monden, Sternen
20 Vorgezeichnet ihren Lauf.

„Als ich größer wurde, Kindchen,
Noch viel mehr begriff ich schon,
Und begriff, und ward vernünftig,
Und ich glaub'[6] auch an den Sohn;

25 „An den lieben Sohn, der liebend
Uns die Liebe offenbart,
Und zum Lohne, wie gebräuchlich,
Von dem Volk gekreuzigt ward.

„Jetzo,[7] da ich ausgewachsen,
30 Viel gelesen, viel gereist,
Schwillt mein Herz, und ganz von Herzen
Glaub' ich an den heil'gen Geist.[8]

„Dieser tat die größten Wunder,
Und viel größre tut er noch;
Er zerbrach die Zwingherrnburgen,
Und zerbrach des Knechtes Joch.

„Alte Todeswunden heilt er   5
Und erneut das alte Recht:
Alle Menschen, gleichgeboren,
Sind ein adliges Geschlecht.

„Er verscheucht die bösen Nebel,
Und das dunkle Hirngespinst,[1]   10
Das uns Lieb' und Lust verleidet,
Tag und Nacht uns angegrinst.

„Tausend Ritter, wohl gewappnet,[2]
Hat der heil'ge Geist erwählt,
Seinen Willen zu erfüllen,   15
Und er hat sie mutbeseelt.

„Ihre teuern Schwerter blitzen,
Ihre guten Banner wehn;
Ei, du möchtest wohl, mein Kindchen,
Solche stolze[3] Ritter sehn?   20

„Nun, so schau mich an, mein Kindchen,
Küsse mich und schaue dreist;
Denn ich selber bin ein solcher
Ritter von dem heil'gen Geist."[4]

III

Still versteckt der Mond sich draußen   25
Hinterm grünen Tannenbaum,
Und im Zimmer unsre Lampe
Flackert matt und leuchtet kaum.

Aber meine blauen Sterne
Strahlen auf in hellerm Licht,   30
Und es glüht die Purpurrose,
Und das liebe Mädchen spricht:

„Kleines Völkchen, Wichtelmännchen,
Stehlen unſer Brot und Speck,
Abends liegt es noch im Kaſten,
Und des Morgens iſt es weg.[1]

„Kleines Völkchen, unſre Sahne
Naſcht es von der Milch und läßt
Unbedeckt die Schüſſel ſtehen,
Und die Katze ſäuft den Reſt.

„Und die Katz' iſt eine Hexe,
Denn ſie ſchleicht, bei Nacht und Sturm,
Drüben nach dem Geiſterberge,[2]
Nach dem altverfallnen Turm.

„Dort hat einſt ein Schloß geſtanden,
Voller[3] Luſt und Waffenglanz;
Blanke Ritter, Fraun und Knappen
Schwangen ſich im Fackeltanz.[4]

„Da verwünſchte Schloß und Leute
Eine böſe Zauberin,
Nur die Trümmer blieben ſtehen,
Und die Eulen niſten drin.

„Doch die ſel'ge Muhme[5] ſagte:
Wenn man ſpricht das rechte Wort,
Nächtlich zu der rechten Stunde,
Drüben an dem rechten Ort,

„So verwandeln ſich die Trümmer
Wieder in ein helles Schloß.
Und es tanzen wieder luſtig
Ritter, Fraun und Knappentroß;

„Und wer jenes Wort geſprochen,
Dem gehören Schloß und Leut',
Pauken und Trompeten huld'gen
Seiner jungen Herrlichkeit."

Also blühen Märchenbilder
Aus des Mundes Röselein,
Und die Augen gießen drüber
Ihren blauen Sternenschein.[1]

Ihre goldnen Haare wickelt   5
Mir die Kleine um die Händ',
Gibt den Fingern hübsche Namen,[2]
Lacht und küßt, und schweigt am End'.

Und im stillen Zimmer alles
Blickt mich an so wohlvertraut;   10
Tisch und Schrank, mir ist, als hätt' ich
Sie schon früher mal geschaut.

Freundlich ernsthaft schwatzt die Wanduhr,
Und die Zither, hörbar kaum,
Fängt von selber an zu klingen,   15
Und ich sitze wie im Traum.

„Jetzo ist die rechte Stunde,
Und es ist der rechte Ort;
Staunen würdest du, mein Kindchen,
Spräch' ich aus das rechte Wort.   20

„Sprech' ich jenes Wort, so dämmert
Und erbebt die Mitternacht,
Bach und Tannen brausen lauter,
Und der alte Berg erwacht.

„Zitherklang und Zwergenlieder   25
Tönen aus des Berges Spalt,
Und es sprießt, wie'n toller Frühling,
Draus hervor ein Blumenwald;

„Blumen, kühne Wunderblumen,
Blätter, breit und fabelhaft,   30
Duftig bunt und hastig regsam,[3]
Wie gedrängt von Leidenschaft.

„Rosen, wild wie rote Flammen,
Sprühn aus dem Gewühl hervor;
Lilien, wie kristallne Pfeiler,
Schießen himmelhoch empor.

5 „Und die Sterne, groß wie Sonnen,
Schaun herab mit Sehnsuchtglut;
In der Lilien Riesenkelche
Strömet ihre Strahlenflut.

„Doch wir selber, süßes Kindchen,
10 Sind verwandelt noch viel mehr;
Fackelglanz und Gold und Seide
Schimmern lustig um uns her.

„Du, du wurdest¹ zur Prinzessin,
Diese Hütte ward zum Schloß,
15 Und da jubeln und da tanzen
Ritter, Fraun und Knappentroß.

„Aber ich, ich hab' erworben
Dich und alles, Schloß und Leut';
Pauken und Trompeten huld'gen
20 Meiner jungen Herrlichkeit!"

Die Sonne ging auf. Die Nebel flohen wie Gespenster
beim dritten Hahnenschrei. Ich stieg wieder bergauf und
bergab, und vor mir schwebte die schöne Sonne, immer neue
Schönheiten beleuchtend. Der Geist des Gebirges begün=
25 stigte mich ganz offenbar; er wußte wohl, daß so ein Dichter=
mensch viel Hübsches wieder erzählen kann, und er ließ
mich diesen Morgen seinen Harz sehen, wie ihn gewiß nicht
jeder sah. Aber auch mich sah der Harz, wie mich nur
wenige gesehen,² in meinen Augenwimpern flimmerten ebenso
30 kostbare Perlen wie in den Gräsern des Tals. Morgentau
der Liebe feuchtete meine Wangen, die rauschenden Tannen

verstanden mich, ihre Zweige taten sich voneinander, bewegten
sich herauf und herab, gleich stummen Menschen, die mit
den Händen ihre Freude bezeigen, und in der Ferne klang's
wunderbar geheimnisvoll, wie Glockengeläute einer verlornen
Waldkirche.[1] Man sagt, das seien die Herdenglöckchen,   5
die im Harz so lieblich, klar und rein gestimmt sind.

Nach dem Stand der Sonne war es Mittag, als ich auf
eine solche Herde stieß, und der Hirt, ein freundlich blonder
junger Mensch, sagte mir, der große Berg, an dessen Fuß
ich stände, sei der alte, weltberühmte Brocken.[2] Viele Stun= 10
den ringsum liegt kein Haus, und ich war froh genug, daß
mich der junge Mensch einlud, mit ihm zu essen. Wir setzten
uns nieder zu einem déjeuner dînatoire,[3] das aus Käse
und Brot bestand; die Schäfchen erhaschten die Krumen,
die lieben, blanken Kühlein sprangen um uns herum und   15
klingelten schelmisch mit ihren Glöckchen und lachten uns an
mit ihren großen, vergnügten Augen. Wir tafelten recht
königlich; überhaupt schien mir mein Wirt ein echter König,
und weil er bis jetzt der einzige König ist, der mir Brot
gegeben hat,[4] so will ich ihn auch königlich besingen.   20

Köng ist der Hirtenknabe,
Grüner Hügel ist sein Thron,
Über seinem Haupt die Sonne
Ist die schwere, goldne Kron'.

Ihm zu Füßen liegen Schafe,   25
Weiche Schmeichler, rotbekreuzt;[5]
Kavaliere sind die Kälber,
Und sie wandeln stolz gespreizt.

Hofschauspieler sind die Böcklein,
Und die Vögel und die Küh',
Mit den Flöten, mit den Glöcklein,
Sind die Kammermusici.[1]

5   Und das klingt und singt so lieblich,
Und so lieblich rauschen drein
Wasserfall und Tannenbäume,
Und der König schlummert ein.

Unterdessen muß regieren
10   Der Minister, jener Hund,
Dessen knurriges Gebelle
Widerhallet in der Rund'.

Schläfrig lallt der junge König:
„Das Regieren ist so schwer,
15   Ach, ich wollt', daß ich zu Hause
Schon bei meiner Kön'gin wär'!

„In den Armen meiner Kön'gin
Ruht mein Königshaupt so weich,
Und in ihren lieben Augen
20   Liegt mein unermeßlich Reich!"

Wir nahmen freundschaftlich Abschied, und fröhlich stieg ich den Berg hinauf. Bald empfing mich eine Waldung himmelhoher Tannen, für die ich in jeder Hinsicht Respekt habe. Diesen Bäumen ist nämlich das Wachsen nicht so ganz
25 leicht gemacht worden, und sie haben es sich in der Jugend sauer werden lassen.[2] Der Berg ist hier mit vielen großen Granitblöcken übersäet, und die meisten Bäume mußten mit ihren Wurzeln diese Steine umranken oder sprengen, und mühsam den Boden suchen, woraus sie Nahrung schöpfen
30 können. Hier und da liegen die Steine, gleichsam ein Tor

bildend, übereinander, und oben darauf stehen die Bäume,
die nackten Wurzeln über jene Steinpforte hinziehend und
erst am Fuße derselben den Boden erfassend, so daß sie
in der freien Luft zu wachsen scheinen. Und doch haben
sie sich zu jener gewaltigen Höhe emporgeschwungen, und 5
mit den umklammerten Steinen wie zusammengewachsen,
stehen sie fester als ihre bequemen Kollegen im zahmen
Forstboden des flachen Landes. So stehen auch im Leben
jene großen Männer, die durch das Überwinden früher
Hemmungen und Hindernisse sich erst recht[1] gestärkt und 10
befestigt haben. Auf den Zweigen der Tannen kletterten
Eichhörnchen, und unter denselben spazierten die gelben
Hirsche. Wenn ich solch ein liebes, edles Tier sehe, so kann
ich nicht begreifen, wie gebildete Leute Vergnügen daran
finden, es zu hetzen und zu töten. Solch ein Tier war 15
barmherziger als die Menschen, und säugte den schmachtenden
Schmerzenreich der heiligen Genoveva.[2]

Allerliebst schossen die goldenen Sonnenlichter durch das
dichte Tannengrün. Eine natürliche Treppe bildeten die
Baumwurzeln. Überall schwellende Moosbänke; denn die 20
Steine sind fußhoch von den schönsten Moosarten, wie mit
hellgrünen Sammetpolstern, bewachsen. Liebliche Kühle
und träumerisches Quellengemurmel. Hier und da sieht
man, wie das Wasser unter den Steinen silberhell hinrieselt
und die nackten Baumwurzeln und Fasern bespült. Wenn 25
man sich nach[3] diesem Treiben hinabbeugt, so belauscht man
gleichsam die geheime Bildungsgeschichte der Pflanzen und

das ruhige Herzklopfen des Berges. An manchen Orten
sprudelt das Wasser aus den Steinen und Wurzeln stärker
hervor und bildet kleine Kaskaden. Da läßt sich gut sitzen.¹
Es murmelt und rauscht so wunderbar, die Vögel singen
5 abgebrochene Sehnsuchtslaute, die Bäume flüstern wie mit
tausend Mädchenzungen, wie mit tausend Mädchenaugen²
schauen uns an die seltsamen Bergblumen, sie strecken nach
uns aus die wundersam breiten, drollig gezackten Blätter,
spielend flimmern hin und her die lustigen Sonnenstrahlen,
10 die sinnigen Kräutlein erzählen sich grüne Märchen, es ist
alles wie verzaubert, es wird immer heimlicher und heim=
licher, ein uralter Traum wird lebendig, die Geliebte erscheint
— ach, daß sie so schnell wieder verschwindet!

Je höher man den Berg hinaufsteigt, desto kürzer, zwerg=
15 hafter werden die Tannen, sie scheinen immer mehr und
mehr zusammenzuschrumpfen, bis nur Heidelbeer= und Rot=
beersträuche und Bergkräuter übrig bleiben. Da wird es
auch schon fühlbar kälter. Die wunderlichen Gruppen der
Granitblöcke werden hier erst recht³ sichtbar; diese sind oft
20 von erstaunlicher Größe. Das mögen wohl die Spielbälle
sein, die sich die bösen Geister einander⁴ zuwerfen in der
Walpurgisnacht,⁵ wenn hier die Hexen auf Besenstielen und
Mistgabeln einhergeritten kommen, und die abenteuerlich
verruchte Lust beginnt, wie die glaubhafte Amme es erzählt,
25 und wie es zu schauen ist auf den hübschen Faustbildern des
Meister Retzsch.⁶ Ja, ein junger Dichter, der auf einer
Reise⁷ von Berlin nach Göttingen in der ersten Mainacht am

Brocken vorbeiritt, bemerkte sogar, wie einige belletristische Damen auf einer Bergecke ihre ästhetische Theegesellschaft hielten, sich gemütlich die „Abendzeitung"[1] vorlasen, ihre poetischen Ziegenböckchen, die meckernd den Theetisch um= hüpften, als Universalgenies priesen und über alle Erschei= nungen in der deutschen Litteratur ihr Endurteil fällten; doch, als sie auch auf den „Ratcliff" und „Almansor"[2] gerieten und dem Verfasser alle Frömmigkeit und Christlichkeit ab= sprachen, da sträubte sich das Haar des jungen Mannes, Entsetzen ergriff ihn — ich gab dem Pferde die Sporen und jagte vorüber.

In der Tat, wenn man die obere Hälfte des Brockens besteigt, kann man sich nicht erwehren, an die ergötzlichen Blocksbergsgeschichten[3] zu denken, und besonders an die große, mystische, deutsche Nationaltragödie vom Doktor Faust.[4] Mir war immer, als ob der Pferdefuß[5] neben mir hinaufklettere, und jemand humoristisch Atem schöpfe. Und ich glaube, auch Mephisto muß mit Mühe Atem holen, wenn er seinen Lieblingsberg ersteigt; es ist ein äußerst erschöpfender Weg, und ich war froh, als ich endlich das langersehnte Brockenhaus zu Gesicht bekam.

Dieses Haus, das, wie durch vielfache Abbildungen be= kannt ist, bloß aus einem Parterre besteht und auf der Spitze des Berges liegt, wurde erst 1800 vom Grafen Stolberg=Wernigerode[6] erbaut, für dessen Rechnung es auch als Wirtshaus verwaltet wird. Die Mauern sind erstaunlich dick, wegen des Windes und der Kälte im

Winter; das Dach ist niedrig, in der Mitte desselben
steht eine turmartige Warte, und bei dem Hause liegen
noch zwei kleine Nebengebäude, wovon das eine in frühern
Zeiten den Brockenbesuchern zum Obdach diente.

5 Der Eintritt in das Brockenhaus erregte bei mir eine
etwas ungewöhnliche, märchenhafte Empfindung.[1] Man ist
nach einem langen, einsamen Umhersteigen durch Tannen
und Klippen plötzlich in ein Wolkenhaus versetzt; Städte,
Berge und Wälder blieben unten liegen, und oben findet
10 man eine wunderlich zusammengesetzte, fremde Gesellschaft,
von welcher man, wie es an dergleichen Orten natürlich
ist, fast wie ein erwarteter Genosse, halb neugierig und
halb gleichgültig, empfangen wird. Ich fand das Haus
voller[2] Gäste, und wie es einem klugen Manne geziemt,
15 dachte ich schon an die Nacht, an die Unbehaglichkeit eines
Strohlagers; mit hinsterbender Stimme verlangte ich gleich
Thee, und der Herr Brockenwirt war vernünftig genug,
einzusehen, daß ich kranker Mensch für die Nacht ein ordent=
liches Bett haben müsse. Dieses verschaffte er mir in
20 einem engen Zimmerchen, wo schon ein junger Kaufmann
sich etabliert hatte.

In der Wirtsstube fand ich lauter Leben und Bewegung.
Studenten von verschiedenen Universitäten. Die einen sind
kurz vorher angekommen und restaurieren sich, andere be=
25 reiten sich zum Abmarsch, schnüren ihre Ranzen, schreiben
ihre Namen ins Gedächtnisbuch, erhalten Brockensträuße[3]
von den Hausmädchen; da wird in die Wangen gekniffen,[4]

gesungen, gesprungen, gejohlt, man fragt, man antwortet,
gut Wetter, Fußweg,[1] Prosit,[2] Abieu. Einige der Abgehen=
den sind auch etwas angesoffen, und diese haben von der
schönen Aussicht einen doppelten Genuß,[3] da ein Betrunkener
alles doppelt sieht.   5

Nachdem ich mich ziemlich refreiert,[4] bestieg ich die Turm=
warte und fand daselbst einen kleinen Herrn mit zwei
Damen, einer jungen und einer ältlichen. Die junge Dame
war sehr schön. Eine herrliche Gestalt, auf dem lockigen
Haupte ein helmartiger, schwarzer Atlashut, mit dessen 10
weißen Federn die Winde spielten, die schlanken Glieder
von einem schwarzseidenen Mantel so fest umschlossen, daß
die edlen Formen hervortraten, und das freie, große Auge
ruhig hinabschauend in die freie, große Welt.

Als ich noch ein Knabe war, dachte ich an nichts als an 15
Zauber= und Wundergeschichten, und jede schöne Dame, die
Straußfedern auf dem Kopfe trug, hielt ich für eine Elfen=
königin. Jetzt denke ich anders, seit ich aus der Natur=
geschichte weiß, daß jene symbolischen Federn von dem
dümmsten Vogel herkommen. Hätte ich mit jenen Knaben= 20
augen die erwähnte junge Schöne, in erwähnter Stellung,
auf dem Brocken gesehen, so würde ich sicher gedacht haben:
Das ist die Fee des Berges, und sie hat eben den Zauber
ausgesprochen, wodurch dort unten alles so wunderbar er=
scheint. Ja, in hohem Grade wunderbar erscheint uns 25
alles beim ersten Hinabschauen vom Brocken, alle Seiten
unseres Geistes empfangen neue Eindrücke, und diese, mei=

stens verschiedenartig, sogar sich widersprechend,[1] verbinden
sich in unserer Seele zu einem großen, noch unentwor=
renen,[2] unverstandenen Gefühl. Gelingt es uns, dieses
Gefühl in seinem Begriffe[3] zu erfassen, so erkennen wir
5 den Charakter des Berges. Dieser Charakter ist ganz
deutsch, sowohl in Hinsicht seiner Fehler, als auch seiner
Vorzüge. Der Brocken ist ein Deutscher. Mit deutscher
Gründlichkeit zeigt er uns, klar und deutlich, wie ein
Riesenpanorama, die vielen hundert Städte, Städtchen und
10 Dörfer, die meistens nördlich liegen, und ringsum alle
Berge, Wälder, Flüsse, Flächen, unendlich weit. Aber eben
dadurch erscheint alles wie eine scharf gezeichnete, rein illu=
minierte Spezialkarte,[4] nirgends wird das Auge durch
eigentlich schöne Landschaften erfreut; wie es denn[5] immer
15 geschieht, daß wir deutschen Kompilatoren wegen der ehr=
lichen Genauigkeit, womit wir alles und alles hingeben
wollen, nie daran denken können, das Einzelne auf eine
schöne Weise zu geben. Der Berg hat auch so etwas
Deutschruhiges, Verständiges, Tolerantes;[6] eben weil er
20 die Dinge so weit und klar überschauen kann. Und wenn
solch ein Berg seine Riesenaugen öffnet, mag er wohl noch
etwas mehr sehen als wir Zwerge, die wir mit unsern
blöden Äuglein auf ihm herumklettern. Viele wollen zwar
behaupten, der Brocken sei sehr philiströse,[7] und Claudius[8]
25 sang: „Der Blocksberg ist der lange Herr Philister!" Aber
das ist Irrtum. Durch seinen Kahlkopf, den er zuweilen
mit einer weißen Nebelkappe bedeckt,[9] gibt er sich zwar

einen Anstrich von Philiströsität;[1] aber, wie bei manchen
andern großen Deutschen, geschieht es aus purer Ironie.[2]
Es ist sogar notorisch, daß der Brocken seine burschikosen,
phantastischen Zeiten hat, z. B. die erste Mainacht.[3] Dann
wirft er seine Nebelkappe jubelnd in die Lüfte und wird, 5
ebensogut wie wir übrigen, recht echtdeutsch[4] romantisch
verrückt.

Ich suchte gleich die schöne Dame in ein Gespräch zu
verflechten; denn Naturschönheiten genießt man erst recht,[5]
wenn man sich auf der Stelle darüber aussprechen kann. 10
Sie war nicht geistreich, aber aufmerksam sinnig. Wahr=
haft vornehme Formen.[6] Ich meine nicht die gewöhnliche,
steife, negative Vornehmheit, die genau weiß, was unter=
lassen werden muß, sondern jene seltnere, freie, positive
Vornehmheit, die uns genau sagt, was wir tun dürfen, und 15
die uns bei aller Unbefangenheit die höchste gesellige
Sicherheit gibt. Ich entwickelte, zu meiner eigenen Verwun=
derung, viele geographische Kenntnisse, nannte der wißbe=
gierigen Schönen[7] alle Namen der Städte, die vor uns
lagen, suchte und zeigte ihr dieselben auf meiner Land= 20
karte, die ich über den Steintisch, der in der Mitte der
Turmplatte steht, mit echter Dozentenmiene ausbreitete.
Manche Stadt konnte ich nicht finden, vielleicht weil ich
mehr mit den Fingern suchte als mit den Augen, die sich
unterdessen auf dem Gesicht der holden Dame orientierten 25
und dort schönere Partien fanden, als „Schierke" und
„Elend."[8] Dieses Gesicht gehörte zu denen, die nie reizen,

selten entzücken, und immer gefallen. Ich liebe solche
Gesichter, weil sie mein schlimmbewegtes[1] Herz zur Ruhe
lächeln.

In welchem Verhältnis der kleine Herr, der die Damen
5 begleitete, zu denselben stehen mochte, konnte ich nicht
erraten. Es war eine dünne, merkwürdige Figur. Ein
Köpfchen, sparsam bedeckt mit grauen Härchen, die über
die kurze Stirn bis an die grünlichen Libellenaugen reich=
ten, die runde Nase weit hervortretend, dagegen Mund
10 und Kinn sich wieder ängstlich nach den Ohren zurück=
ziehend. Dieses Gesichtchen schien aus einem zarten, gelb=
lichen Tone zu bestehen, woraus die Bildhauer ihre ersten
Modelle kneten; und wenn die schmalen Lippen zusammen=
kniffen, zogen sich über die Wangen einige tausend halb=
15 kreisartige, feine Fältchen. Der kleine Mann sprach kein
Wort, und nur dann und wann, wenn die ältere Dame
ihm etwas Freundliches zuflüsterte, lächelte er wie ein
Mops, der den Schnupfen hat.

Jene ältere Dame war die Mutter der jüngeren, und
20 auch sie besaß die vornehmsten Formen. Ihr Auge verriet
einen krankhaft schwärmerischen Tiefsinn, um ihren Mund
lag strenge Frömmigkeit, doch schien mir's, als ob er einst
sehr schön gewesen sei und viel gelacht und viele Küsse
empfangen und viele erwidert habe. Ihr Gesicht glich
25 einem codex palimpsestus,[2] wo unter der neuschwarzen
Mönchsschrift eines Kirchenvatertextes die halberloschenen
Verse eines altgriechischen Liebesdichters hervorlauschen.

Beide Damen waren mit ihrem Begleiter dieses Jahr in
Italien gewesen und erzählten mir allerlei Schönes von
Rom, Florenz und Venedig. Die Mutter erzählte viel
von den Raphaelschen Bildern in der Peterskirche;[1] die
Tochter sprach mehr von der Oper im Theater Fenice.[2]   5

Derweilen wir sprachen, begann es zu dämmern; die
Luft wurde noch kälter, die Sonne neigte sich tiefer, und
die Turmplatte füllte sich mit Studenten, Handwerksbur=
schen und einigen ehrsamen Bürgerleuten samt deren Ehe=
frauen und Töchtern, die alle den Sonnenuntergang sehen 10
wollten. Es ist ein erhabener Anblick, der die Seele zum
Gebet stimmt. Wohl eine Viertelstunde standen alle
ernsthaft schweigend und sahen, wie der schöne Feuerball
im Westen allmählich versank; die Gesichter wurden vom
Abendrot angestrahlt, die Hände falteten sich unwillkürlich; 15
es war, als ständen wir, eine stille Gemeinde, im Schiffe
eines Riesendoms, und der Priester erhöbe jetzt den Leib
des Herrn,[3] und von der Orgel herab ergösse sich Palestri=
nas[4] ewiger Choral.

Während ich so in Andacht versunken stehe, höre ich, 20
daß neben mir jemand ausruft: „Wie ist die Natur doch
im allgemeinen so schön!"[5] Diese Worte kamen aus der
gefühlvollen Brust meines Zimmergenossen, des jungen
Kaufmanns. Ich gelangte dadurch wieder zu meiner
Werkeltagsstimmung,[6] war jetzt im stande, den Damen 25
über den Sonnenuntergang recht viel Artiges zu sagen
und sie ruhig, als wäre nichts passiert, nach ihrem Zim=

mer zu führen. Sie erlaubten mir auch, sie noch eine
Stunde zu unterhalten. Wie die Erde selbst drehte sich
unsre Unterhaltung um die Sonne. Die Mutter äußerte,
die in Nebel versinkende Sonne habe ausgesehen wie eine
5 rotglühende Rose, die der galante Himmel herabgeworfen
in den weit ausgebreiteten, weißen Brautschleier seiner
geliebten Erde. Die Tochter lächelte und meinte,[1] der
öftere Anblick solcher Naturerscheinungen schwäche ihren
Eindruck. Die Mutter berichtigte diese falsche Meinung
10 durch eine Stelle aus Goethes Reisebriefen[2] und frug[3]
mich, ob ich den Werther gelesen? Ich glaube, wir sprachen auch von Angorakatzen, etruskischen Vasen, türkischen
Shawls, Makkaroni und Lord Byron, aus dessen Gedich-
ten die ältere Dame einige Sonnenuntergangsstellen, recht
15 hübsch lispelnd und seufzend, rezitierte. Der jüngern
Dame, die kein Englisch verstand und jene Gedichte kennen
lernen wollte, empfahl ich die Übersetzungen meiner schönen,
geistreichen Landsmännin, der Baronin Elise von Hohenhausen,[4] bei welcher Gelegenheit ich nicht ermangelte, wie
20 ich gegen junge Damen[5] zu tun pflege, über Byrons Gott-
losigkeit, Lieblosigkeit, Trostlosigkeit, und der Himmel weiß
was noch mehr, zu eifern.

Nach diesem Geschäfte ging ich noch auf dem Brocken
spazieren; denn ganz dunkel wird es dort nie. Der Nebel
25 war nicht stark, und ich betrachtete die Umrisse der beiden
Hügel, die man den Hexenaltar und die Teufelskanzel
nennt. Ich schoß meine Pistolen ab, doch es gab kein

Echo. Plötzlich aber höre ich bekannte Stimmen und fühle mich umarmt und geküßt. Es waren meine Landsleute, die Göttingen vier Tage später verlassen hatten und bedeutend erstaunt waren, mich ganz allein auf dem Blocks= berge wiederzufinden. Da gab es ein Erzählen und Ver= wundern und Verabreden, ein Lachen und Erinnern, und im Geiste waren wir wieder in unserem gelehrten Sibirien, wo die Kultur so groß ist, daß die Bären in den Wirts= häusern angebunden werden.[1]

Im großen Zimmer wurde eine Abendmahlzeit gehalten. Ein langer Tisch mit zwei Reihen hungriger Studenten. Im Anfange gewöhnliches Universitätsgespräch: Duelle, Duelle und wieder Duelle. Die Gesellschaft bestand mei= stens aus Hallensern,[2] und Halle wurde daher Haupt= gegenstand der Unterhaltung. Hernach kamen die zwei Chinesen aufs Tapet, die sich vor zwei Jahren in Berlin sehen ließen[3] und jetzt in Halle zu Privatdozenten der chinesischen Ästhetik abgerichtet werden. Nun wurden Witze gerissen. Man setzte den Fall, ein Deutscher ließe sich in China für Geld sehen; und zu diesem Zwecke wurde ein Anschlagzettel geschmiedet, worin die Mandarinen Tsching= Tschang=Tschung und Hi=Ha=Ho begutachteten, daß es ein echter Deutscher sei, worin ferner seine Kunststücke[4] aufge= rechnet wurden, die hauptsächlich in Philosophieren, Tabak= rauchen und Geduld bestanden, und worin noch schließlich bemerkt wurde, daß man um zwölf Uhr, welches die Füt= terungsstunde sei, keine Hunde mitbringen dürfe, indem

diese dem armen Deutschen die besten Brocken wegzu=
schnappen pflegten.

Ein junger Burschenschafter, der kürzlich zur Purifikation[1]
in Berlin gewesen, sprach viel von dieser Stadt, aber sehr
einseitig. Er hatte Wisotzki[2] und das Theater besucht;
beide beurteilte er falsch. „Schnell fertig ist die Jugend
mit dem Wort u. s. w.“[3] Er sprach von Garderobeauf=
wand, Schauspieler= und Schauspielerinnenskandal u. s. w.
Der junge Mensch wußte nicht, daß, da in Berlin über=
haupt der Schein der Dinge am meisten gilt,[4] was schon
die allgemeine Redensart „man so duhn“[5] hinlänglich an=
deutet, dieses Scheinwesen auf den Brettern erst recht[6]
florieren muß, und daß daher die Intendanz[7] am meisten
zu sorgen hat für die „Farbe des Barts, womit eine Rolle
gespielt wird,“ für die Treue der Kostüme, die von
beeidigten Historikern vorgezeichnet[8] und von wissenschaft=
lich gebildeten Schneidern genäht werden. Und das ist
notwendig. Denn trüge mal Maria Stuart[9] eine Schürze,
die schon zum Zeitalter der Königin Anna gehört,[10] so
würde gewiß der Bankier Christian Gumpel[11] sich mit Recht
beklagen, daß ihm dadurch alle Illusion verloren gehe;
und hätte mal Lord Burleigh[12] aus Versehen die Hosen
von Heinrich IV. angezogen, so würde gewiß die Kriegs=
rätin von Steinzopf,[13] geb. Lilientau, diesen Anachronis=
mus den ganzen Abend nicht aus den Augen lassen.[14]
Solche täuschende[15] Sorgfalt der Generalintendanz erstreckt
sich aber nicht bloß auf Schürzen und Hosen, sondern auch

auf die darin verwickelten Personen. So soll künftig der
Othello von einem wirklichen Mohren gespielt werden, den
Professor Lichtenstein[1] schon zu diesem Behufe aus Afrika
verschrieben hat.

Hatte nun oben erwähnter junger Mensch die Verhält= 5
nisse des Berliner Schauspiels schlecht begriffen, so merkte
er noch viel weniger, daß die Spontinische Janitscharenoper,[2]
mit ihren Pauken, Elefanten,[3] Trompeten und Tamtams,
ein heroisches Mittel ist, um unser erschlafftes Volk krie=
gerisch zu stärken, ein Mittel, das schon Plato[4] und Cicero 10
staatspfiffig empfohlen haben. Am allerwenigsten begriff
der junge Mensch die diplomatische Bedeutung des Balletts.
Mit Mühe zeigte ich ihm, wie in Hoguets[5] Füßen mehr
Politik sitzt als in Buchholz'[6] Kopf, wie alle seine Tanz=
touren diplomatische Verhandlungen bedeuten, wie jede 15
seiner Bewegungen eine politische Beziehung habe, so z. B.,
daß er unser Kabinett meint, wenn er, sehnsüchtig vorge=
beugt, mit den Händen weit ausgreift; daß er den Bun=
destag[7] meint, wenn er sich hundertmal auf einem Fuße
herumdreht, ohne vom Fleck zu kommen; daß er die kleinen 20
Fürsten[8] im Sinne hat, wenn er wie mit gebundenen
Beinen herumtrippelt; daß er das europäische Gleichge=
wicht bezeichnet, wenn er wie ein Trunkener hin= und
herschwankt; daß er einen Kongreß andeutet, wenn er die
gebogenen Arme knäuelartig ineinander verschlingt; und 25
endlich, daß er unsern allzu großen Freund im Osten[9]
darstellt, wenn er in allmählicher Entfaltung sich in die

Höhe hebt, in dieser Stellung lange ruht und plötzlich in
die erschrecklichsten Sprünge ausbricht. Dem jungen Manne
fielen die Schuppen von den Augen, und jetzt merkte er,
warum Tänzer besser honoriert[1] werden als große Dich-
5 ter, und warum das Ballett beim diplomatischen Korps
ein unerschöpflicher Gegenstand des Gesprächs ist. Beim
Apis![2] wie groß ist die Zahl der exoterischen[3] und wie
klein die Zahl der esoterischen[3] Theaterbesucher! Da steht
das blöde Volk und gafft und bewundert Sprünge und
10 Wendungen, und schwatzt von Grazie und Harmonie —
und keiner merkt, daß er in getanzten Chiffern das Schicksal des deutschen Vaterlandes vor Augen hat.

　　Während solcherlei Gespräche hin- und herflogen, verlor
man doch das Nützliche nicht aus den Augen, und den
15 großen Schüsseln, die mit Fleisch, Kartoffeln u. s. w. ehrlich angefüllt waren, wurde fleißig zugesprochen. Jedoch
das Essen war schlecht. Dieses erwähnte ich leichthin gegen
meinen Nachbar, der aber mit einem Accente, woran ich
den Schweizer erkannte, gar unhöflich antwortete, daß wir
20 Deutschen, wie mit der wahren Freiheit, so auch mit der
wahren Genügsamkeit unbekannt seien. Ich zuckte die
Achseln und bemerkte, daß die eigentlichen Fürstenknechte[4]
und Leckerkramverfertiger überall Schweizer sind und vor-
zugsweise so genannt werden,[5] und daß überhaupt die
25 jetzigen schweizerischen Freiheitshelden, die so viel Politisch-
Kühnes ins Publikum hineinschwatzen, mir immer vorkom-
men wie Hasen, die auf öffentlichen Jahrmärkten Pistolen

abschießen, alle Kinder und Bauern durch ihre Kühnheit
in Erstaunen setzen und dennoch Hasen sind.

Der Sohn der Alpen hatte es gewiß nicht böse gemeint,
„es war ein dicker Mann, folglich ein guter Mann," sagt
Cervantes.[1] Aber mein Nachbar von der andern Seite, 5
ein Greifswalder,[2] war durch jene Äußerung sehr pikiert;
er beteuerte, daß deutsche Tatkraft und Einfältigkeit noch
nicht erloschen sei, schlug sich dröhnend auf die Brust und
leerte eine ungeheure Stange Weißbier.[3] Der Schweizer
sagte: „Nu! Nu!"[4] Doch, je beschwichtigender er dieses 10
sagte, desto eifriger ging der Greifswalder ins Geschirr.[5]
Dieser war ein Mann aus jenen Zeiten, als die Friseure
zu verhungern fürchteten. Er trug herabhängend langes
Haar, ein ritterliches Barett, einen schwarzen, altdeutschen
Rock,[6] ein schmutziges Hemd, das zugleich das Amt einer 15
Weste versah, und darunter ein Medaillon mit einem
Haarbüschel von Blüchers[7] Schimmel. Er sah aus wie
ein Narr in Lebensgröße. Ich mache mir gern einige
Bewegung beim Abendessen und ließ mich daher von ihm
in einen patriotischen Streit verflechten. Er war der 20
Meinung, Deutschland müsse in dreiunddreißig Gauen[8]
geteilt werden. Ich hingegen behauptete, es müßten achtund=
vierzig[9] sein, weil man alsdann ein systematischeres Hand=
buch über Deutschland schreiben könne, und es doch
notwendig sei, das Leben mit der Wissenschaft zu verbin= 25
den. Mein Greifswalder Freund war auch ein deutscher
Barde,[10] und wie er mir vertraute, arbeitete er an einem

Nationalheldengedicht zur Verherrlichung Hermanns und
der Hermannsschlacht.[1] Manchen nützlichen Wink gab ich
ihm für die Anfertigung dieses Epos. Ich machte ihn
darauf aufmerksam, daß er die Sümpfe und Knüppelwege[2]
des Teutoburger Waldes sehr onomatopöisch[3] durch wässrige
und holprige Verse andeuten könne, und daß es eine pa=
triotische Feinheit wäre, wenn er den Varus und die
übrigen Römer lauter Unsinn sprechen ließe. Ich hoffe,
dieser Kunstkniff wird ihm, ebenso erfolgreich wie andern
Berliner Dichtern, bis zur bedenklichsten[4] Illusion gelingen.

An unserem Tische wurde es immer lauter und traulicher,
der Wein verdrängte das Bier, die Punschbowlen dampften,
es wurde getrunken, schmolliert[5] und gesungen. „Der alte
Landesvater"[6] und herrliche Lieder von W. Müller,[7]
Rückert,[8] Uhland[9] u. s. w. erschollen. Schöne Meth=
fesselsche[10] Melodien. Am allerbesten erklangen unseres
Arndts[11] deutsche Worte: „Der Gott, der Eisen wachsen
ließ, der wollte keine Knechte!" Und draußen brauste es;[12]
als ob der alte Berg mitsänge, und einige schwankende
Freunde behaupteten sogar, er schüttle freudig sein kahles
Haupt, und unser Zimmer werde dadurch hin und her
bewegt. Die Flaschen wurden leerer und die Köpfe voller.
Der eine brüllte, der andere fistulierte, ein dritter dekla=
mierte aus der „Schuld,"[13] ein vierter sprach Latein, ein
fünfter predigte von der Mäßigkeit, und ein sechster stellte
sich auf den Stuhl und dozierte: „Meine Herren! Die
Erde ist eine runde Walze, die Menschen sind einzelne Stift=

chen darauf, scheinbar arglos zerstreut; aber die Walze
dreht sich, die Stiftchen stoßen hier und da an, und tönen,
die einen oft, die andern selten, das gibt eine wunder=
bare, komplizierte Musik, und diese heißt Weltgeschichte.
Wir sprechen also erst von der Musik, dann von der Welt 5
und endlich von der Geschichte; letztere aber teilen wir ein
in Positiv und spanische Fliegen.[1]—" Und so ging's weiter
mit Sinn und Unsinn.

Ein gemütlicher Mecklenburger, der seine Nase im Punsch=
glase hatte und selig lächelnd den Dampf einschnupfte, machte 10
die Bemerkung, es sei ihm zu Mute, als stände er wieder
vor dem Theaterbüffett in Schwerin! Ein anderer hielt
sein Weinglas wie ein Perspektiv vor die Augen und schien
uns aufmerksam damit zu betrachten, während ihm der rote
Wein über die Backen ins hervortretende Maul hinablief. 15
Der Greifswalder, plötzlich begeistert, warf sich an meine
Brust und jauchzte: „O, verständest du mich, ich bin ein
Liebender, ich bin ein Glücklicher, ich werde wieder geliebt,
und es ist ein gebildetes Mädchen, denn sie trägt ein weißes
Kleid und spielt Klavier!" — Aber der Schweizer weinte 20
und küßte zärtlich meine Hand und wimmerte beständig:
„O Bäbeli! O Bäbeli!"[2]

In diesem verworrenen Treiben, wo die Teller tanzen
und die Gläser fliegen lernten, saßen mir gegenüber zwei
Jünglinge, schön und blaß[3] wie Marmorbilder, der eine 25
mehr dem Adonis, der andere mehr dem Apollo ähnlich.
Kaum bemerkbar war der leichte Rosenhauch, den der Wein

über ihre Wangen hinwarf. Mit unendlicher Liebe sahen
sie sich einander an, als wenn einer lesen könnte in den
Augen des andern, und in diesen Augen strahlte es, als
wären einige Lichttropfen hineingefallen aus jener Schale
5 voll lobernder Liebe, die ein frommer Engel dort oben
von einem Stern zum andern hinüberträgt. Sie sprachen
leise, mit sehnsuchtbebender Stimme, und es waren traurige
Geschichten, aus denen ein wunderschmerzlicher Ton her=
vorklang. „Die Lore ist jetzt auch tot!" sagte der eine
10 und seufzte, und nach einer Pause erzählte er von einem
Halleschen Mädchen, das in einen Studenten verliebt war
und, als dieser Halle verließ, mit niemand mehr sprach,
und wenig aß, und Tag und Nacht weinte, und immer
den Kanarienvogel betrachtete, den der Geliebte ihr einst
15 geschenkt hatte. „Der Vogel starb, und bald darauf ist
auch die Lore gestorben!" so schloß die Erzählung, und
beide Jünglinge schwiegen wieder und seufzten, als wollte
ihnen das Herz zerspringen. Endlich sprach der andere:
„Meine Seele ist traurig! Komm mit hinaus in die dunkle
20 Nacht! Einatmen will ich den Hauch der Wolken und die
Strahlen des Mondes. Genosse meiner Wehmut! ich liebe
dich, deine Worte tönen wie Rohrgeflüster, wie gleitende
Ströme, sie tönen wider¹ in meiner Brust, aber meine
Seele ist traurig!"

25 Nun erhoben sich die beiden Jünglinge, einer schlang den
Arm um den Nacken des andern, und sie verließen das
tosende Zimmer.² Ich folgte ihnen nach und sah, wie sie

m eine dunkle Kammer traten, wie der eine, statt des
Fensters, einen großen Kleiderschrank öffnete, wie beide
vor demselben mit sehnsüchtig ausgestreckten Armen stehen
blieben und wechselweise sprachen. „Ihr Lüfte der däm-
mernden Nacht!" rief der erste, „wie erquickend kühlt ihr 5
meine Wangen! Wie lieblich spielt ihr mit meinen flat-
ternden Locken! Ich steh' auf des Berges wolkigem Gipfel,
unter mir liegen die schlafenden Städte der Menschen und
blinken die blauen Gewässer. Horch! dort unten im Tale
rauschen die Tannen! Dort über die Hügel ziehen, in 10
Nebelgestalten, die Geister der Väter. O, könnt' ich mit
euch jagen, auf dem Wolkenroß, durch die stürmische Nacht,
über die rollende See, zu den Sternen hinauf! Aber ach!
ich bin beladen mit Leid, und meine Seele ist traurig!"
— Der andere Jüngling hatte ebenfalls seine Arme sehn- 15
suchtsvoll nach dem Kleiderschrank ausgestreckt, Tränen
stürzten aus seinen Augen, und zu einer gelbledernen Hose,
die er für den Mond¹ hielt, sprach er mit wehmütiger
Stimme: „Schön bist du, Tochter des Himmels! Holdselig ist deines Antlitzes Ruhe! Du wandelst einher in 20
Lieblichkeit! Die Sterne folgen deinen blauen Pfaden im
Osten. Bei deinem Anblick² erfreuen sich die Wolken, und
es lichten sich ihre düstern Gestalten. Wer gleicht dir am
Himmel, Erzeugte der Nacht? Beschämt in deiner Gegenwart sind die Sterne und wenden ab die grünfunkelnden 25
Augen. Wohin, wenn des Morgens dein Antlitz erbleicht,
entfliehst du von deinem Pfade? Hast du gleich mir deine

Halle?¹ Wohnst du im Schatten der Wehmut? Sind deine
Schwestern vom Himmel gefallen? Sie, die freudig mit
dir die Nacht durchwallten, sind sie nicht mehr? Ja, sie
fielen herab, o schönes Licht, und du verbirgst dich oft, sie
5 zu betrauern. Doch einst wird kommen die Nacht, und du,
auch du bist vergangen und hast deine blauen Pfade dort
oben verlassen. Dann erheben die Sterne ihre grünen
Häupter; die einst deine Gegenwart beschämt, sie werden
sich freuen. Doch jetzt bist du gekleidet in deiner Strahlen=
10 pracht und schaust herab aus den Toren des Himmels.
Zerreißt die Wolken, o Winde, damit die Erzeugte der
Nacht hervorzuleuchten vermag, und die buschigen Berge
erglänzen, und das Meer seine schäumenden Wogen rolle
in Licht!"

15 Ein wohlbekannter,² nicht sehr magerer Freund, der mehr
getrunken als gegessen hatte, obgleich er auch heute abend,
wie gewöhnlich, eine Portion Rindfleisch verschlungen, wo=
von sechs Gardeleutnants und ein unschuldiges Kind satt
geworden wären, dieser kam jetzt vorbeigerannt, schob die
20 beiden elegischen Freunde etwas unsanft in den Schrank
hinein, polterte nach der Haustüre und wirtschaftete drau=
ßen ganz mörderlich.³ Der Lärm im Saal wurde auch
immer verworrener und dumpfer. Die beiden Jünglinge
im Schranke jammerten und wimmerten, sie lägen⁴ zer=
25 schmettert am Fuße des Berges; und der eine sprach zum
andern: „Lebe wohl! Ich fühle, daß ich verblute.⁵ Warum
weckst du mich, Frühlingsluft? Du buhlst und sprichst: ich

betaue dich mit Tropfen des Himmels. Doch die Zeit
meines Welkens ist nahe, nahe, der Sturm, der meine
Blätter herabstört![1] Morgen wird der Wanderer kommen,
kommen, der[2] mich sah in meiner Schönheit, ringsum wird
sein Auge im Felde mich suchen und wird mich nicht fin= 5
den. —" Aber alles übertobte die wohlbekannte Baß=
stimme,[3] die draußen vor der Türe, unter Fluchen und
Jauchzen, sich gottläſterlich beklagte, daß auf der ganzen
dunkeln Weenderstraße keine einzige Laterne brenne, und
man nicht einmal sehen könne, bei wem man die Fenster= 10
scheiben[4] eingeschmissen habe.

Ich kann viel[5] vertragen.— die Bescheidenheit erlaubt
mir nicht, die Bouteillenzahl zu nennen — und ziemlich gut
konditioniert gelangte ich nach meinem Schlafzimmer. Der
junge Kaufmann lag schon im Bette, mit seiner kreideweißen 15
Nachtmütze und safrangelben Jacke von Gesundheitsflanell.
Er schlief noch nicht und suchte ein Gespräch mit mir anzu=
knüpfen. Er war ein Frankfurt=am=Mainer,[6] und folglich
sprach er gleich von den Juden, die alles Gefühl für das
Schöne und Edle verloren haben und die englischen Waren 20
25 Prozent unter dem Fabrikpreise verkaufen. Es ergriff
mich die Lust, ihn etwas zu mystifizieren; deshalb sagte ich
ihm, ich sei ein Nachtwandler und müsse im voraus um
Entschuldigung bitten für den Fall, daß ich ihn etwa im
Schlafe stören möchte. Der arme Mensch hat deshalb, wie 25
er mir den andern Tag gestand, die ganze Nacht nicht
geschlafen, da er die Besorgnis hegte, ich könnte mit meinen

Seelenergüssen, die altdeutschen Revolutionsdilettanten mit
ihren Turngemeinplätzen,[1] die Berliner Schullehrer mit ihren
verunglückten Entzückungsphrasen u. f. w. Herr Johan=
nes Hagel[2] will sich auch mal als Schriftsteller zeigen. Hier
5 wird des Sonnenaufgangs majestätische Pracht beschrieben;
dort wird geklagt über schlechtes Wetter, über getäuschte
Erwartungen, über den Nebel, der alle Aussicht versperrt.
„Benebelt[3] heraufgekommen und benebelt hinuntergegangen!"
ist ein stehender Witz, der hier von Hunderten nachgerissen
10 wird. Das ganze Buch riecht nach Käse, Bier und Tabak;
man glaubt einen Roman von Clauren[4] zu lesen.

Während ich nun besagtermaßen[5] Kaffee trank und im
Brockenbuche blätterte, trat der Schweizer mit hochroten
Wangen herein, und voller Begeisterung erzählte er von dem
15 erhabenen Anblick, den er oben auf dem Turm genossen, als
das reine, ruhige Licht der Sonne, Sinnbild der Wahrheit,
mit den nächtlichen Nebelmassen gekämpft; daß es ausgesehen
habe wie eine Geisterschlacht, wo zürnende Riesen ihre langen
Schwerter ausstrecken, geharnischte Ritter auf bäumenden
20 Rossen einherjagen, Streitwagen, flatternde Banner, aben=
teuerliche Tierbildungen aus dem wildesten Gewühle hervor=
tauchen, bis endlich alles in den wahnsinnigsten Verzerrungen
zusammenkräuselt, blasser und blasser zerrinnt und spurlos
verschwindet. Diese demagogische[6] Naturerscheinung hatte
25 ich versäumt, und ich kann, wenn es zur Untersuchung[7]
kommt, eidlich versichern, daß ich von nichts weiß, als vom
Geschmack des guten braunen Kaffees. Ach, dieser war so=

gar schuld, daß ich meine schöne Dame vergessen, und jetzt
stand sie vor der Tür, mit Mutter und Begleiter, im Begriff
den Wagen zu besteigen. Kaum hatte ich noch Zeit, hin=
zueilen und ihr zu versichern, daß es kalt sei. Sie schien
unwillig, daß ich nicht früher gekommen; doch ich glättete 5
bald die mißmütigen Falten ihrer schönen Stirn, indem ich
ihr eine wunderliche Blume schenkte, die ich den Tag vorher
mit halsbrechender Gefahr von einer steilen Felsenwand
gepflückt hatte. Die Mutter verlangte den Namen der
Blume zu wissen, gleichsam als ob sie es unschicklich fände, 10
daß ihre Tochter eine fremde, unbekannte Blume vor die
Brust stecke — denn wirklich, die Blume erhielt diesen benei=
denswerten Platz, was sie sich gewiß gestern auf ihrer ein=
samen Höhe nicht träumen ließ.[1] Der schweigsame Begleiter
öffnete jetzt auf einmal den Mund, zählte die Staubfäden der 15
Blume und sagte ganz trocken: „Sie gehört zur achten Klasse."

Es ärgert mich jedesmal, wenn ich sehe, daß man auch
Gottes liebe Blumen, ebenso wie uns, in Kasten geteilt hat,
und nach ähnlichen Äußerlichkeiten, nämlich nach Staubfäden=
verschiedenheit. Soll doch mal eine Einteilung[2] stattfinden, 20
so folge man dem Vorschlage Theophrasts,[3] der die Blumen
mehr nach dem Geiste, nämlich nach ihrem Geruch, einteilen
wollte. Was mich betrifft, so habe ich in der Naturwissen=
schaft mein eigenes System, und demnach teile ich alles ein
in dasjenige, was man essen kann, und in dasjenige, was 25
man nicht essen kann.

Jedoch der ältern Dame war die geheimnisvolle Natur

der Blumen nichts weniger als verschlossen, und unwillkürlich
äußerte sie, daß sie von den Blumen, wenn sie noch im
Garten oder im Topfe wachsen, recht erfreut werde, daß
hingegen ein leises Schmerzgefühl traumhaft beängstigend
5 ihre Brust durchzittere, wenn sie eine abgebrochene Blume
sehe — da eine solche doch eigentlich eine Leiche sei, und so
eine gebrochene, zarte Blumenleiche ihr welkes Köpfchen
recht traurig herabhängen lasse, wie ein totes Kind. Die
Dame war fast erschrocken über den trüben Widerschein ihrer
10 Bemerkung, und es war meine Pflicht, denselben mit einigen
Voltaireschen Versen zu verscheuchen. Wie doch ein paar
französische Worte[1] uns gleich in die gehörige Konvenienz-
stimmung zurückversetzen können! Wir lachten, Hände wurden
geküßt, huldreich wurde gelächelt, die Pferde wieherten, und
15 der Wagen holperte langsam und beschwerlich den Berg
hinunter.

Nun machten auch die Studenten Anstalt zum Abreisen,
die Ranzen wurden geschnürt, die Rechnungen, die über
alle Erwartung billig ausfielen, berichtigt; die Hausmädchen
20 brachten, wie gebräuchlich ist, die Brockensträußchen, halfen
solche auf die Mützen befestigen, wurden dafür mit einigen
Küssen oder Groschen honoriert, und so stiegen wir alle den
Berg hinab, indem die einen, wobei der Schweizer und
Greifswalder, den Weg nach Schierke einschlugen, und die
25 andern, ungefähr zwanzig Mann, wobei auch meine Landsleute und ich, angeführt von einem Wegweiser, durch die
sogenannten Schneelöcher[2] hinabzogen nach Ilsenburg.

Das ging über Hals und Kopf. Hallesche Studenten marschieren schneller als die östreichische Landwehr.[1] Ehe ich mich dessen versah, war die kahle Partie[2] des Berges mit den darauf zerstreuten Steingruppen schon hinter uns, und wir kamen durch einen Tannenwald, wie ich ihn den Tag vorher gesehen. Die Sonne goß schon ihre festlichsten Strahlen herab und beleuchtete die humoristisch buntgeklei= deten Burschen, die so munter durch das Dickicht drangen, hier verschwanden, dort wieder zum Vorschein kamen, bei Sumpfstellen über die quergelegten Baumstämme liefen, bei abschüssigen Tiefen an den rankenden Wurzeln kletter= ten, in den ergötzlichsten Tonarten emporjohlten und ebenso lustige Antwort zurückerhielten von den zwitschernden Wald= vögeln, von den rauschenden Tannen, von den unsichtbar plätschernden Quellen und von dem schallenden Echo. Wenn frohe Jugend und schöne Natur zusammenkommen, so freuen sie sich wechselseitig.

Je tiefer wir hinabstiegen, desto lieblicher rauschte das unterirdische Gewässer, nur hier und da, unter Gestein und Gesträppe, blinkte es hervor und schien heimlich zu lauschen, ob es ans Licht treten dürfe, und endlich kam eine kleine Welle entschlossen hervorgesprungen. Nun zeigt sich die gewöhnliche Erscheinung: ein Kühner macht den Anfang, und der große Troß der Zagenden wird plötzlich zu seinem eigenen Erstaunen von Mut ergriffen und eilt, sich mit jenem ersten zu vereinigen. Eine Menge anderer Quellen hüpften jetzt hastig aus ihrem Versteck, verbanden

sich mit der zuerst hervorgesprungenen, und bald bildeten
sie zusammen ein schon bedeutendes Bächlein, das in un=
zähligen Wasserfällen und in wunderlichen Windungen das
Bergtal hinabrauscht. Das ist nun die Ilse, die liebliche,
5 süße Ilse. Sie zieht sich durch das gesegnete Ilsetal, an
dessen beiden Seiten sich die Berge allmählich höher erheben,
und diese sind bis zu ihrem Fuße meistens mit Buchen,
Eichen und gewöhnlichem Blattgesträuche bewachsen, nicht
mehr mit Tannen und anderm Nadelholz. Denn jene
10 Blätterholzart[1] wird vorherrschend auf dem „Unterharze,“
wie man die Ostseite des Brockens nennt, im Gegensatz
zur Westseite desselben, die der „Oberharz“ heißt und
wirklich viel höher ist, und also auch viel geeigneter zum
Gedeihen der Nadelhölzer.

15　　Es ist unbeschreibbar, mit welcher Fröhlichkeit, Naivetät
und Anmut die Ilse sich hinunterstürzt über die abenteuer=
lich gebildeten Felsstücke, die sie in ihrem Laufe findet, so
daß das Wasser hier wild emporzischt oder schäumend über=
läuft, dort aus allerlei Steinspalten, wie aus tollen[2] Gieß=
20 kannen, in reinen Bögen sich ergießt, und unten wieder
über die kleinen Steine hintrippelt, wie ein munteres
Mädchen. Ja, die Sage ist wahr, die Ilse ist eine Prin=
zessin, die lachend und blühend den Berg hinabläuft. Wie
blinkt im Sonnenschein ihr weißes Schaumgewand! Wie
25 flattern im Winde ihre silbernen Busenbänder! Wie funkeln
und blitzen ihre Diamanten! Die hohen Buchen stehen dabei
gleich ernsten Vätern, die verstohlen lächelnd dem Mut=

willen des lieblichen Kindes zusehen; die weißen Birken
bewegen sich tantenhaft vergnügt,[1] und doch zugleich ängst=
lich über die gewagten Sprünge; der stolze Eichbaum
schaut drein[2] wie ein verdrießlicher Oheim, der das schöne
Wetter bezahlen[3] soll; die Vögelein in den Lüften jubeln 5
ihren Beifall, die Blumen am Ufer flüstern zärtlich: „O,
nimm uns mit,[4] nimm uns mit, lieb Schwesterchen!" —
aber das lustige Mädchen springt unaufhaltsam weiter, und
plötzlich ergreift sie den träumenden Dichter, und es strömt
auf mich herab ein Blumenregen von klingenden Strahlen 10
und strahlenden Klängen,[5] und die Sinne vergehen mir
vor lauter Herrlichkeit, und ich höre nur noch die flöten=
süße Stimme:

> „Ich bin die Prinzessin Ilse,
> Und wohne im Ilsenstein;
> Komm mit nach meinem Schlosse, 15
> Wir wollen selig sein.

> „Dein Haupt will ich benetzen
> Mit meiner klaren Well',
> Du sollst deine Schmerzen vergessen,
> Du sorgenkranker Gesell'! 20

> „In meinen weißen Armen,
> An meiner weißen Brust,
> Da sollst du liegen und träumen
> Von alter Märchenlust.
> 25
> „Ich will dich küssen und herzen,
> Wie ich geherzt und geküßt
> Den lieben Kaiser Heinrich,[6]
> Der nun gestorben ist.

„Es bleiben tot die Toten,[1]
Und nur der Lebendige lebt;[2]
Und ich bin schön und blühend,
Mein lachendes Herze bebt.

5   „Und bebt mein Herz dort unten,
So klingt mein kristallenes Schloß,
Es tanzen die Fräulein und Ritter,
Es jubelt der Knappentroß.

„Es rauschen die seidenen Schleppen,
10   Es klirren die Eisenspor'n,
Die Zwerge trompeten und pauken,
Und fiedeln und blasen das Horn.

„Doch dich soll mein Arm umschlingen,
Wie er Kaiser Heinrich umschlang;
15   Ich hielt ihm zu die Ohren,
Wenn die Trompet' erklang.“[3]

Unendlich selig ist das Gefühl, wenn die Erscheinungswelt[4]
mit unserer Gemütswelt zusammenrinnt, und grüne Bäume,
Gedanken, Vögelgesang, Wehmut, Himmelsbläue, Erin=
20 nerung und Kräuterduft sich in süßen Arabesken ver=
schlingen. Die Frauen kennen am besten dieses Gefühl,
und darum mag auch ein so holdselig ungläubiges Lächeln
um ihre Lippen schweben, wenn wir mit Schulstolz unsere
logischen Taten rühmen, wie wir alles so hübsch eingeteilt
25 in objektiv und subjektiv, wie wir unsere Köpfe apotheken=
artig mit tausend Schubladen versehen, wo in der einen
Vernunft, in der andern Verstand, in der dritten Witz, in
der vierten schlechter Witz und in der fünften gar nichts,
nämlich die Idee, enthalten ist.

30   Wie im Traume fortwandelnd, hatte ich fast nicht be=

Der Ilsenstein.

merkt, daß wir die Tiefe des Ilsetales verlassen und
wieder bergauf stiegen. Dies ging sehr steil und mühsam,
und mancher von uns kam außer Atem. Doch wie unser
seliger Vetter,[1] der zu Mölln[2] begraben liegt, dachten wir
im voraus ans Bergabsteigen und waren um so vergnügter. 5
Endlich gelangten wir auf den Ilsenstein.[3]

Das ist ein ungeheurer Granitfelsen, der sich lang und
keck aus der Tiefe erhebt. Von drei Seiten umschließen
ihn die hohen, waldbedeckten Berge, aber die vierte, die
Nordseite, ist frei, und hier schaut man das unten liegende 10
Ilsenburg und die Ilse weit hinab ins niedere Land.
Auf der turmartigen Spitze des Felsens steht ein großes,
eisernes Kreuz,[4] und zur Not ist da noch Platz für vier
Menschenfüße.

Wie nun die Natur durch Stellung und Form den 15
Ilsenstein mit phantastischen Reizen geschmückt, so hat
auch die Sage ihren Rosenschein darüber ausgegossen.
Gottschalk[5] berichtet: „Man erzählt, hier habe ein ver=
wünschtes Schloß gestanden, in welchem die reiche, schöne
Prinzessin Ilse gewohnt, die sich noch jetzt jeden Morgen 20
in der Ilse bade; und wer so glücklich ist, den rechten
Zeitpunkt zu treffen, werde von ihr in den Felsen, wo ihr
Schloß sei, geführt und königlich belohnt!" Andere erzählen
von der Liebe des Fräuleins Ilse und des Ritters von
Westenberg eine hübsche Geschichte, die einer unserer be= 25
kanntesten Dichter[6] romantisch in der „Abendzeitung" besun=
gen hat. Andere wieder erzählen anders: es soll der

altsächsische Kaiser Heinrich gewesen sein, der mit Ilse,
der schönen Wasserfee, in ihrer verzauberten Felsenburg
die kaiserlichsten Stunden genossen.   Ein neuerer Schrift=
steller, Herr Niemann, Wohlgeb.,[1] der ein Harzreisebuch
5 geschrieben, worin er die Gebirgshöhen, Abweichungen[2] der
Magnetnadel, Schulden der Städte und dergleichen mit
löblichem Fleiße und genauen Zahlen angegeben, behauptet
indes: „Was man von der schönen Prinzessin Ilse erzählt,
gehört dem Fabelreiche an."   So sprechen alle diese Leute,
10 denen eine solche Prinzessin niemals erschienen ist, wir
aber, die wir von schönen Damen besonders begünstigt
werden, wissen das besser.   Auch Kaiser Heinrich mußte
es.   Nicht umsonst hingen die altsächsischen Kaiser so sehr
an ihrem heimischen Harze.   Man blättere nur in der
15 hübschen „Lüneburger Chronik",[3] wo die guten alten Herren
in wunderlich treuherzigen Holzschnitten abkonterfeit sind,
wohlgeharnischt, hoch auf ihrem gewappneten Schlachtroß,
die heilige Kaiserkrone auf dem teuren Haupte, Scepter
und Schwert in festen Händen; und auf den lieben, knebel=
20 bärtigen Gesichtern kann man deutlich lesen, wie oft sie
sich nach den süßen Herzen ihrer Harzprinzessinnen und
dem traulichen Rauschen der Harzwälder zurücksehnten,
wenn sie in der Fremde weilten, wohl gar in dem zitronen=
und giftreichen Welschland,[4] wohin sie und ihre Nachfolger
25 so oft verlockt wurden von dem Wunsche, römische Kaiser[5]
zu heißen, einer echtdeutschen Titelsucht, woran Kaiser und
Reich zu Grunde gingen.

Ich rate aber jedem, der auf der Spitze des Ilsensteins steht, weder an Kaiser und Reich, noch an die schöne Ilse, sondern bloß an seine Füße zu denken. Denn als ich dort stand, in Gedanken verloren, hörte ich plötzlich die unterirdische Musik des Zauberschlosses, und ich sah, wie sich die Berge ringsum auf die Köpfe stellten, und die roten Ziegeldächer zu Ilsenburg anfingen zu tanzen, und die grünen Bäume in der blauen Luft herumflogen, daß es mir blau und grün vor den Augen wurde,[1] und ich sicher, vom Schwindel erfaßt, in den Abgrund gestürzt wäre, wenn ich mich nicht in meiner Seelennot ans eiserne Kreuz festgeklammert hätte. Daß ich in so mißlicher Stel= lung dieses letztere getan habe, wird mir gewiß niemand verdenken.[2]

———————

Die „Harzreise" ist und bleibt Fragment, und die bunten Fäden, die so hübsch hineingesponnen sind, um sich im Ganzen harmonisch zu verschlingen, werden plötzlich, wie von der Schere der unerbittlichen Parze,[3] abgeschnitten. Vielleicht verwebe ich sie weiter in künftigen Liedern, und was jetzt kärglich verschwiegen ist, wird alsdann vollauf gesagt. Am Ende kommt es auch auf eins heraus, wann und wo man etwas ausgesprochen hat, wenn man es nur überhaupt einmal ausspricht.[4] Mögen die einzelnen Werke immerhin[5] Fragmente bleiben, wenn sie nur in ihrer Ver= einigung ein Ganzes bilden. Durch solche Vereinigung mag hier und da das Mangelhafte ergänzt, das Schroffe aus=

geglichen und das Allzuherbe gemildert werden. Dieses
würde vielleicht schon bei den ersten Blättern der „Harzreise" der Fall sein, und sie könnten wohl einen minder
sauern Eindruck hervorbringen, wenn man anderweitig[1]
5 erführe, daß der Unmut, den ich gegen Göttingen im allgemeinen hege, obschon er noch größer ist, als ich ihn
ausgesprochen, doch lange nicht so groß ist wie die Verehrung, die ich für einige Individuen dort empfinde. Und
warum sollte ich es verschweigen: ich meine hier ganz
10 besonders jenen vielteuren Mann, der schon in frühern
Zeiten sich so freundlich meiner annahm, mir schon damals
eine innige Liebe für das Studium der Geschichte ein-
flößte, mich späterhin in dem Eifer für dasselbe bestärkte
und dadurch meinen Geist auf ruhigere Bahnen führte,
15 meinem Lebensmute heilsamere Richtungen anwies und
mir überhaupt jene historischen Tröstungen bereitete, ohne
welche ich die qualvollen Erscheinungen des Tages[2] nimmermehr ertragen würde. Ich spreche von Georg Sartorius,[3]
dem großen Geschichtsforscher und Menschen, dessen Auge
20 ein klarer Stern ist in unserer dunkeln Zeit, und dessen
gastliches Herz offen steht für alle fremde[4] Leiden und
Freuden, für die Besorgnisse des Bettlers und des Königs,
und für die letzten Seufzer untergehender Völker und
ihrer Götter.

25   Ich kann nicht umhin, hier ebenfalls anzudeuten, daß
der Oberharz, jener Teil des Harzes, den ich bis zum
Anfang des Ilsetals beschrieben habe, bei weitem keinen

so erfreulichen Anblick wie der romantisch malerische Un=
terharz gewährt, und in seiner wildschroffen, tannendüstern
Schönheit gar sehr mit demselben kontrastiert; so wie
ebenfalls die drei von der Ilse, von der Bode und von
der Selke gebildeten Täler des Unterharzes gar anmutig 5
untereinander kontrastieren, wenn man den Charakter jedes
Tales zu personifizieren weiß. Es sind drei Frauenge=
stalten, wovon man nicht so leicht zu entscheiden vermag,
welche die schönste sei.

Von der lieben, süßen Ilse, und wie süß und lieblich 10
sie mich empfangen, habe ich schon gesagt und gesungen.[1]
Die düstere Schöne, die Bode, empfing mich nicht so gnädig,
und als ich sie im schmiedebunkeln Rübeland[2] zuerst er=
blickte, schien sie gar[3] mürrisch und verhüllte sich in einen
silbergrauen Regenschleier. Aber mit rascher Liebe warf 15
sie ihn ab, als ich auf die Höhe der Roßtrappe[4] gelangte;
ihr Antlitz leuchtete mir entgegen in sonnigster Pracht, aus
allen Zügen hauchte eine kolossale[5] Zärtlichkeit, und aus
der bezwungenen Felsenbrust drang es hervor wie Sehn=
suchtseufzer und schmelzende Laute der Wehmut. Minder 20
zärtlich, aber fröhlicher, zeigte sich mir die schöne Selke,
die schöne, liebenswürdige Dame, deren edle Einfalt und
heitre Ruhe alle sentimentale Familiarität entfernt hält,
die aber doch durch ein halbverstecktes Lächeln ihren necken=
den Sinn verrät; und diesem möchte ich es wohl zuschrei= 25
ben, daß mich im Selketal gar mancherlei kleines Ungemach
heimsuchte, daß ich, indem ich über das Wasser springen

wollte, just in die Mitte hineinplumpfte, daß nachher, als
ich das naſſe Fußzeug mit Pantoffeln vertauſcht hatte,
einer derſelben mir abhanden oder vielmehr abfüßen kam,[1]
daß mir ein Windſtoß die Mütze entführte, daß mir
5 Waldborne die Beine zerſetzten, und leider ſo weiter. Doch
all dieſes Ungemach verzeihe ich gern der ſchönen Dame,
denn ſie iſt ſchön. Und jetzt ſteht ſie vor meiner Ein=
bildung, mit all ihrem ſtillen Liebreiz und ſcheint zu ſagen:
„Wenn ich auch lache, ſo meine ich es doch gut mit Ihnen,
10 und ich bitte Sie, beſingen Sie mich!“ Die herrliche Bode
tritt ebenfalls hervor in meiner Erinnerung, und ihr
dunkles Auge ſpricht: „Du gleichſt mir im Stolz und im
Schmerze, und ich will, daß du mich liebſt.“ Auch die
ſchöne Ilſe kommt herangeſprungen, zierlich bezaubernd in
15 Miene, Geſtalt und Bewegung; ſie gleicht ganz dem
holden Weſen, das meine Träume beſeligt, und ganz wie
Sie[2] ſchaut ſie mich an, mit unwiderſtehlicher Gleichgültig=
keit und doch zugleich ſo innig, ſo ewig, ſo durchſichtig
wahr. — Nun, ich bin Paris,[3] die drei Göttinnen ſtehen
20 vor mir, und den Apfel gebe ich der ſchönen Ilſe.

Es iſt heute der erſte Mai;[4] wie ein Meer des Lebens
ergießt ſich der Frühling über die Erde, der weiße Blüten=
ſchaum bleibt an den Bäumen hängen, ein weiter, warmer
Nebelglanz verbreitet ſich überall; in der Stadt blitzen
25 freudig die Fenſterſcheiben der Häuſer, an den Dächern
bauen die Spatzen wieder ihre Neſtchen, auf der Straße
wandeln die Leute und wundern ſich, daß die Luft ſo an=

greifend und ihnen selbst so wunderlich zu Mute ist; die
bunten Vierländerinnen[1] bringen Veilchensträuße; die Wai=
senkinder[2] mit ihren blauen Jäckchen und ihren lieben
Gesichtchen ziehen über den Jungfernstieg[3] und freuen sich,
als sollten sie heute einen Vater wiederfinden; der Bettler[4]
an der Brücke schaut so vergnügt, als hätte er das große
Los[5] gewonnen; sogar den schwarzen, noch ungehenkten
Makler,[6] der dort mit seinem spitzbübischen Manufaktur=
waren=Gesicht einherläuft, bescheint die Sonne mit ihren
tolerantesten Strahlen, — ich will hinauswandern vor das
Tor.

Es ist der erste Mai, und ich denke deiner, du schöne
Ilse — oder soll ich dich "Agnes"[7] nennen, weil dir dieser
Name am besten gefällt? — ich denke deiner, und ich
möchte wieder zusehen, wie du leuchtend den Berg hinab=
läufst. Am liebsten aber möchte ich unten im Tale stehen
und dich auffangen in meine Arme. — Es ist ein schöner
Tag! Überall sehe ich die grüne Farbe, die Farbe der
Hoffnung. Überall, wie holde Wunder, blühen hervor die
Blumen, und auch mein Herz will wieder blühen. Dieses
Herz ist auch eine Blume, eine gar wunderliche. Es ist
kein bescheidenes Veilchen, keine lachende Rose, keine reine
Lilie oder sonstiges Blümchen, das mit artiger Lieblichkeit
den Mädchensinn erfreut und sich hübsch vor den hübschen
Busen stecken läßt, und heute welkt und morgen wieder
blüht. Dieses Herz gleicht mehr jener schweren,[8] abenteuer=
lichen Blume aus den Wäldern Brasiliens, die der Sage

nach alle hundert Jahre nur einmal blüht. Ich erinnere
mich, daß ich als Knabe eine solche Blume gesehen. Wir
hörten in der Nacht einen Schuß, wie von einer Pistole,
und am folgenden Morgen erzählten mir die Nachbars=
5 kinder, daß es ihre „Aloe"[1] gewesen, die mit solchem
Knalle plötzlich aufgeblüht sei. Sie führten mich in ihren
Garten, und da sah ich zu meiner Verwunderung, daß
das niedrige, harte Gewächs mit den närrisch breiten,
scharfgezackten Blättern, woran man sich leicht verletzen
10 konnte, jetzt ganz in die Höhe geschossen war und oben,
wie eine goldene Krone, die herrlichste Blüte trug. Wir
Kinder konnten nicht mal[2] so hoch hinaufsehen, und der
alte, schmunzelnde Christian,[3] der uns lieb hatte, baute
eine hölzerne Treppe um die Blume herum, und da klet=
15 terten wir hinauf wie die Katzen und schauten neugierig
in den offenen Blumenkelch, woraus die gelben Strahlen=
fäden und wildfremden Düfte mit unerhörter Pracht her=
vordrangen.

Ja, Agnes, oft und leicht kommt dieses Herz nicht zum
20 Blühen; soviel ich mich erinnere, hat es nur ein einziges
Mal[4] geblüht, und das mag schon lange her sein, gewiß
schon hundert Jahr. Ich glaube, so herrlich auch damals
seine Blüte sich entfaltete, so mußte sie doch aus Mangel
an Sonnenschein und Wärme elendiglich verkümmern, wenn
25 sie nicht gar[5] von einem dunkeln Wintersturme gewaltsam
zerstört worden. Jetzt aber regt und drängt es sich wie=
der in meiner Brust, und hörst du plötzlich den Schuß —

Mädchen, erschrick nicht! ich hab' mich nicht totgeschossen, sondern meine Liebe sprengt ihre Knospe und schießt empor in strahlenden Liedern, in ewigen Dithyramben, in freu= digster Sangesfülle.

Ist dir aber diese hohe Liebe zu hoch, Mädchen, so 5 mach' es dir bequem und besteige die hölzerne Treppe, und schaue von dieser hinab in mein blühendes Herz.

Es ist noch früh am Tage, die Sonne hat kaum die Hälfte ihres Weges zurückgelegt, und mein Herz duftet schon so stark, daß es mir betäubend zu Kopfe steigt, daß 10 ich nicht mehr weiß, wo die Ironie[1] aufhört und der Him= mel anfängt, daß ich die Luft mit meinen Seufzern be= völkere, und daß ich selbst wieder zerrinnen möchte in süße Atome, in die unerschaffene Gottheit; — wie soll das erst[2] gehen, wenn es Nacht wird, und die Sterne am Himmel 15 erscheinen, „die unglücksel'gen Sterne, die dir sagen können — —"

Es ist der erste Mai, der lumpigste Ladenschwengel hat heute das Recht, sentimental zu werden, und dem Dichter wolltest du es verwehren? 20

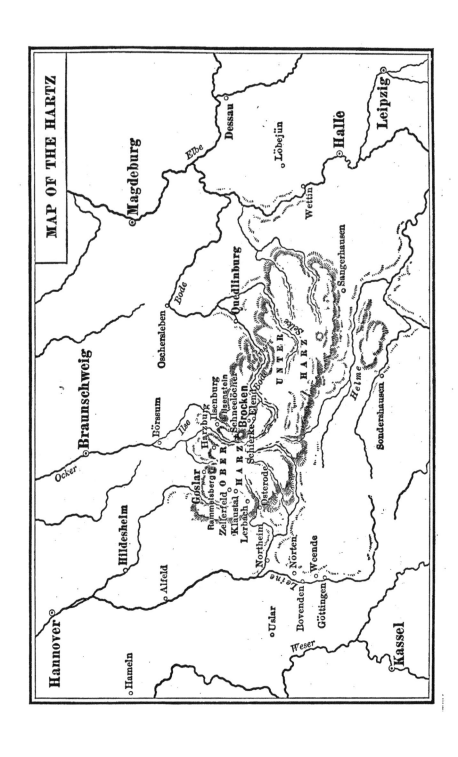

MAP OF THE HARTZ

NOTES

The references to Heine's works are to the edition of Elster: *Heinrich Heines sämtliche Werke. Mit Einleitungen, erläuternden Anmerkungen und Verzeichnissen sämtlicher Lesarten.* Von Dr. Ernst Elster. 7 vols. Leipzig. Bibliographisches Institut.

Page 2. —1. From Ludwig Börne's *Denkrede auf Jean Paul*, delivered at Frankfurt, December 2, 1825. Rhythmically the sentences here quoted are perhaps the most striking of a piece that abounds in brilliant passages. While it can hardly be maintained that this motto strikes in any real sense — the dissonance with the opening paragraphs is especially noticeable — the key-note of the *Harzreise*, it at least serves as an indication that the latter is less an objective account of the poet's foot-tour than a blending of Dichtung und Wahrheit.

Ludwig Börne (1786–1837), born in Frankfurt of Jewish parents, was a prominent journalist and radical politician. Like Heine he was baptized a Christian, and spent the later years of his life in Paris. In contrast with Heine, Börne was a thoroughly consistent character, zealously devoted to the cause of political reform; a man, in fact, whose judgments of contemporaries were throughout determined by the color of his political spectacles. It is hence not surprising that his relations with Heine, in whom the artistic temperament was predominant, though at first friendly, should at last have become strained and openly hostile. The first break between them came in 1832, six years after the publication of the *Harzreise*.

Instances of literary indebtedness of Heine to Börne are pointed out below, page 58, note 2, and page 25, note 3.

Page 3. — 1. Embraffieren (pron. the first syllable as in French), for the German umar'men, the foreign word aptly expressing the conventional character of the embraces, which are to be understood as exchanged between men, a common enough custom in Germany. The whole of the first stanza (Röcke, Strümpfe) has reference to men.

2. frommen. The meaning is that, in contrast with conventional society, the Hütten have remained close to nature's heart.

3. The personal side of his resentment against Göttingen and its university Heine indicates on page 4, line 6. In reality the antipathy was far more deeply rooted; cf. page 84, line 5 ff.

4. Hanno'ver. Notice the pronunciation and spelling as compared with the English *Han'over.*

5. Feuerstellen, *fire-places* or *hearths,* an old-fashioned way of designating the total number of dwellings in a town. The whole characterization of Göttingen is a parody on a style of description that is even now met with in German encyclopedias and guide-books.

6. Karzer (from the Latin *carcer,* '*prison*'). University students in Germany formerly constituted a privileged class, subject only to the jurisdiction of the University Court. Hence the designation *civis academicus,* akademischer Bürger.

7. Ratskeller, the basement of the town hall (Rathaus) leased or conducted by the municipality as an establishment for the sale of wine and beer. Do not translate the word.

Page 4. — 1. Lüder, probably a fellow student. The authorized French version has *mon ami Luder.*

2. vor fünf Jahren. Heine matriculated at Göttingen in the autumn of 1820; his rustication followed in January, 1821.

3. Schnurren, *university police.* The nickname alludes to the rattle (die Schnurre) carried by night watchmen.

4. Pudeln, *poodles,* a re-christening of Pedell', "beadle."

5. Guelfenorden (*pron.* Gw—), founded in 1815 by George IV, then Prince Regent of England and Hanover. The royal house of England and the former royal house of Hanover both belong to the Guelf family. In present German politics the Guelf party (Welfen) favors the restoration to the Hanoverian throne of the descendants of the king deposed in 1866.

6. Promotionskutschen, *graduation carriages,* used by candidates for the doctorate in making a formal call upon the examiners just before proceeding to the degree.

7. **Relegationsräten,** a play upon the word Legationsrat (councilor of legation). The word is of course coined by Heine and designates the officers of the university having the matter of rustication (Relegation) in charge.

8. **Profaxen,** Göttingen students' slang for *pro-rector,* who is in reality the governing rector, the nominal rector (magnificentissimus) being a reigning prince, formerly the king of Hanover. Cf. page 6, note 7.

9. **Völkerwanderung,** *migration of nations,* the German term for those vast movements of barbaric peoples that began A. D. 375, when the Huns forced the West Goths across the Danube, and continued for nearly two hundred years.

10. **ungebundenes;** the pun consists in a play upon the meanings *unbound* (of books) and *unbridled, wild, dissolute.* Similarly, **Exemplar** may denote a *copy* (of a book) or a *specimen.*

11. **Vandalen . . . Thüringer.** Such names, representing in the main ethnic divisions of the German race, are common with students' societies (Landsmannschaften). Heine himself joined the Westfalia.

12. **Farben.** Society *colors* appear, as here indicated, on caps and pipe cords; on festive occasions also in the form of a ribbon slung across the shoulder and chest.

13. **Weenderstraße,** the principal street of Göttingen, so named because it leads to the village of Weende.

14. The **Rasenmühle** (old *mills* frequently serve as resorts) and the Ritschenkrug (Krug = Schenke, *tavern*) are resorts, Bovden (= Bovenden) is a village in the neighborhood of Göttingen.

15. **Duces** (Latin), *leaders.* The Latin term is used to keep up the parallelism with the age of migrations, the equivalent in the student vernacular being Haupthähne.

16. **uraltes,** i.e. handed down, the author implies, from the time of the migrations.

17. **Komment** (from the French *comment,* 'how,' and pronounced as in French), the code of student usage in regard to dueling, drinking, etc.

18. **legibus barbarorum** (Latin), *Laws of the Barbarians,* i.e. the body of old Teutonic law as opposed to Roman law.

Page 5. — 1. $\mathfrak{Phili'fter}$, *Philistines*, i.e. all the townspeople not connected with the university. In the more general sense, . which Matthew Arnold in his essay on Heine was the first to introduce into English, it applies to the materialistic, narrow-minded classes as opposed to those with whom the ideal interests of life are paramount.

2. $\mathfrak{nichts weniger als}$, *anything but.*

3. $\mathfrak{unordentlichen.}$ There are two classes of professors at German universities: the $\mathfrak{ordentliche}$ or *ordinarii* (*full, regular*) and the $\mathfrak{außerordentliche}$ or *extraordinarii*. By substituting $\mathfrak{unordentlich}$ for $\mathfrak{außerordentlich}$ Heine makes a division into *regular and irregular* or *orderly and disorderly.*

4. $\mathfrak{wäre zu weitläuftig}$, *would carry us too far afield.*

5. $\mathfrak{die \ldots haben}$, *who haven't made a name as yet.*

6. $\mathfrak{beffer gesagt}$, *rather.*

7. $\mathfrak{Kot}$, *dirt;* in view of their $\mathfrak{schmußige Gesichter}$ (line 11).

8. $\mathfrak{Rechnungen}$, *bills,* i.e. against students.

9. $\mathfrak{nur}$, *possibly.*

10. $\mathfrak{Topographie.}$ The work referred to is *Göttingen in medizinischer, physischer und historischer Hinsicht geschildert* von Dr. K. F. H. Marx, Göttingen, 1824. Marx was a professor of medicine in the university.

11. $\mathfrak{widerfpricht.}$ The passage in Marx here referred to is in part as follows: „$\mathfrak{Hübfch gebildete Füße will mancher Tadelfüchtige unferen Schönen abfprechen; gewiß mit Unrecht.}$"

12. $\mathfrak{feit Jahr und Tag}$, *for a year and more, for a considerable time.*

13. $\mathfrak{gehört}$; $\mathfrak{hören}$, *to follow a course of lectures on;* so $\mathfrak{lefen}$, of professors, *to lecture.*

Page 6. — 1. $\mathfrak{fo}$, as relative, *which;* an archaic use, in perfect keeping with the pedantically learned outline of the podological monograph.

2. $\mathfrak{Ullrichs Garten}$, a students' resort.

3. In a letter of 1826, Heine professes in this characterization to have had in mind Eduard Gans (1798–1839), professor of jurisprudence at the University of *Berlin*. The French version, however, has *le savant Eichhorn*. Eichhorn was professor of jurisprudence

at Göttingen. — The professor's dream reflects the nature of his daily work: the mechanical collecting and sorting öf material.

4. **nidjt mal** = nidjt einmal', *not even.*

5. **mensa,** *table,* the regular paradigm of the first declension in Latin.

6. **die Jungen piepen, wie die Alten pfeifen,** another form of the adage:

> Wie die Alten fungen (= fangen),
> So zwitschern die Jungen.

i.e. our "Like sire, like son."

7. **hochgelahrten,** archaic and pompous for **hochgelehrt,** *highly learned.* — **Georgia Augusta,** so named from its founder, George (Augustus) II of England and Hanover. The reigning sovereign was ex officio *rector magnificentissimus* of the university. Elsewhere Heine wittily refers to the „Rektor von Göttingen, der in London eine Anstellung als König von England hat."

Page 7. — 1. **die letzte Zeit,** *recently, for some time.*

2. **Pandek'tenstall,** *pandect stable.* The pandects (or the digest) in Roman law are a compilation from the writings of early Roman jurists made by the direction of the emperor Justinian and completed in A. D. 533. Tribonian was president of the commission that drew it up. The word *pandect* is of Greek origin and means 'all-receiving,' i.e. an encyclopedic treatise.

3. **Hermogenian,** the author of the Hermogenian Code, promulgated about A. D. 365.

4. **Dummerjahn,** *Stupidian, Assinian.* The word, not however of Heine's coinage, is formed on the basis of **dumm,** *stupid,* and is cleverly used to travesty the names of the learned jurists immediately preceding. Jahn (or more properly Jan, i.e. 'John') in itself carries the suggestion of dulness.

5. **Doris . . . Gessner** (1730–1788), a Swiss, the author of pastoral idyls in prose that in their day enjoyed a European reputation. Of his *Death of Abel* more particularly there were some six English translations, of which at least seventeen reprints are known to have been made in the United States up to the year 1815. — Schäfer — a common family-name in German — may have been the actual name of the one Pedell, this giving rise to the students

dubbing his comrade Doris, a conventional name of the shepherdess
in pastoral poetry, although not actually occurring in Gessner.

6. **wohlbeſtallte** (= wohlbeſtellte), an archaic form of a word that
is itself no longer in current use. Cf. Schiller's *Wilhelm Tell*, ll.
1859–60:

> ich bin dein Waffenknecht
> Und wohlbeſtellter Wächter bei dem Hut.

7. **Privat'dozen'ten,** *privatdocent,* a lecturer in German universities, lowest in official rank and receiving no salary other than the
fees paid by students. Young and eager to win a reputation, such
men frequently do the most notable scientific work. Hence the
fear that they might smuggle in new ideas.

8. **halbjährigen Schriften,** presumably official *semi-annual reports*
on infractions by students of university regulations or of arrests
made by the Pedell.

9. **citiert,** in the double sense of *quoted* and *summoned* (to appear
before the university authorities). The double meaning does not
extend to Citation below.

Page 8. — 1. **Semesterwelle,** *semestral wave;* the university
year is divided into semesters, the summer semester extending from
the middle of April to the middle of August, the winter semester
from the middle of October to the middle of March. There is
a constant migration from one university to another, and length of
residence is reckoned in semesters, not in years.

2. **unreife,** after alle the weak form of the adjective is now usual.
Heine uses both the strong and weak.

3. **Wirtshausſonne,** *the tavern sun,* i.e. the inn at the sign of the
'Sun.'

4. **Northeim,** for this and other proper names see map.

5. **wollten,** *could not but.*

6. **die akademiſchen Gerichte,** i.e. the academic *hash* dished up at
the university lectures.

7. **alten,** i.e. *warmed over.*

Page 9. — 1. **Salat',** *salad;* a humorous variation of the biblical account, Daniel 4, 30: er aß Gras wie Ochſen. The same jest is
found in Heine's *Geständnisse (Confessions),* Elster VI, 53.

2. **dem erſten beſten Studenten,** idiomatic for *the first student he met.*

3. **Frau** (**Gemahlin, Schweſter**) before names of relationship is not to be translated.

4. **auch ordentliche Leute,** *really nice people.*

5. **Hotel de Brühbach,** perhaps named, as was the custom, from its first occupant or, as Kluge suggests, from the jailer. — The French designation *Hotel de* is common before names of hostelries in Germany. — Notice how the host's smile is cleverly made the occasion for furnishing the clue to the mystification.

6. **Braunſchweiger Meſſe;** as the *Brunswick fair* falls in the week of August 10, and Heine made his tour through the Hartz in September, what follows is a bit of fiction inserted for the sake of the humorous turn of the last sentence of the paragraph.

7. **eingefangene,** *captured, caught in snares.* The reference is not to canaries but to native song-birds, such as finches, linnets, thrushes.

Page 10. — 1. **Oſtero'be,** notice the accentuation.

2. **wie ein Gott,** our *like a top,* which destroys however the Heinesque juxtaposition of **Hund** and **Gott.**

3. **und zwar** introduces a clause that makes a preceding state-ment more specific; so here the meaning is *to be more specific,* or *that is to say.*

4. **des juriſtiſchen Saals,** i.e. the part of the library devoted to law.

5. **Themis,** in Greek mythology, is a personification of custom and unwritten law. Hesiod calls her a Titan (hence **Titanin**), i.e. one of the daughters of Sky and Earth. In more modern times, as in the present passage, she is regarded as symboliz-ing law and justice and her attributes are accordingly the sword and a pair of scales. With these emblems she is now frequently seen above the entrances of court houses in the United States.

6. **Doctores juris** (Latin), *doctors of law.*

7. **Ruſticus,** a latinization of **Bauer.** Anton Bauer was professor of criminal law at Göttingen.

8. **Lykurg,** *Lycurgus,* the celebrated lawgiver of Sparta.

9. **Cavaliere servente** (Italian) = **dienender Ritter,** *attendant cavalier.* In translating, the Italian expression (*pron.* **Cavalje're ſerwen'te**) may be retained.

10. **Cujacius,** a celebrated French jurist of the sixteenth century. The name stands for Gustav Hugo, an adherent of the historical school of jurisprudence founded by Savigny.

Page 11. — 1. **beſchneidet.** The reference is to a dispute as to the interpretation of a passage in the Corpus Juris that deals with the trimming of trees overhanging a neighbor's property. Hugo maintained that all of the top exceeding fifteen feet in height was to be cut off, while others contended that the tree should be trimmed from the base upwards to a height of fifteen feet.

2. **Syſtemchen . . . Köpfchens,** notice the humorous effect of the diminutive endings cleverly capped by **Köpfchen**; *puny* may perhaps be used to render **-chen.**

3. **illuſtren = hochſtehenden,** *illustrious.* The unusual foreign word is employed to characterize the pedantry. So **regardierte** below (l. 17).

4. **drauf los definierten,** *glibly put forth their definitions.*

5. **Prometheus,** the benefactor and champion of mankind, whom Aeschylus, the Greek tragedian, in his drama *Prometheus Bound,* represents as chained, at the command of Zeus, to a rock by Force (**Kraft**) and Violence (**Gewalt**). Here a vulture gnaws at his vitals to punish him for having stolen fire for man from the gods. The reference is to the long sufferings of the German nation (Prometheus) under the reactionary policy of the Holy Alliance.[1]

Page 12. — 1. **Münchhauſen** (1688-1770), influential statesman, curator of the University of Göttingen at the time of its foundation. The fame early won by the university was largely due to his efforts. His portrait hung in the hall.

2. **in ihrem Anblick,** *at the sight of her.*

---

[1] The fact that the French version of 1858 (published two years after the poet's death) here has " La force insultante et la violence muette de la sainte alliance ont enchaîné le héros sur un rocher dans l'océan" does not militate against this view. The earlier edition of 1834 reads *l'innocent* (= **den Schuldloſen**) instead of *le héros,* and the very substitution of the latter expression, with its obvious reference to Napoleon I, indicates the existence of a feeling that **der Schuldloſe** is an epithet that cannot properly be applied to Napoleon. To Heine Napoleon was *imperator* and *liberator,* not ein **Schuldloſer.** The *rock* as such (**Marterfelſen**) is of course part and parcel of the Prometheus legend and has no necessary connection with the historical or legendary Napoleon.

3. **hochgebenedeiten,** *blessed;* the use of this adjective, which properly applies to the Virgin Mary, imparts a religious coloring to the rhapsody. The poet takes sanctuary with the god and goddess that typify eternal beauty. — The contrast here drawn between arid juridical speculations and the Hellenic world of beauty is in Heine's best vein. The dream further symbolizes his turning from his legal studies in Göttingen to the poetry and nature of the Hartz.

4. **Lyrahlänge,** *strains of the lyre;* the lyre was Apollo's attribute as god of music.

5. **Glöckchen,** i.e. *bells* hung around the necks of the cattle.

6. **Befreiungskriege,** the *War of Liberation* against Napoleon (1813–15). Heine's admiration for Napoleon causes him repeatedly to speak disparagingly of the achievements of the nation in the Befreiungskrieg.

7. With this a passage from Heine's *Lutezia* (Elster VI, 288) may be contrasted: Bürgersleute, welche . . . sich gern erbauen an dem Anblick gefallener Größe, im süßen Bewußtsein, daß sie von dergleichen Katastrophen gesichert sind in der bescheidenen Dunkelheit einer arrière-boutique der Rue St. Denis.

Page 13. — 1. **gar liebe, kindliche,** *childlike in its beauty and loveliness.*

2. **Von,** *of,* not "from." The reference is to the ruins of the Ostero'der Burg.

3. **Handwerksburschen,** *journeyman;* under the old system of guilds an apprentice upon completing his term of apprenticeship became journeyman, i.e. he traveled about seeking to perfect himself still further in his craft through the instruction of masters in other cities.

4. **dortiges,** *there current.*

5. **der junge Herzog,** i.e. of Brunswick.

6. **Herzog Ernst,** an epic poem of the twelfth century. Duke Ernst of Swabia, when his stepfather puts him under the ban of the empire, makes a crusade to the Holy Land. The epic tells of the marvelous adventures he met with.

Page 14. — 1. **Ossians Nebelgeister.** The poems compiled and composed in English by James MacPherson, published in 1760–63, were at the time of their appearance considered renderings from

Keltic originals by Ossian. In Germany especially, these Ossianic poems created a furore. Heine's term Nebelgeister finds its best commentary in a modern critic's characterization of Ossian's heroes: "The actors ... are like figures *seen through a mist*, barely sketched in outline, whose dress, ornaments, and arms are so generally and vaguely described as to lose all peculiar and distinctive character." Cf. page 67, note 3.

2. The first two stanzas of the *Volkslied* run as follows:

Ein Käfer auf dem Zaune saß; brumm, brumm!
Die Fliege, die darunter saß, summ, summ!

„Fliege, willst du mich heiraten? brumm, brumm!
Ich hab' noch drei Dukaten," summ, summ!

3. das Goethesche Wort, i.e. *sayings* (*lines, words*) *of Goethe.*

4. The original is the famous song of Klärchen in *Egmont:*

Freudvoll
Und leidvoll,
Gedankenvoll sein,
Langen
Und bangen
In schwebender Pein,
Himmelhoch jauchzend,
Zum Tode betrübt—
Glücklich allein
Ist die Seele, die liebt.

5. Lottchen bei dem Grabe ihres Werthers, a sentimental poem forming a sequel to Goethe's novel *The Sorrows of Young Werther* (Die Leiden des jungen Werthers), which closes with the suicide of Werther.

6. Herberge, here *guild house*, the house of the guild (of tailors in this case), in which meetings were held and at which journeymen of the guild put up; hence the expression Wir haben.

Page 15. — 1. Ziegenhainer, name of a cane carried by students, so called from the village Ziegenhain near Jena, where they are made. Translate *spindle legs.* It is barely possible that there also is in the word a reference to the standing association in German of tailors with goats (Ziegen).

2. namentlich, not 'namely,' but *especially.*

3. den Weg zwischen die Beine nehmen, colloquial for *push on, make headway.*

4. A most amusing commentary on this whole episode as related by Heine is contained in a letter addressed by Karl Dörne, the

original of the Schneidergesell in question, to the *Gesellschafter*, the Berlin periodical in which the *Harzreise* first made its appearance. According to this account Dörne first inquired as to the name and business of his fellow traveler. Heine answered that his name was Peregrinus and that he was a cosmopolite traveling as a recruiting officer in the service of the Sultan of Turkey. Dörne, who in reality was a commercial traveler, in his turn passed himself off as a journeyman tailor and told the tale of the capture of the Duke of Brunswick by the Turks. Heine thereupon promised to do his utmost to intercede in the duke's behalf with his Majesty the Sultan. The mutilation of the texts of the *Volkslieder* appears to have been wholly conscious and intentional. Heine furthermore misrepresents the meaning of doppelte Poesie. Dörne explains how his friend when tipsy saw everything double and hence also made *double poetry!* On this latter point compare page 55, note 3. The change here made by Heine in the interpretation of doppelte Poesie is probably due to the fact that the figure of the Schneidergesell is throughout conceived in a vein of caricature, and the anecdote as originally told was out of keeping with this conception.

Page 16. — 1. Ernst Theodor Amadäus Hoffmann (1776–1822), of the later Romantic school, a writer to whom the grotesque and fantastic appealed very strongly.

2. **bemalt** (different from gemalt, *painted*), *would* (*if he had had a free hand*) *have given them* (*in nature*) *motley colors.*

3. **über eine halbe Stunde ;** expressing shorter distances in terms of the time taken to cover them on foot is usual in German.

4. **Kropfleute.** Goitre seems to be peculiarly prevalent in valleys and elevated plains of mountainous districts.

5. **Albinos,** found in all parts of the globe, peculiar in having a perfectly white skin (hence the name, from the Latin *albus* = white), white hair, and eyes with bright-red pupil and pink iris..

Page 17. — 1. **schlechte Verse.** In the letter referred to above Dörne cleverly suggests that these are other poets' verses.

2. **blauäugig und flachshaarig,** *blue eyed and flaxen-haired;* the pure Teutonic type.

3. **Klosterschule,** the Düsseldorf Lycée, on which see the Introduction. Heine entered it at the age of ten.

4. **den ganzen lieben Vormittag,** *the whole precious forenoon.*

5. **Krone,** now **Die Goldene Krone** and proud of the fact that Heine once lodged there.

6. **gestorben :** supply **ist.**

7. **Bievlied.** Biervliet is the correct form. By **Zeeland** (*pron.* Seeland) the Dutch province of that name is meant, of which Middelburg is the capital.

8. **schmeckt doch,** *does taste.*

Page 18. — 1. **Handlungsbeflissener** "has a tinge of irony about it . . . and may be rendered . . . *votary of commerce*" (Buchheim).

2. **Kleider machen Leute,** *Fine feathers make fine birds.*

3. **bei,** *on pain of.*

4. **doch,** *after all.*

5. **Silberblick,** a technical term in silver smelting : the gleam that silver emits at the moment it solidifies. By adding **wie oft im Leben** Heine humorously makes this ill luck symbolic of his failure to catch sight of (much) silver in life.

6. **weiter . . . können,** true also of his subsequent business relations with his publishers, the firm of Hoffmann und Campe in Hamburg, which grew rich on the sales of Heine's works.

7. **hatte . . . das Zusehen,** *had to be content with looking on.*

8. **mal,** *some day.*

Page 19. — 1. **die Kinder Israel,** not necessarily *the Jews,* but 'the chosen people,' that are gifted with the **Silberblick.**

2. **Tugend,** i. e. the kind of virtue that is a little the worse for wear and needs patching.

3. **Schurzfell,** *leather apron,* fastened about the waist and worn behind.

Page 20. — 1. **Kamin'fegeloch,** *chimney-sweeping hole.* "Such holes are usual in the breastwork of the chimney above the roof in German houses ; the sweep mounts to the leads, opens the hole, and sweeps upwards and downwards" (Colbeck).

2. **nichts weniger als,** see page 5, note 2.

3. **Es gibt,** *it causes ;* **schon,** *in itself.*

4. **von,** *of* or *having.*

5. **fotig naß,** *dirty and wet.*

6. **Da unten,** *down below,* i.e. at the bottom of the mine.

Page 21. — 1. Lafayette, as 'guest of the nation,' paid a visit to the United States in 1824–25. He was most enthusiastically received and congress voted him a gift of $200,000.00.

2. **unter uns gesagt,** *between you and me.*

3. **im vorigen Jahre,** in making a trip from Kuxhaven to Helgoland on August 22, 1823.

Page 22. — 1. **Glückauf',** the usual miner's greeting, for which there is no parallel expression in English. The meaning is 'luck on the way up.' In rendering retain the German expression. Notice the accent.

2. **Cicerone** (*pron.* Tsitsero'ne), *guide,* an Italian word, literally 'a Cicero.' The connection in thought between a guide and the great Roman orator is apparently that of talkativeness, volubility.

3. **pudeldeutsche,** a compound of Heine's coinage. By 'poodle-German' Heine satirizes the unquestioning, docile devotion (to the reigning house) that he thinks characteristic of the Germans of his day.

4. **Herzog von Cambridge:** Adolphus Frederick, seventh son of George III of England and Hanover, and at this time stadholder of Hanover.

5. **bleibe,** subjunctive of indirect statement: *the latter, he said, would remain,* etc.

Page 23. — 1. **Abref'senflostel,** *flourish, phrase.* The term **Abresse** is here used of an address or petition to the throne, in which the expressions of loyalty and devotion are apt to be mere conventional phrases.

2. **dem getreuen Eckart** (= Eckhardt), as treated in Tieck's tale (interspersed with verse) of that name, which may be conveniently read in Carlyle's translation.

3. **glaubt:** as shown by the policy of repression of liberal ideas pursued by German governments after the War of Liberation.

4. **geheiligten,** a reference to either the 'Holy' Alliance or the 'divine right' of kings.

Page 24. — 1. ©o . . . au&, *placid and stationary as.*

2. **Märchenfabel,** *fairy-tale.* It should be remembered that the *Kinder- und Hausmärchen* of the brothers Grimm, which gave the German fairy-tale its classical literary form, had appeared in 1812-15, and were therefore at the time Heine wrote the *Harzreise* a comparatively recent publication.

3. **sprechen und handeln.** Heine's explanation seems entirely plausible. It was among the peasant and working classes that the *Märchen*, before their collection by the Grimms, had been preserved and cherished.

Page 25. — 1. The examples are all taken from the first volume of Grimm's *Kinder- und Hausmärchen* (1812) and are cited in the order in which they occur in that volume: No. 10. *Das Lumpengesindel* (The Riffraff); No. 18. *Strohhalm, Kohle und Bohne auf der Reise;* No. 42. *Der Herr Gevatter* (The Godfather); No. 53. *Sneewittchen* (Little Snow White); No. 56. *Der Liebste Roland.* As is shown also by close resemblances in phraseology, Heine, to gather his illustrations, gave the volume a careful scrutiny.

2. **Aus demselben Grunde,** *for the same reason,* i. e. on account of the direct touch with nature.

3. **statt daß,** *whereas.* The thought of these lines is quite the same as that contained in Börne's essay *Die Kunst, in drei Tagen ein Original-Schriftsteller zu werden,* from which Heine also borrows a conceit further on. See page 58, note 2.

4. **Isaak,** i. e. the (Jewish) second-hand dealer. **Hans** may perhaps be rendered by *Jack,* **Isaak** (pron. J=sa=ak) by *Ike.*

Page 26. — 1. **die liebe Hand der Geliebten so lieblich ruhte.** The combination of humor and pathos is thoroughly Heinesque. Notice the cumulative effect of liebe — Geliebten — lieblich.

2. **wieder erzählt,** *tells in his turn.*

3. **hinterm Ofen.** How these lives form an eternal cycle is finely indicated by the repetition at the end of the paragraph of the words with which it opened: dem großen Schranke gegenüber, hinterm Ofen.

4. **Hofrat B.,** perhaps Friedrich Bouterwek, professor at Göttingen, known especially as the author of *Geschichte der Poesie und*

Beredsamkeit seit dem Ende des dreizehnten Jahrhunderts, Göttingen, 1801-1819.

5. **Schlemihl'**, i. e. *Peter Schlemihl*, the famous story of the man who sold his shadow to the devil. The point about Chamisso's (*pron.* Schamis'so) arrival and departure in a downpour is that he herein resembles Schlemihl, who in order that his lack of a shadow might not be observed chose rainy days for traveling.

Page 27. — 1. **hob auf . . . und ging,** a parody (hence also hob auf meine Füße for hob meine Füße auf) of the biblical Da hob Jakob seine Füße auf, und ging in das Land, das gegen Morgen liegt, Genesis 29, 1. For the pertinency of this style in connection with Goslar see page 29, note 3. The Land of Promise proves a disappointment (p. 29, l. 12 ff.).

2. **das alte Märchen.** Reminiscent in a general way of such a story as *Dat Erdmänneken* (The Dwarf) in the Grimm collection.

3. **mehr und mehre,** unusual for mehr und mehr. Heine frequently uses mehre for mehrere, *several.*

4. **ihre breiten Häupter,** a characteristic of dwarfs in German folklore.

5. **darauf,** *at them.*

Page 28. — 1. **Es werde Licht,** i.e. Genesis 1, 3, Und Gott sprach: Es werde Licht. Und es ward Licht.

2. **Wie doch,** *Alas, how* (Buchheim).

Page 29. — 1. **just,** colloquial for gerade, here employed for its humorous effect in connection with the travesty of the Märchen style.

2. **eigenes,** *peculiar.*

3. **Goslar,** a quaint old town with many historical associations. It was founded by Henry the Fowler about 920. Numerous diets were held there, and it was frequently the residence of the early emperors.

4. **allwo,** archaic for wo, purposely used here as in keeping with quaint old Goslar; verfallen and dumpfig apply to *Goslar*, not to the *Gose.*

5. **Berliner Hexameter.** It is not clear to just what writers Heine is referring.

6. **Schützenhof** (= Schützenfest), here the *rifle-match ;* below (page 43, line 3), the place of resort itself.

7. **es,** i. e. das Metallbecken.

Page 30. — 1. **Rathaus,** *town hall,* dating from 1134, recently restored.

2. **Gildenhaus,** i. e. *guild hall* of the tailors, now called die Kaiserworth and used as hotel. See the illustration and compare page 14, note 6.

3. **sehen aus;** observe the droll effect of the omission of sie, which can perhaps be imitated in English.

4. **gebratene,** *roasted,* because räucherig schwarz.

5. **sagen soll,** *means.*

6. **niedergerissen,** *torn down ;* it was condemned and demolished in 1820.

7. The Kaiserstuhl is now in the Kaiserhaus, which although not mentioned by Heine, is since its restoration in 1873 the most noteworthy structure in Goslar. It dates from the year 1050 and was the imperial palace.

8. **Kaiserstühle . . . geworfen,** symbolizing the political changes that were, or were thought to be, impending.

9. **seligen,** *defunct,* humorously applied to Dom. Its natural use (*deceased, late*) is seen on page 16, line 2.

Page 31. — 1. **Lukas Cranach** (1472–1553), an eminent German painter and engraver of the period of the Reformation.

2. **ein heidnischer Opferaltar,** now generally regarded as of Christian, not pagan, origin. It is probably a reliquary, i. e., a repository for relics.

3. **Karyati'den,** *Caryatids,* i. e. sculptured female figures in the place of supporting columns.

4. **quis . . . quando,** a mnemonic Latin dactylic hexameter (Quis'? quid? ubi'? quibus au'xiliis'? cur? quo'modo? quan'do? *Who? what? where? by what means? why? how? when?*) containing suggestions for the treatment of any given theme.

5. **abgetragener,** *worn out,* an adjective that is properly speaking applicable to clothing only.

6. **Batavia,** the capital of Java in the Dutch East Indies. Here used for Java, the island.

Page 32. — 1. aufgeklärte, '*enlightened*,' *rationalistic*.

2. ich will . . . gesagt haben, *I didn't mean to say*.

3. ordentlich, adverb, but render by adjective: *regular*.

4. beturbanten, i.e. with a turban sculptured on them.

5. bei den Chine′sen gar, *as for the Chinese*; gar, *even*, implies that the Chinese even outdo the Turks.

Page 33. — 1. Mäuler, properly used of animals; hence insulting when applied to men. The use of Maul for Mund is however usual in the *Studentensprache*, being merely symptomatic of the bluntness or coarseness which the latter affects.

2. Rot= und Blauröcke, i.e. the military.

Page 34. — 1. schnurrbärtige Liebenswürdigkeit, *fascination of their mustaches*.

2. Logis, pronounce as in French.

3. Rammelsberg, rich in minerals, a mile south of Goslar.

4. mit Brettern zugenagelt, *nailed up with boards*, an idea frequently met with in German children's stories.

5. Petrischlüssel: *Petri* is the Latin genitive of *Petrus*. St. Peter has charge of the keys of heaven.

6. Spießbürger, not essentially different in meaning from Philister; cf. page 5, note 1.

7. Maule: the designation is in keeping with Spießbürger.

Page 35. — 1. Unsterblichkeitsgedanken. For a similar thought compare Goethe, *Hermann und Dorothea* IX, 222–225:

> Und es schaute das Mädchen mit tiefer Rührung zum Jüngling
> Und vermied nicht Umarmung und Kuß, den Gipfel der Freude,
> Wenn sie den Liebenden sind die lang ersehnte Versicherung
> Künftigen Glücks im Leben, das nun ein unendliches scheinet.

2. stärker fühlt, *feels more intensely*. This idea that the night intensifies the inner life of plant as of man is not infrequent in Heine's writings.

3. sinnig verschämt, *with charming diffidence*.

4. so ist es, i. e. her smile is in itself a prayer.

5. ich schnüre den Ranzen, *I pack my knapsack;* notice the anti-climax, of a kind with the final ironical turn (Stimmungsbrechung) that Heine often gives his finest poems.

Page 36.—1. der Öſtreichiſche Beobachter, *the Austrian Observ-er*, a Vienna newspaper that appeared from 1810–32. As the official publication of the reactionary Austrian government, it would naturally be ultra-conservative, including in its conservatism, Heine seems to imply, a belief in, and fear of, ghosts.

2. Aſcher, a Jewish friend of Heine; in philosophy a disciple of Kant.

3. höchſte Prinzip', i.e. in controlling our actions.

4. tranſcendentalgrauen; tranſcendental' is a technical term in Kantian philosophy meaning *transcending experience.*

Page 37.— 1. überhaupt, *in fact;* überhaupt regularly intro-duces a statement more sweeping or of wider application than what has preceded.

2. Vernunft, *reason.* By rationalism Heine here understands a system of philosophy which regards reason as the sole arbiter of opinion and guide of life, repudiates all belief in the supernatural and denies that the emotions play any important part in controlling human action. Such an attitude of mind is diametrically opposed to that of the child, hence the remark in ll. 9–10.

3. **Varnhagen von Ense** (1785–1858), not a writer of importance, but well-known through the brilliant Berlin salon over which his Jewish wife, Rahel Levin, presided. To this salon Heine had ac-cess during his stay in Berlin. Heine's friendship with the author has doubtless colored the expression of his opinion (l. 22) on the story.

4. jene entſetzliche Geſchichte. The title of the story is Das warnende Geſpenſt.

5. Auch, *besides.*

6. des Nachts, an adverbial genitive of time formed in analogy with such masculine nouns as Tag, Abend, etc.

Page 38. — 1. und zwar, *and that too;* cf. page 10, note 3.

2. volle, inflected adjective; translate as adverb, *fully.*

3. Winkel, i.e. at the corners.

Page 39. — 1. Dialekte, *speech.*

2. Bedingungen der Möglichkeit, *conditions of the possibility*, the phraseology is that of current philosophy.

3. Substituting Abteilung for Abſchnitt the reference is an actual one. The section deals with the distinction between *phenomena* and *noumena*. In Kantian philosophy *phenomena* are objects as they present themselves to our senses, *noumena* as they are in themselves. We have no guarantee that the two are identical. In the present instance Ascher is to be understood as insisting upon the unreality of this 'phenomenal' ghost, i.e. of this ghost as seen and heard, on the ground of its logical inadmissibility as *noumenon*. — This idea of a ghost arguing against the admissibility of ghosts would seem to have been suggested to Heine by the Walpurgisnacht scene of Goethe's *Faust*, where the Proktophantasmist (*Faust* I, ll. 4158-67) — also a caricature of a Berlin rationalist — plays a somewhat similar part. Cf. page 57, note 8.

Page 40. — 1. Glockenblümchen, i.e. those purloined from the window sill (p. 33, l. 4). He still wore them in his cap.

2. Ich mochte . . . haben, *it seemed that I had actually lost my way.*

3. näher ("nearer"), here to be rendered *sooner*.

4. überhaupt, see page 37, note 1. The reflections that follow refer primarily to *life's* experiences.

5. wohlwollend, *generously.*

6. große : modern usage requires großen.

7. konnten: könnten or hätten . . . können would be expected.

Page 41. — 1. daß die wimmernden Stimmen . . . Sau, sc. herrührten.

2. den eben geworfenen Jungen, *the new litter.* Wild boars are still found in the Hartz.

3. was . . . anbelange, *so far as his humble self was concerned.* Wenigkeit is said with the tone of conventional self depreciation.

4. nüchternem, i.e. saliva secreted *on an empty stomach.*

5. auf . . . Natur, *how everything in nature was useful and adapted to an end.*

6. und sei er noch so groß, *however great he be.*

Page 42. — 1. die alte Weiſ', *the old tune;* its content is indicated in the last stanza of I, p. 43, ll. 21-24.

Page 43. — 1. Schützenhof : cf. page 29, note 6.

2. uns einander = einander or uns. This pleonastic use of the

reciprocal is not infrequent in the fairy tale and popular ballad. Heine employs it repeatedly.

Page 44. — 1. **gar zu oft,** *any too often.* — The next three stanzas are of course addressed by the girl to the poet. The entire dialogue is reminiscent of that between Faust and Margarete in the scene Marthens Garten of Goethe's *Faust.*

2. **Zucken,** *quiver, twitch;* compare the description of Heine by a Göttingen friend (quoted by Gregor): „Er hatte . . . einen Mund, der in steter, zuckender Bewegung war." The Zucken and der Augen frommer Strahl symbolize the dualism of Heine's nature.

3. **was so . . . heißt,** *what is properly called.*

4. **Mutters:** colloquial for der Mutter.

5. **Der da waltet,** *who rules the world.*

6. **glaub':** the change to the present tense is significant, the reference being to Heine's impending formal acceptance of Christianity. See Introduction.

7. **Jetzo,** archaic form of jetzt.

8. **den heil'gen Geist.** In Heine's interpretation of the creed the 'holy ghost' stands for the modern spirit of emancipation, political, social and religious.

Page 45. — 1. **das dunkle Hirngespinst,** *the gloomy phantom,* i.e. superstition.

2. **gewappnet,** poetic for gewaffnet, *armed.*

3. **solche stolze,** the more correct modern form is solche stolzen.

4. **ein solcher Ritter von dem heil'gen Geist,** i.e. as poet, championing the cause of liberty and emancipation. The term Ritter vom Geist became a watchword of 'Young Germany.'

Page 46. — 1. **weg;** the pronunciation of this adverb, as here shown by the rime with Speck, is *wĕk.*

2. **Geisterberge.** The reference is not to the Brocken but to the Grosse Burgberg, just south of the town Harzburg, on which the ruins of the famous old castle, the Harzburg (built 1065–1069), are still to be seen.

3. **Voller,** a variant form of voll; the -er is not felt as a declensional ending.

4. **Fackeltanz,** at present a dance or march in which the leaders carry torches. It is still customary at marriages in the royal family

of Prussia, and was for example danced on the occasion of the wedding of the crown prince and the princess Cecilie of Mecklenburg. — Here the word is used in a more general sense.

5. ſel'ge Muhme: cf. page 43, line 1.

Page 47. — 1. A stanza of wonderful melody.

2. The German 'Mother Goose' has a number of 'finger rimes', in which the individual fingers are given various fanciful names.

3. haſtig regſam, *quivering with life.*

Page 48. — 1. wurdeſt zur, *hast become a.*

2. wie mich nur wenige geſehen, i.e. with tears in his eyes, a sentiment with which the opening lines of Heine's sonnet to his mother („Ich bin's gewohnt, den Kopf recht hoch zu tragen") may be compared.

Page 49. — 1. einer verlornen Waldkirche, alluding to legends everywhere current in Germany of edifices or towns that have mysteriously vanished, and from which sounds such as the ringing of bells may at times reach the upper air. In literature this conception of a 'vanished church' has found its classic expression in Uhland's ballad *Die verlorene Kirche* (1812), which Heine probably had in mind here, and of which the first lines are:

> Man höret oft im fernen Wald
> Von obenher ein dumpfes Läuten,
> Doch niemand weiß, von wann es hallt,
> Und kaum die Sage kann es deuten.

2. Brocken, the highest peak of the Hartz range, much frequented by tourists. A railway now runs up its summit. It has been made weltberühmt by Goethe's *Faust*, in which the Walpurgisnacht scene (see page 52, note 5) is laid on the Brocken.

3. déjeuner dinatoire, "an ample second breakfast taken about noon, which might be considered as taking the place of a regular dinner. The expression is used ironically" (Van Daell).

4. Brot gegeben hat. That Heine should make this remark, even in jest, indicates at once the consciousness on the part of the young poet of his great power and his inherent tendency to look to outsiders for patronage.

5. rotbekreuzt; the sheep are the fawning courtiers and the red cross marks on their foreheads are their orders and decorations. — The poem is a wonderful blending of humor, satire and pathos.

Page 50. — 1. $\mathfrak{Kammermuſici}$ (*pron.* =mu'ſitſi), the Latin plural of *musicus; musicians of the royal household.*

2. **unb ſie . . . laſſen,** *and their youth has been a period of toil and drudgery.*

Page 51. — 1. **erſt recht,** *only the more* or *all the more.*

2. The legend of Genovefa and Schmerzenreich ('rich in sorrows') is best known through the *Volksbuch* and Tieck's drama, *Leben und Tod der heiligen Genoveva.* The story runs that while Genovefa's husband, the palsgrave Siegfried, is away from home fighting the Moors, she is through the machinations of the villainous Golo, to whose keeping she had been entrusted, accused of unfaithfulness and condemned to die. Spared through the mercy of the servants to whom the execution of the sentence had been committed, she lives with her infant son for seven years in a. cave in the forest. She herself subsists on roots and herbs, while her babe through the grace of God. is twice a day suckled by a doe. Siegfried returns, detects Golo's treachery and some time afterwards while hunting discovers his wife and child, whom he had thought dead.

Elsewhere (Elster III, 103) Heine expresses his views on hunting as follows:

Der Sinn für das Edle, Schöne und Gute läßt sich oft durch Erziehung den Menſchen beibringen; aber der Sinn für die Jagd liegt im Blute. Wenn die Ahnen ſchon ſeit undenklichen Zeiten Rehböcke geſchoſſen haben, ſo findet auch der Enkel ein Vergnügen an dieſer legitimen Beſchäftigung. Meine Ahnen gehörten aber nicht zu den Jagenden, viel eher zu den Gejagten.

3. **nach:** *to listen to, to examine.*

Page 52. — 1. **Da läßt ſich gut ſitzen,** *it is pleasant to sit there.*

2. Notice the fine effect of the chiasm (parallelism in reverse order): bie Bäume flüſtern wie mit tauſend Mädchenzungen, wie mit tauſend Mädchenaugen ſchauen uns an bie ſeltſamen Bergblumen. The effort to heighten this effect explains also the position of **an,** which would otherwise stand last.

3. **erſt recht,** *more than ever.*

4. **ſich . . . einander,** see page 43, note 2.

5. **Walpurgisnacht,** the night between April 30 and May 1, when according to old German tradition witches gathered on the Brocken to celebrate their annual festival. That this latter should bear

the name of the saintly Walpurga, a niece of St. Boniface and the abbess of a Bavarian nunnery, is solely due to the circumstance that May 1 is St. Walpurga's day in the Roman Catholic calendar.

6. $\Re e\mathfrak{t}\mathfrak{fch}$, well-known as illustrator of Goethe's *Faust* and other German classics.

7. $\Re e\mathfrak{ife}$. Heine made a trip from Göttingen to Berlin toward the end of March, 1824, remained in Berlin four weeks and, as stated in the text, returned to Göttingen at the beginning of May.

Page 53. — 1. $\mathfrak{Abendzeitung}$, a periodical of considerable influence appearing at Dresden from 1817 onward. Contributors mentioned elsewhere in the *Harzreise* are H. Clauren, Kotzebue and Elise von Hohenhausen.

2. $\Re atcliff$ und $\mathfrak{Almanfor}$, Heine's two tragedies, written, the former in 1822, the latter in 1820 and 1821. They were published together in 1823. The order in which they are mentioned is the one they occupied in this volume. Heine was not a dramatist and neither play is of any real importance.

3. $\mathfrak{Blocksbergsgeschichten}$. $\mathfrak{Blocksberg}$ (i.e. 'boulder-mountain') is a name given the Brocken more particularly in connection with its character as the rendezvous of witches.

4. That $\mathfrak{Fauft}$ is a $\mathfrak{deutfche}$ $\Re ationaltragödie$ is among other things shown by the many writers who either planned or composed a *Faust:* Goethe, Lessing, Maler Müller, Klinger, Lenau, Heine, etc.

5. $\mathfrak{der}$ $\mathfrak{Pferdefuß}$, i.e. Mephistopheles (Mephisto), just as Faust and Mephistopheles in the Walpurgisnacht scene of Goethe's *Faust* ascend the Blocksberg together. In a sense therefore Heine here identifies himself with Faust.

6. $\mathfrak{Stolberg\text{-}Wernigerode}$, a wealthy old family, still the owners of the Brockenhaus.

Page 54. — 1. $\mathfrak{ungewöhnliche}$, $\mathfrak{märchenhafte}$ $\mathfrak{Empfindung}$, *a strange sensation as if I had been transported to fairyland.*

2. $\mathfrak{voller}$: see page 46, note 3.

3. $\mathfrak{Brockenfträuße}$, i.e. nosegays of flowers growing on the Brocken. Owing to its height, the Brocken formerly had a rich flora peculiar to itself. The annual swarms of marauding tourists

have almost totally extirpated it, and at present there is a law forbidding the picking of any flower or plant on the Brocken.

4. **da wird . . . gekniffen,** u. f. w., *there is a pinching*, etc.

Page 55. — 1. **Fußweg,** i.e. guten Fußweg : the French version has *bon chemin*.

2. **Profit,** Latin, *may it do you good*. Profit (or the shortened Pröft) is the usual expression in pledging before drinking. The term may be retained in rendering into English.

3. **doppelten Genuß,** *double enjoyment;* it will be noticed that Heine here turns to account the authentic explanation of the Schneidergeſell as to the meaning of doppelte Poeſie. See page 15, note 4.

4. **refreiert,** pronounce refre=iert.

Page 56. — 1. **ſich widerſprechend,** *mutually contradictory.*

2. **noch unentworrenen,** lit. 'not yet disentangled,' i.e. *still confused.*

3. **Begriffe,** *essence.*

4. **ſcharf gezeichnete, rein illuminierte,** *sharply outlined, clearly colored.* The term Spezialkarte is often applied to a small map, on a larger scale than the principal one, which it accompanies, and a portion of which it treats.

5. **wie es denn,** *just as it.*

6. **Deutſchruhiges, Verſtändiges, Tolerantes.** The *German calmness, intelligence and tolerance* of the Brocken are due to its wide outlook and clear view.

7. **philiſtrö'ſe:** philiſterhaft is the usual adjective. Compare Philiſtröſität (= Philiſterei) below, words ending in =tät being characteristic of students' slang.

8. **Claudius,** i.e. the poet Matthias Claudius in his *Rheinwein-lied*, in which the vine-clad slopes of the Rhine are contrasted with various distant mountains. Two of the stanzas are :

Thüringens Berge, zum Exempel, bringen
Gewächs, ſieht aus wie Wein,
Iſt's aber nicht : man kann dabei nicht ſingen,
Dabei nicht fröhlich ſein.

Der Blocksberg iſt der lange Herr Philiſter,
Er macht nur Wind, wie der ;
Drum tanzen auch der Kuckuck und ſein Küſter
Auf ihm die Kreuz und Quer.

9. **mit . . . Nebelkappe bedeckt,** i.e. to hide its baldness. The Nebelkappe, *cap of mist*, resembles a Nachtmütze and the latter is regarded as the very essence of Philiströsität. So the Nürnberger Spießbürger . . . mit weißer Nachtmütze of page 34, line 22.

Page 57.— 1. **Philiströsität,** see page 56, note 7.

2. **Ironie** is a term that plays a great rôle in Romantic literature. Hence the reference to manchen andern großen Deutschen. The Stimmungsbrechung found in so many of Heine's poems, to which reference has before been made (page 35, note 5), merely carried this principle of ' Romantic Irony ' to its legitimate conclusion.

3. **die erste Mainacht,** i.e. the Walpurgisnacht.

4. **recht echtdeutsch,** *in the most orthodox German fashion.*

5. **genießt man erst recht, wenn,** *one doesn't really begin to enjoy fully until.*

6. **Formen,** *manners.*

7. **der wißbegierigen Schönen,** *the fair one with her thirst for knowledge.*

8. **Schierke und Elend,** villages at the foot of the Brocken. The collocation of these two names is doubtless a reminiscence from the Walpurgisnacht scene of *Faust* which Goethe places in the Gegend von Schierke und Elend. The names themselves (Schurke, ' scoundrel '; Elend, ' misery ') also have an ominous sound.

Page 58. — 1. **schlimmbewegtes,** *tempest-tossed;* schlimm= = severely.

2. **codex palimpsestus,** a parchment written upon twice, the original writing having been wholly or partially erased to make room for the second. As has been recently pointed out this striking comparison is not original with Heine but is borrowed from Börne:

„Wie die Welt jetzt beschaffen, gleichen die Köpfe der Gelehrten, und also auch ihre Werke den alten Handschriften, von welchen man die langweiligen Zänkereien eines Kirchenstiefvaters oder die Faseleien eines Mönches erst abkratzen muß, um zu einem römischen Klassiker zu kommen."

Compare page 25, note 3.

Page 59. — 1. **in der Peterskirche,** a slip for *in the Vatican,* there being no paintings by Raphael in St. Peter's.

2. **Theater Feni'ce** (pron. =ce as *cha* in *chase*), the *Phœnix Theatre* in Venice.

3. **Leib des Herrn**, i.e. the consecrated wafer or host.

4. **Palestri'na** (about 1524–1594), the famous Italian composer of church music. The reference is probably to the mass known as the Missa Papae Marcelli, regarded as Palestrina's greatest work.

5. **„Wie ist . . . so schön"** : a characteristic example of Heinesque Stimmungsbrechung.

6. **Werkeltagsstimmung**, *workaday-mood*. The word is the more appropriate as what was depicted at the end of the preceding paragraph is a Sonntagsstimmung in the literal sense.

Page 60. — 1. **meinte**, *expressed as her opinion*.

2. **eine Stelle aus Goethes Reisebriefen.** The passage referred to occurs in Goethe's *Letters from Switzerland*, under date of October 3, 1779 (Weimar Ed. IV, 4, 71).

3. **frug**, a common colloquial form for fragte.

4. **Elise von Hohenhausen** (1791–1857) translated Byron's *Corsair* (1820) and a number of lyrics. Heine had met her in Berlin. Although she was born at Kassel, her father had been a Westphalian general and her own home had largely been in Westphalia. It is in this sense that she is called Landsmännin.

5. **gegen junge Damen :** Heine was in reality a great admirer of Byron. The two poets had much in common. Elise von Hohenhausen called Heine the German-Byron.

Page 61. — 1. **die Bären . . . angebunden werden.** Einen Bären anbinden is students' slang for Schulden machen. So einen Bären losbinden = Schulden bezahlen. The 'learned Siberia' is, of course, Göttingen.

2. **Hallen'fern.** Next to Göttingen, Halle is the university town nearest to the Hartz.

3. **sich . . . sehen ließen**, *were on exhibition*. The price of admission was six Groschen (15 cents).

4. **Kunststücke ;** the whole passage is a satire on the impracticality of the Germans and their supposed incapacity for the affairs of politics, both home and foreign.

Page 62. — 1. **Purifikation**, i.e. to clear himself of the charge of high treason. The Burschenschaften — students' societies that were the centre of liberal political thought and agitation — had in Prussia been suppressed in 1820.

2. **Wiſotzki,** the proprietor of a popular restaurant.

3. **Schnell fertig u. ſ. w.,** a frequently quoted sentiment taken from Schiller's *Wallensteins Tod,* Act II, Scene 2 :

> Schnell fertig iſt die Jugend mit dem Wort,
> Das ſchwer ſich handhabt, wie des Meſſers Schneide;
> Aus ihrem heißen Kopfe nimmt ſie keck
> Der Dinge Maß, die nur ſich ſelber richten.

4. **am meiſten gilt,** *is most regarded.*

5. **man ſo duhn,** Berlin dialect for bloß ſo tun, *merely act so, merely pretend.*

6. **erſt recht,** *most of all.*

7. The **Intendant'** (*manager*) here ridiculed is Count von Brühl. The clause in quotation-marks refers to Bottom's "What beard were I best to play it in?" *Midsummer Night's Dream,* I, 2 (Mod. Lang. Notes, 24, 123). — 8. **vorgezeichnet,** *drawn.*

9. **Maria Stuart,** i.e. in Schiller's play of that name.

10. **ſchon . . . gehört,** *belongs to as late a period as.*

11. **Christian Gumpel.** Lazarus Gumpel, a Jewish banker of Hamburg, is meant. In another part of the *Reisebilder* (*Die Bäder von Lucca* and *Die Stadt Lucca*) he is burlesqued under the name of Gumpelino.

12. **Lord Burleigh,** again a character in Schiller's *Maria Stuart.*

13. **Steinzopf.** The Zopf (*cue*) is symbolical of the formalism of a bygone age, a notion that is enforced by Stein (i.e. petrified). Like Gumpel, the lady is, as the name Lilientau shows, of Jewish birth and may be assumed to belong to the uncultured *nouveaux riches.* — The abbreviation **geb.** = geborene, *née.*

14. **aus den Augen laſſen,** *lose sight of.*

15. **täuſchende.** The meaning is that the care as respects historical accuracy of costume is so great that the observer is *deceived,* i.e. regards as real what is merely illusion.

Page 63. — 1. **Lichtenſtein,** professor of zoology at the University of Berlin.

2. **Spontiniſche Janitſcha'renoper.** Spontini, an Italian by birth, one of the prominent composers of that day, was made

Director General of Music at Berlin in 1820. The janizaries are the old Turkish standing army — unruly and turbulent — sup-. pressed after a fierce struggle in 1826. The Janitſcharenmuſik which Spontini favored is therefore music of the noisy, deafening kind, Pauten= und Trompetenſpektakel, as Heine elsewhere calls it.

3. Elefan'ten ; an elephant actually appeared on the stage in one of the pieces (Elster VII, 184). — Tamtams, *tam-tams*, a species of drum.

4. Plato, in his *Republic* (IV, 424). Cicero in his *De Legibus* (II, 15, 38) refers to this passage in Plato.

5. Hoguet, a celebrated dancer of the time.

6. Buchholz, a Berlin historian, attacked in the press of the day (1823) for his shifting attitude toward Napoleon. He subsequently wrote a Geſchichte Napoleon Buonapartes.

7. The Bundestag, formed in 1815 and meeting at Frankfurt on the Main under the presidency of Austria, consisted of delegates of all the German states. It possessed little real authority.

8. die kleinen Fürſten. Some of these, as for instance the duke of Weimar, were politically liberally minded, and the greater re-actionary powers frequently brought pressure to bear upon them.

9. allzu großen Freund im Oſten, i.e. Russia. Fear of Russia, of a Slavic invasion, has long been a potent factor in German politics.

Page 64. — 1. honoriert. The terms honorieren and das Honorar' apply to the pay of professional men.

2. Apis, the sacred bull of the Egyptians.

3. exote'riſch, eſote'riſch (Greek terms), *belonging to the outer circle, belonging to the inner circle,* i.e. fully initiated into all the mysteries, that, as Heine elsewhere puts it, are nur den Schülern der erſten Klaſſe bekannt. — A similar interpretation of dance as pantomime will be found Elster VI, 299.

4. Fürſtenknechte, since the 15th century the Swiss have served foreign powers as *mercenaries,* often forming the body guard of reigning princes. The papal guard is still Swiss.

5. ſo genannt werden, i.e. 'Schweizer' came to stand for *mercenary* or *confectioner* without reference to the nationality of the individual.

Page 65. — 1. Cervantes, see *Don Quixote*, Chapter 2.

2. **Greifswalder,** i.e. a student at the University of Greifswald (in Pomerania).

3. **Weißbier,** a thin whitish beer brewed and drunk especially in Berlin.

4. **Nu! Nu!** colloquial for **Nun! Nun!** said in a conciliatory tone.

5. **desto . . . Geschirr,** *into all the greater passion did the Greifswalder work himself.*

6. **altdeutschen Rock.** Students, especially the **Burschenschafter,** affected old-German costume.

7. **Blücher,** Prussian field-marshall, who perhaps saved the day at Waterloo, the idol of his men and of the nation. To the **Burschenschafter** he was the type of the old German.

8. **Gauen** (= Latin *pagi*), the old historic divisions of Germany, still seen in such designations as Freiburg im Breisgau, Thurgau, etc.

9. **achtundvierzig,** i.e. on account of the greater divisibility of this number, allowing division and subdivision.

10. **Barde,** applied more particularly to a poet dealing with a (trite) patriotic subject. In the last quarter of the 18th century the word acquired an ironical coloring.

Page 66. — 1. **Hermanns und der Hermannsschlacht.** The same inspiration that the legend of Faust afforded 18th century German idealism, the story of Arminius (Hermann) furnished the German patriotic muse. The **Hermannsschlacht** is the battle of the Teutoburg forest, A. D. 9, in which a large force of Romans under Varus were routed by the Germans under Arminius.

2. **Knüppelweg,** a road made of fagots through marshy land. Translate *corduroy-road.*

3. **onomatopöisch,** i.e. the sound of the verses suggesting the character of the **Sümpfe** and **Knüppelwege.**

4. **bedenklichsten,** *questionable, equivocal.* The meaning is that such an illusion has its dangers.

5. **schmollieren** is to drink fraternity, bringing with it the use of the familiar **du.**

6. **„Der alte Landesvater,"** reserved at present for especial occasions, such as a **Stiftungsfest** or the **Kaisers Geburtstag.** At its con-

clusion a rapier goes the rounds which is thrust through caps of
the participants.   The first three stanzas are as follows:

Alles schweige!   Deutschlands Söhne,
Jeder neige   Laut ertöne
Ernsten Tönen nun sein Ohr!   Euer Vaterlandsgesang!
Hört, ich sing das Lied der Lieder!   Vaterland! du Land des Ruhmes,
Hört es, meine deutschen Brüder!   Weih zu deines Heiligtumes
Hall es wieder, froher Chor!   Hütern uns und unser Schwert!

Hab' und Leben
Dir zu geben,
Sind wir allesamt bereit,—
Sterben gern zu jeder Stunde
Achten nicht der Todeswunde,
Wenn das Vaterland gebeut.

7. **Wilhelm Müller** (1794–1827), a gifted lyric poet to whom
Heine elsewhere acknowledges his indebtedness.   He is particularly
known by a cycle of love-songs entitled Die schöne Müllerin, which
Franz Schubert set to music.

8. **Rückert** (1788–1866), a writer of great productivity both as
translator and original poet; noted especially for his virtuosity in
the handling of verse and rime.

9. **Uhland** (1787–1862), poet and scholar, master of the ballad.

10. **Methfessel**, a popular composer and author of a Kommers=
buch, with whom Heine was personally acquainted and of whom he
had written an appreciative notice in the Gesellschafter.

11. **Arndt** (1769–1860), the virile poet of the War of Liberation.
The famous lines here quoted are from the *Vaterlandslied*, of which
the complete first stanza is as follows:

Der Gott, der Eisen wachsen ließ,
Der wollte keine Knechte,
Drum gab er Säbel, Schwert und Spieß
Dem Mann in seine Rechte;
Drum gab er ihm den kühnen Mut,
Den Zorn der freien Rede,
Daß er bestände bis aufs Blut,
Bis in den Tod die Fehde.

12. **brauste es**, a reference to the opening lines of the last three
stanzas of Arndt's poem, which are respectively: Laßt brausen, was
nur brausen kann! — Laßt klingen, was nur klingen kann! — Laßt wehen
was nur wehen kann!

13. „𝕾𝖈𝖍𝖚𝖑𝖇" (1813), by Müllner, the best known of the *Schick-salstragödien* ('fate tragedies'), and immensely popular in its day.

Page 67. — 1. **ſpaniſche Fliegen**, extensively employed as a blister and irritant. The collocation is in Heine's vein.

2. **Bä'beli**, a Swiss diminutive form of the name Barbara.

3. **ſchön und blaß.** The parody of Ossianic situation and style, which from here on is gradually worked up to, first becomes pronounced page 68, line 19 (**Meine Seele iſt traurig! u. ſ. w.**), to culminate in the paragraphs following.

Page 68. — 1. **tönen wider**, *strike a responsive chord.*

2. **das toſende Zimmer**, *the turmoil of the room* (Gregor).

Page 69. — 1. **Mond.** The apostrophe to the moon that follows (p. 69, l. 19 to p. 70, l. 14) is an exact version of a passage from Ossian's Darthula. The original reads:

> Daughter of heaven, fair art thou! the silence of thy face is pleasant. Thou comest forth in loveliness: the stars attend thy blue steps in the east. The clouds rejoice in thy presence, O moon, and brighten their dark-brown sides. Who is like thee in heaven, daughter of the night? The stars are ashamed in thy presence, and turn aside their green, sparkling eyes. — Whither dost thou retire from thy course, when the darkness of thy countenance grows? Hast thou thy hall like Ossian? Dwellest thou in the shadow of grief? Have thy sisters fallen from heaven? Are they who rejoiced with thee, at night, no more? — Yes! they have fallen, fair light! and thou dost often retire to mourn. — But thou thyself shalt fail, one night; and leave thy blue path in heaven. The stars will then lift their green heads: they who were ashamed in thy presence, will rejoice.
>
> Thou art now clothed with thy brightness: look from thy gates in the sky. Burst the cloud, O wind, that the daughter of night may look forth, that the shaggy mountains may brighten, and the ocean roll its blue waves, in light.

2. **deinem Anblick.** See page 12, note 2.

Page 70. — 1. **Haſt du gleich mir deine Halle**, for the original *Hast thou thy hall like Ossian?* the ecstatic youth identifying himself with Ossian.

2. **Ein wohlbekannter**, one of the **Göttinger Landsleute** (p. 61, l. 2), as appears from page 71, line 9.

3. **wirtſchaftete . . . mörderlich**, *made an infernal racket.*

4. **ſie lägen**, *that they were lying.*

5. **daß ich verblute**, *that my life is ebbing away.*

Page 71. — 1. **der . . . herabſtört,** *that will strip me. of my leaves.* The lines **Warum wedſt . . . finden** are from Ossian's *Berrathon,* in Goethe's version, *Werthers Leiden,* Weimar Ed. 19, 175–6.

2. **kommen, der,** *he will come who.*

3. **Baßſtimme,** subject of übertobte; **alles** is object. The **Baßſtimme** belongs, of course, to the **wohlbekannter, nicht ſehr magerer Freund.**

4. **bei wem . . . die Fenſterſcheiben,** *whose window-panes.*

5. **viel,** i.e. much liquor. As a matter of fact, Heine was, as much from choice as necessity, extremely moderate in his use of alcoholic drinks.   •

6. Frankfurt am Main had a large Jewish population and was one of the centres of anti-Semitism.

Page 72. — 1. **Aus dieſem Lärmen.** The reference is to a short passage omitted in this edition, in which a wildly fantastic dream is described. — 2. **die ſtille Gemeinde.** See page 59, line 16.

3. **karmoiſinrote** (pron. oi as in French), *crimson.*

Page 73. — 1. **Bulbul=Lieder.** **Bulbul** (also written **Bülbül**) is a Persian-Arabic word designating an eastern bird, of the thrush family. On account of its sweet song it has been called the 'nightingale of the East.'

2. **Kame′le,** *camels;* there is perhaps a play upon the word, **Kamel** in university slang meaning a) a student not belonging to any of the students' societies and hence b) a student taking no part in the jovial and hilarious side of student life, i.e. a 'dig.'

3. **Congreviſchen Blicken.** The allusion is to the military rocket invented in 1808 by Sir William Congreve, and named, after him, the Congreve rocket.

4. **Houris,** according to the Mohammedan tradition the beauteous maidens that are the companions of the faithful in paradise.

5. **Brockenbuch,** the same as the **Gedächtnisbuch** of page 54, line 26.

6. **in Ermangelung derſelben,** *in default of such.*

7. **des Prinzen von Pallagonia.** The palace of the prince of Pallagonia is described by Goethe in his *Italienische Reise* in the letter dated Palermo, April 9, 1787. The name has come to symbolize the bizarre and monstrous.

Page 74. — 1. **Turngemeinplätzen.** The reference is to the **Turner** organized by 'father' Jahn in 1811 and to the **Burſchenſchaft**

founded in 1815. In the case of both these associations an attitude of protest against the reaction as personified in Metternich developed into more or less clearly defined revolutionary tendencies. They both also affected ancient German (altdeutſch) dress. By Turnge= meinplätze *commonplace patriotic sentiments* are meant. The word itself is a playful compound of Turngemein, *gymnastic association,* Turnplatz, *open place for gymnastics* and Gemeinplatz, *commonplace.*

2. Johannes Hagel = Jan Hagel, a Dutch designation of the plebs, the rabble. The change from Jan to Johannes makes the combination approximate a real name.

3. benebelt is also used in the sense of *befuddled, the worse for liquor.* The play upon the word may perhaps be rendered by *foggy going up, groggy coming down.*

4. **Clauren.** H. Clauren, anagram and pseudonym of Carl Heun (1771–1854), the immensely popular author of a prodigious output of vapid, sentimental, commonplace fiction.

5. besagtermaßen, *as aforesaid;* this pedantically stiff expression serves to heighten the contrast with the ecstacies of the Schweizer.

6. demagogiſche: inasmuch as the light, emblematic of truth, is conceived as vanquishing the medievalism represented by the armor-clad knights. — It was dangerous to be suspected of Dema= gogie. A highly entertaining account of the trial of a student on this accusation before the academic senate may be found in Hauff's *Memoiren des Satan* I, Chapter 10.

7. Unterſuchung, i.e. a judicial inquiry into this desperate *Geisterschlacht.*

Page 75. — 1. ſich (*dat.*) nicht träumen ließ, *did not dream.*

2. Soll ... Einteilung, *if a classification must.*

3. Theophraſts: usually thought to refer to the Greek Theo- phrastus, — from whom George Eliot's series of essays *Theophras- tus Such* takes its title — the pupil of Aristotle. The sixth book of his *Principles of Vegetable Life* treats of the smell and taste of plants. According to Elster VII, 414 and IV, 226, however, Heine has in mind Theophrastus Paracelsus Bombast (1493–1541), physician and scholar, an author well-known to German romanticists.

Page 76. — 1. franzöſiſche Worte. Even during the Parisian residence of the second half of his life Heine adhered to this view of the essentially unpoetic character of French verse.

2. Schneelöcher, ravines north of the Brocken, so callèd because the snow remains there later in the season than elsewhere.

Page 77. — 1. die öſtreichiſche Landwehr, *the Austrian militia* had acquired a reputation for slowness; hence the familiar lines:

Nur immer langſam voran! Nur immer langſam voran!
Daß die öſtreich'ſche Landwehr auch nachkommen kann.

2. die kahle Partie, *the bare portion*, embracing the last hundred feet of the elevation.

Page 78. — 1. Blätterholzart, *leaf-bearing trees, deciduous trees;* i.e. the Buchen and Eichen in contrast with the Nadelholz.

2. tollen, *freakish, giddy.*

Page 79. — 1. tantenhaft vergnügt, *like delighted aunts.*

2. ſchaut drein, *watches it all.*

3. das ſchöne Wetter bezahlen, *foot the bill, pay the piper.* The figure of the verdrießlicher Oheim is doubtless suggested by Heine's relations to his uncle Salomon, who also periodically had to 'foot the bill.'

4. nimm uns mit; reminiscent of Goethe's poem *Mahomets Gesang*, ll. 35–37:

Bruder, nimm die Brüder mit,
Mit zu deinem alten Vater,
Zu dem ew'gen Ozean.

5. von . . . Klängen, *of resounding beams and beaming sounds.*

6. Kaiſer Heinrich, probably Henry the Fowler (919–936).

Page 80. — 1. Es bleiben tot die Toten, motivating her turning from the *dead* emperor to the *living* poet. The last line of this stanza is perhaps the finest of the poem.

2. Und nur der Lebendige lebt; slightly reminiscent of Schiller's

Wir, wir leben! Unſer ſind die Stunden,
Und der Lebende hat Recht.

(*An die Freunde.*)

3. Ich hielt . . . erklang, another instance of the Stimmungsbrechung, that became a mannerism with Heine.

4. **Erſcheinungswelt** (*world of phenomena*) is the world without, **Gemütswelt** (*world of feeling*) the world within.

Page 81. — 1. **unſer ſeliger Vetter,** *our lamented cousin*, i.e. Till Eulenspiegel, the traditional wag, still alive in the mouths of the people. He is the hero of a sixteenth century *Volksbuch*. The story in question is frequently alluded to: Eulenspiegel is in a merry mood whenever *ascending* a mountain because he has in mind the *descent* that follows.

2. **Mölln,** some distance south of Lübeck. The tombstone is still shown there.

3. **Ilſenſtein,** rising some 600 ft. above the Ilse. See illustration.

4. **Kreuz;** erected in 1814 by Count Stolberg-Wernigerode in memory of comrades that had fallen in the War of Liberation.

5. **Gottſchalk;** compare page 13, lines 5–6.

6. **einer unſerer bekannteſten Dichter;** the reference, as Archivrat Jacobs at Wernigerode informs me, is to Theodor Hell's poem *Der Ilsenstein und Westerberg im Ilsentale*, which appeared in the *Abendzeitung* for September 8 and 9, 1824. For the *Abendzeitung* see page 53, note 1. Theodor Hell (pseudonym for K. G. Th. Winkler), editor of the *Abendzeitung*, was once *well-known* as lyric and dramatic poet, translator and publicist, but is now forgotten.

Page 82. — 1. **Wohlgeb.** = **Wohlgeboren,** *Esquire*, humorously added: the eminently respectable author lacks imagination.

2. **Abweichungen der Magnet′nadel;** the Ilsenstein, like some other rocks in the Hartz, actually causes such a *variation of the magnetic needle*.

3. **Lüneburger Chronik,** a chronicle of the city of Lüneburg, southeast of Hamburg. It is the work of the provost Jakob Schomaker (1499–1563) and is of especial value for the period of the Reformation. Heine's parents had moved to Lüneburg in 1822.

4. **Welſchland.** The expeditions to *Italy*, which virtually began with Otto I (936–973) are in their consequences generally thought to have been disastrous to the German empire.

5. **römiſche Kaiſer zu heißen;** the crowning as Roman Emperor was a function of the pope.

Page 83. — 1. baß . . . wurde, *things began to swim.*

2. Heine's baptism — it was of course in no sense a conversion — falls between the time of his tour through the Hartz (1824) and the date of the publication of the *Harzreise* (1826). It took place in June, 1825. The words in ſo mißlicher Stellung symbolize the plight Heine was in, the obtaining of the desired official appointment being dependent upon his apostasy.

3. Parze. Of the three *Parcæ*, or Fates, Clotho spins the thread, Lachĕsis determines its length, and Atrŏpos (= 'not to be averted') cuts it.

4. wenn . . . ausſpricht, *if only one does say it some time.*

5. Mögen . . . immerhin, *no matter whether.*

Page 84. — 1. anderweitig, i.e. *elsewhere* in his published works.

2. Erſcheinungen des Tages, *facts of everyday existence.*

3. Georg Sartorius, professor of history at Göttingen.

4. alle fremde: see page 8, note 2.

Page 85. — 1. geſagt und geſungen, *said and sung,* the old traditional formula in German, ſagen referring to epic narrative, ſingen to lyric song. Notice the alliteration.

2. Rübeland, a village that is somewhat of an industrial centre, but which is now visited chiefly on account of the two large natural caves that are found in its vicinity. — The epithet ſchmiede= dunkeln has the Homeric ring.

3. gar = ſogar, *even.*

4. Roßtrappe, a rock rising, almost perpendicularly, some 650 ft. above the bed of the Bode.

5. koloſſa'le, a favorite adjective with students.

Page 86. — 1. abhanden . . . kam, *was no longer on hand or rather on foot.*

2. Sie, *she,* i.e. his beloved. The initial capital is intended to indicate the peculiar emphasis that falls on the word.

3. Paris; the reference is, of course, to the judgment of Paris.

4. der erſte Mai: May 1, 1826 is meant.

Page 87. — 1. Vierländerinnen; *die Vierlande* is a district south of Hamburg, on the east bank of the Elbe. It supplies

Hamburg with fruit and flowers.   The women wear a striking costume.

2. **Waiſenkinder.** "The first of May used to be the special fête-day of the *foundling* or *orphan-children* at Hamburg.   They marched in procession through the town, receiving numerous small gifts of money from the charitable Hamburghers.   All the schools were closed, and the whole town took part in the festival" (Buchheim).

3. **Jungfernſtieg,** *Maiden Lane,* the fashionable promenade of Hamburg, an imposing wide street fronting the basin of the Inner Alster.   Heine describes it at length (Elster IV, 103).

4. **der Bettler.** "Heine alludes here to the *old beggar,* who, in his days, used to have his stand at the *Lombardsbrücke* — the principal bridge of Hamburg — and who was one of the most familiar figures in the town" (Buchheim).

5. **das groſße Los,** *the first prize (in the lottery).*

6. **Makler.** The reference seems to be to a certain Joseph Friedländer, who shortly after the publication of the *Harzreise* actually sought to revenge himself by attacking the poet on the streets of Hamburg.

7. **Agnes,** i.e. the poet's cousin, Therese Heine, a younger sister of Amalie.   Heine's passion for her dates from the summer of 1823.

8. **ſchweren** is in contrast with *artiger Lieblichkeit* and seems to combine the two notions of *heavy* and *melancholy* (ſchwermütig).

Page 88. — 1. **Aloe :** pronounce as three syllables. "The plant often delays flowering for many years, and then pushes up a flowering stalk with great rapidity, sometimes at the rate of 1 foot or even 2 feet in twenty-four hours" (Encycl. Brit.).   The statement that it bursts into flower with a loud report, though more or less traditional, has no basis in fact : it was needed here for the effective climax that follows (p. 89, l. 1).

2. **nicht mal** = nicht einmal', *not even.*

3. **Chriſtian,** a servant.

4. **ein einziges Mal,** a reference to his early love for Amalie, Therese's sister.   This love met with no response (Mangel an Sonnenſchein und Wärme).

5. **gar** = ſogar, *even.*

Page 89.—1. **Ironie.** Heine elsewhere (Elster III, 104; 322; 423; V, 288) repeatedly speaks of the world and of man as products of the Ironie of God, in this sense the 'poet' of irony *par excellence.* Ironie would here accordingly seem to stand for die Welt, *the world,* and the contrast with der Himmel becomes obvious.

2. **erſt :** i.e. if the fragrance is so overpowering during the *day,* what will it be when *night* comes. For the sentiment compare page 35, note 2.

VOCABULARY

The endings of both the genitive singular and nominative plural of nouns are given, except in the case of feminines, where the plural alone is given. Strong verbs are followed by the vowels of the preterit and past participle. In the case of compound verbs the sign *S.* indicates that the verb in question is strong or irregular, and that the vowels of the principal parts will be found under the simple verb. All verbs not marked *S.*, or not accompanied by the vowels of the principal parts, are weak. Separable compounds are indicated by a hyphen between adverb and verb (ab-brechen). Accent is marked wherever a misconception of the German pronunciation seemed liable.

A

Abbildung, *f.*, –en, picture.

ab-blühen, to cease blossoming, fade.

ab-brechen, *S.*, to tear down; pluck.

Abend, *m.*, –s, –e, evening.

Abendessen, *n.*, –s, supper.

Abendmahlzeit, *f.*, –en, supper.

Abendrot, *n.*, –es, sunset glow.

Abendzeitung, *f.*, Evening News.

abenteuerlich, fantastic, rom'antic.

aber, but; however.

ab-fahren, u, a, to drive off, depart.

abgebrochen, broken (off), disjointed.

ab-gehen, *S.*, to leave, depart.

abgeschmackt, insipid.

Abgeschmacktheit, *f.*, –en, insipidity.

abgetragen, worn out.

Abgrund, *m.*, –es, ᵘe, abyss.

Abhandlung, *f.*, –en, treatise.

ab-kappen, to truncate.

abkonterfeien, to depict, portray.

Abmarsch, *m.*, –es, ᵘe, start, departure.

ab-pflücken, to pick, pluck.

Abreise, *f.*, –n, departure.

ab-reisen, to depart.

ab-richten, to train (*of animals*).

Abschied, *m.*, –s, –e, leave, parting.

ab-schießen, *S.*, to shoot off, discharge.

ab-schlagen, *S.*, to strike, cut off.

ab-schneiden, *S.*, to cut off.

Abschnitt, *m.*, –s, –e, section.

abschüssig, precipitous.

Absicht, *f.*, –en, purpose.

absichtlich, deliberate, with conscious purpose.

ab=ſprechen, *S.*, to deny.

abſtrakt′, abstract.

Abſurdität′, *f.*, -en, absurdity.

Abweichung, *f.*, -en, variation.

ab=wenden, wandte, gewandt, to turn away.

ab=werfen, *S.*, to throw off.

Abweſenheit, *f.*, absence.

Accent′, *m.*, -es, -e, accent.

Acci′ſeeinnehmer, *m.*,-s, —, excise (internal revenue) gatherer; die Herren —, the gentlemen of the excise.

ach! ah! oh! alas!

Achſel, *f.*, -n, shoulder.

achtundvierzig, forty-eight.

Achtung, *f.*, esteem, respect.

Adieu, *n.*, -s, -s, adieu.

adlig, noble.

Adreſ′ſenfloskel, *f.*, -n, flourish.

Affe, *m.*, -n, -n, ape.

Ägyp′ten, *n.*, -s, Egypt.

ähnlich, similar, resembling.

akade′miſch, academic.

Albi′no, *m.*, -s, -s, albino.

all, all, every; alldort′, there.

allerbeſt′, best of all.

Allerhei′ligſte, *n.*, -n, holy of holies.

allerlei, all kinds of.

allerliebſt′, most charming.

allerſchönſt′, most beautiful.

allertap′ferſt, most valiant.

allerwe′nigſt, least of all.

allgemein, general, (generally) current.

allmäh′lich, gradual.

Allongeperücke (*pron.* Allonge- as *in French, but with three syllables*), *f.*, -n, full-bottomed wig.

allwo′, where, in which.

allzu, too, all too.

allzuherb, over bitter, over harsh.

Aloe, *f.*, -n, aloe.

Alp, *f.*, -en, the Alps.

als, when; as, as if; than.

alsdann′, then, thereupon.

alſo, accordingly, therefore.

alt, old; die Alten, the ancients.

altdeutſch, Old German, Teutonic.

Altertümlichkeit, *f.*, -en, antiquity, ancient remains (*pl.*).

altgriechiſch, ancient Greek.

altklug, ('old-wise'), precocious.

ältlich, elderly.

altſächſiſch, Old Saxon.

altverfallen, long ago decayed.

Amme, *f.*, -n, nurse.

Amt, *n.*, -es, ˮer, office, duty.

an, at, in, on.

Anachronis′mus, *m.*, —, -men, anachronism.

Analy′ſe, *f.*, -n, analysis.

Anatomie′, *f.*, -n, anatomy.

anato′miſch, anatomical.

an=belangen, to concern.

an=binden, *S.*, to tie.

Anblick, *m.*, -s, -e, sight, view.

an=blicken, to look at.

an=bringen, *S.*, to apply.

Andacht, *f.*, devotion.

Andenken, *n.*, -ß, —, remembrance, commemoration, memorial.

ander, other; next.

anders, different.

anderweitig, in another connection.

an=deuten, to indicate.

• Anekdo'te, *f.*, -n, anecdote.

Anfang, *m.*, -ß, "e, beginning.

an=fangen, *S.*, to begin.

Anfertigung, *f.*, preparation.

Anflug, *m.*, -es, "e, beginning, semblance, trace.

an=freſſen, a, e, to eat into, scar.

an=führen, to lead.

an=füllen, to fill.

an=geben, *S.*, to state, report, indicate.

an=gehören, to belong to.

angenehm, pleasant.

angeſoffen, fuddled, tipsy.———

Angorakatze, *f.*, -n, Angora cat.

angreifend, over-powering, fatiguing, intoxicating.

an=grinſen, to grin at.

Angſt, *f.*, "e, fear, terror.

ängſtlich, terrified, fearful, anxious, timid.

angſtlos, fearless, without fear.

Anhänger, *m.*, -ß, —, adherent, associate.

Anhöhe, *f.*, -n, height.

an=knüpfen, to start.

an=kommen, *S.*, to arrive.

Ankunft, *f.*, "e, arrival.

an=lachen, to laugh at.

Anlauf, *m.*, -ß, "e, start, run.

Anmut, *f.*, charm, grace.

anmutig, charming, pretty.

an=nehmen, *S.* (ſich), *w.gen.*, to show an interest in.

an=richten, to cause.

an=ſchauen, to gaze upon, look at.

Anſchauung, *f.*, -en, contemplation, intuition.

Anſchauungsleben, *n.*, -ß, —, life of contemplation (intuition).

Anſchlagzettel, *m.*, -ß, —, poster.

an=ſehen, *S.*, to view, look at.

Anſehen, *n.*, -ß, appearance.

an=ſprechen, *S.*, to appeal to.

Anſtalt, *f.*, -en, preparation.

an=ſtoßen, *S.*, to strike.

an=ſtrahlen, to shine upon, illumine.

an=ſtreichen, *S.*, to paint.

Anſtrich, *m.*, -ß, -e, air, touch, dash.

Antlitz, *n.*, -es, -e, countenance.

an=treffen, *S.*, to meet with.

Antwort, *f.*, -en, answer.

antworten, to answer.

an=vertrauen, to confide, entrust.

an=weiſen, ie, ie, to point out.

an=ziehen, *S.*, to put on; ſich —, to dress.

an=zünden, to light.

Apfel, *m.*, -ß, ", apple.

Apoll', *m.*, -ß, Apollo.

apothe′kenartig, like an apothecary's shop.

Appetit′, *m.*, –8, appetite.

Äqua′tor, *m.*, –8, equator.

Arabes′ke, *f.*, –n, arabesque.

ara′bisch, Arabic.

arbeiten, to work.

ärgerlich, vexed.

ärgern, to vex.

arglos, without design, at random.

Arm, *m.*, –es, –e, arm.

arm, poor.

Art, *f.*, –en, kind, species.

artig, nice, pretty, pleasant.

Arzt, *m.*, –es, ″e, physician.

Ästhe′tik, *f.*, aesthetics.

ästhe′tisch, aesthetic.

Atem, *m.*, –8, breath.

Atlashut, *m.*, –es, ″e, satin hat.

atmen, to breathe.

Atom′, *n.*, –8, –e, atom.

auch, also, besides, moreover.

auf, upon, on, at, in.

auf=binden, *S.*, to tie on.

auf=blühen, to blossom forth.

auf=fangen, *S.*, to catch.

auf=gehen, *S.*, to rise.

aufgeklärt, enlightened.

aufgepflanzt, planted, arrayed.

auf=heben, *S.*, to lift up.

auf=hören, to cease.

aufmerksam, attentive; — machen, to call attention.

auf=passen, to watch, look out.

auf=räumen, to put in order.

auf=rechnen, to enumerate.

auf=richten (sich), to sit up.

auf=schlagen, *S.*, to open.

auf=schließen, *S.*, to open.

auf=schreien, *S.*, to cry out.

auf=sperren, to open wide; auf= gesperrt, gaping.

auf=stehen, *S.*, to get up, rise.

auf=steigen, *S.*, to rise, mount.

auf=stellen, to set up, exhibit.

auf=strahlen, to light up, brighten up.

auf=suchen, to look up.

Auftrag, *m.*, –8, ″e, commission, message.

auf=treiben, ie, ie, to procure (after diligent search).

Aufwartung, *f.*, –en, attendance; seine — machen, to pay one's respects.

Auge, *n.*, –8, –n, eye; aus den Augen verlieren, to lose sight of.

Äug(e)lein, *n.*, –8, —, little eye.

Augenblick, *m.*, –8, –e, instant, moment.

Augenkreis, *m.*, –es, –e, orbit (of the eye).

Augenwimper, *f.*, –n, eyelash.

aus, out, from.

aus=brechen, *S.*, to break out.

aus=breiten, to spread out.

Ausdruck, *m.*, –8, ″e, expression.

aus=drücken, to express.

ausdrücklich, expressly.

aus=fallen, *S.*, to turn out to be, prove.

ausführ′lich, detailed; Ausführ= licheres, further details.

aus=gehen, S., to go out.

ausgewachsen, grown up, adult.

aus=gießen, S., to pour, shed.

aus=gleichen, S., to smooth, adjust.

aus=greifen, i, i, to reach out.

aus=halten, S., to stand, endure.

aus=hauchen, to breathe forth.

aus=hauen, S., to hew out

aus=rufen, S., to call out.

ausschließlich, exclusive.

aus=sehen, S., to look, appear.

außer, out of; äußer, outward.

außerdem, besides.

Äußerlichkeit, f., –en, external.

äußern, to express, remark.

außeror'dentlich, extraordinary.

äußerst, extreme.

Äußerung, f., –en, remark.

Aussicht, f., –en, view.

aus=sprechen, S., to express, pronounce; sich —, to find its expression, manifest itself; to talk about (p. 57, l. 10).

aus=stehen, S., to stand, endure, put up with.

aus=strecken, to stretch out.

aus=trinken, S., to drain, drink.

auswendig, by heart.

aus=ziehen, S., to move; sich —, to undress.

Autor, m , –s, –en, author.

B

Bach, m., –es, "e, brook.

Bache, f., –n, wild sow.

Bächlein, n., –s, —, little brook.

Backe, f., –n, cheek.

baden, to bathe.

Bahn, f., –en, path.

bald, soon.

Balken, m., –s, —, beam.

Ballett', n., –s, –s, ballet.

bang, fearful, timid, afraid.

Bank, f., "e, bench.

Bankier' (pron. Bankje'), m., –s, –s, banker.

Banner, n., –s, —, banner.

Bär, m., –en, –en, bear.

Barde, m., –n, –n, bard.

Barett', n., –s, –e, cap.

barmher'zig, merciful, compassionate.

barock', baroque, grotesque.

Baro'nin, f., –nen, baroness.

Bart, m., –es, "e, beard.

Baßstimme, f., –n, bass voice.

Bauch, m., –es, "e, belly, stomach.

bauen, to build.

Bauer, m., –n, (–s), –n, peasant.

Baum, m., –es, "e, tree.

bäumen, to rear, prance.

Baumstamm, m., –es, "e, trunk of a tree.

Baumwurzel, f., –n, tree root.

beängstigend, oppressive.

beben, to quiver, tremble.

Becken, n., –s, —, basin.

bedecken, to cover.

bedenken, S., to consider.

bedenk'lich, questionable, dubious.

bedeuten, to signify; inform, indicate.

bedeutend, important, significant, considerable.

Bedeutung, *f.*, –en, significance, importance.

bedeutungſchwer, portentous.

Bediente, *m.*, –n, –n, servant.

Bedingung, *f.*, –en, condition, necessary assumption.

beei'digt, sworn, under oath.

Beet, *n.*, –es, –e, bed (in a garden).

befahren, u, a, to enter, visit; das B—, the descent (into).

befeſtigen, to fasten, establish.

befinden, *S.*, to find.

befragen, to interrogate.

Befreiungskrieg, *m.*, –s, –e, war of liberation.

befreundet, familiar.

begegnen, to meet; happen to.

begeiſtern, to inspire, enrapture.

Begeiſterung, *f.*, enthusiasm.

beginnen, a, o, to begin.

begleiten, to accompany.

Begleiter, *m.*, –s, companion.

begraben, u, a, to bury.

begreifen, i, i, to comprehend, understand.

begrenzt', limited.

Begriff, *m.*, –s, –e, concept; essence; im — ſein, to be on the point of.

begünſtigen, to favor.

begut'achten, to report professionally, certify.

begütigend, conciliatory.

behagen, to please, suit.

behag'lich, comfortable.

Behältnis, *n.*, –ſes, –ſe, receptacle, cage.

behaupten, to maintain, assert.

Behuf, *m.*, –s, purpose.

bei, at, among, upon.

beide, both, two.

Beifall, *m.*, –s, applause.

beilei'be, on one's life.

beim = bei dem.

Bein, *n.*, –es, –e, bone, limb.

Beinchen, *n.*, –s, —, little (thin) leg.

bejahen, to answer in the affirmative.

bejahrt', advanced in years.

bekannt, known, well known; der Bekannte, acquaintance.

beklagen (ſich), to complain.

bekommen, *S.*, to get, receive; be served with.

beladen, u, a, to load, burden.

belauſchen, to watch, spy, overhear.

beleuchten, to illuminate, light up.

Beleuchtung, *f.*, –en, illumination; dämmernde —, twilight.

belletri'ſtiſch, literary.

belohnen, to reward.

belvede'riſch, Belvedere.

bemalen, to paint upon, paint.

bemerkbar, noticeable.

bemerken, to notice, observe. state.

Bemerkung, *f.*, –en, remark.
bene'belt, befogged, fuddled.
benei'denswert, enviable.
benennen, *S.*, to call.
benetzen, to sprinkle, bathe.
Beob'achter, *m.*, –s, —, observer.
bequem', convenient, indolent, easy going.
bereit, ready.
bereiten, to prepare, get ready.
bereits, already.
Berg, *m.*, –es, –e, mountain, hill.
bergab', down-hill.
Bergabsteigen, *n.*, –s, going down-hill.
Bergarbeiter, *m.*, –s, —, mineworker.
bergauf', up-hill.
Bergblume, *f.*, –n, mountain flower.
Bergecke, *f.*, –n, corner of a mountain, mountain ridge.
Bergesgeist, *m.*, –es, -er, mountain spirit.
Bergesgipfel, *m.*, –s, —, mountain top.
Bergeshöhe, *f.*, –n, mountain height.
Berghütte, *f.*, –n, mountain hut, miner's hut.
Bergknappe, *m.*, –n, –n, miner.
Bergkraut, *n.*, –es, "er, mountain plant.
Bergmann, *m.*, –s ; *pl.*, –leute, miner.

Bergmärchen, *n.*, –s, —, mountain legend.
Bergnacht, *f.*, "e, night (darkness) of the mine.
Bergschacht, *m.*, –es, –e, mineshaft.
Bergstädtchen, *n.*, –s, —, (mountain town), mining town.
Bergtal, *n.*, –s, "er, mountain valley.
Bergwerkswesen, *n.*, –s, mining.
berichten, to report, inform.
berichtigen, to correct; adjust.
Berichtiger, *m.*, –s, —, rectifier, monitor.
Berli'ner, of Berlin.
berühmt, famous; *subst.*, celebrity.
besagterma'ßen, as aforesaid, as set forth above.
beschäftigen (sich), to busy oneself, be engaged upon.
beschämen, to put to shame; beschämt, abashed.
Beschauer, *m.*, –s, —, beholder.
bescheiden, modest.
Bescheidenheit, *f.*, modesty.
bescheinen, *S.*, to shine upon.
beschneiden, *S.*, to trim, clip.
beschreiben, *S.*, to write upon; describe.
beschützen, to protect.
beschwer'lich, difficult.
beschwichtigen, to appease, soothe, calm, conciliate; beschwichtigend, conciliatory.
besehen, *S.*, to view.

beſe'ligen, to enrapture, delight.
Beſen, *m.*, -$, —, broom.
Beſenſtiel, *m.*, -$, -e, broomstick.
beſingen, *S.*, to celebrate in song.
beſitzen, *S.*, to possess.
beſonder, special, especial.
beſonders, especially, particularly.
beſorglich, anxious, solicitous.
Beſorgnis, *f.*, -ſe, fear, care.
beſpülen, to wash.
beſſer, better.
beſtändig, permanent, constant.
beſtärken, to confirm.
beſtehen, *S.*, to consist.
beſteigen, *S.*, to climb, ascend; enter (Wagen).
beſuchen, to visit; der Beſuchende, visitor.
betäuben, to stupefy.
betauen, to bedew.
beten, to pray.
beteuern, to asseverate.
betrachten, to view, gaze upon.
betrauern, to mourn.
betreffen, *S.*, to concern.
betrübt, melancholy, disconsolate.
betrunken, drunken.
Betſtunde, *f.*, -n, hour of prayer, matins.
Bett, *n.*, -es, -en, bed.
Bettchen, *n.*, -$, —, little bed.
Bettler, *m.*, -$, —, beggar.
betur'bant, turbaned.
beur'teilen, to judge.

bevölkern, to people.
bewachſen, *S.*, to overgrow.
bewegen, to move, wag.
Bewegung, *f.*, -en, motion, exertion, exercise, commotion, movement.
Beweis, *m.*, -es, -e, proof, conclusion.
beweiſen, ie, ie, to prove, demonstrate.
bewirken, to effect, bring about.
Bewohner, *m.*, -$, —, inhabitant.
bewundern, to admire.
bezahlen, to pay, pay for.
bezaubern, to charm, fascinate.
bezeichnen, to mark, indicate, characterize.
bezeigen, to show, indicate.
beziehen, *S.*, to remove to.
Beziehung, *f.*, -en, allusion, reference, import.
bezweifeln, to doubt.
bezwingen, a, u, to conquer, vanquish.
Bibel, *f.*, -n, Bible.
Bibliothek', *f.*, -en, library.
biegen, o, o, to bend.
Bier, *n.*, -es, -e, beer.
Bild, *n.*, -es, -er, image, statue, picture.
bilden, to form, constitute, be; educate.
Bildhauer, *m.*, -$, —, sculptor.
Bildſäule, *f.*, -n, statue.
Bildungsgeſchichte, *f.*, -n, story of growth.

billig, reasonable.

binden, a, u, to bind, tie.

Biograph', m., –en, –en, biographer.

Birke, f., –n, birch.

bis, until, to.

bitten, a, e, to beg, ask, request.

bizarr', bizarre, fantastic.

blank, bright, resplendent, sleek.

Blase, f., –n, blister.

blasen, ie, a, to blow.

blaß, pale.

Blatt, n., –es, "er, leaf.

Blätterholzart, f., –en, (species of) leaf-bearing trees.

blättern, to turn the leaves (of a book).

Blattgesträuch, n., –s, –e, brushwood, copsewood.

blau, blue.

blauäugig, blue-eyed.

Blaurock, m., –s, "e, blue-coat.

blauseiden, of blue silk. —

bleiben, ie, ie, to remain.

bleich, pale, dim.

blendend, dazzling.

Blick, m., –es, ⌣e, glance.

blinken, to glisten.

Blitz, m., –es, –e, lightning.

blitzäugig, with flashing eyes, bright eyed.

blitzen, to lighten, sparkle.

Blocksberggeschichte, f.,–n, story of the Brocken.

blöde, dull, stupid, purblind.

blond, fair-haired, blond.

bloß, simply, merely, only.

blühen, to bloom, blossom.

Blümchen, n., –s, —, little flower.

Blume, f., –n, flower.

Blumenkelch, m., –es, –e, calix of a flower.

Blumenleiche, f., –n, flower corpse.

Blumenregen, m.,–s, —, flowery rain.

Blumenwald, m.,–es, "er, forest of flowers.

Blut, n., –es, blood.

blutbeschmiert, blood-smeared.

Blüte, f., –n, blossom.

Blütenschaum, m., –es, "e, foam of blossoms.

blutig, bloody, sanguinary.

blutrot, blood-red.

Blutstropfen, m., –s, —, drop of blood.

Böcklein, n., –s, —, kid.

Boden, m., –s, ", soil; attic.

Bogen, m., –s, ", arch, curve.

Bord, m., –s, –e, board.

böse, bad, evil.

Bouteil'lenzahl, f., number of bottles.

bramarbasie'ren, to rant, brag, bluster.

Brasi'lien, n., –s, Brazil.

braten, ie, a, to fry, roast.

braun, brown.

Braunschweiger, of Brunswick.

brausen, to rush, roar.

Brautkleid, n., –es, –er, wedding dress.

Brautſchleier, *m.* -s, —, bridal veil.

brechen, a, o, to break.

breit, broad.

brennen, brannte, gebrannt, to burn.

Brett, *n.*, -es, -er, board, shelf; *pl.*, boards, *i.e.* the stage.

Brille, *f.*, -n, *sing.*, spectacles.

bringen, brachte, gebracht, to bring.

Brocken, *m.*, -s, —, bit, morsel; *proper name*, the Brocken.

Brockenbeſucher, *m.*, -s, —, visitor to the Brocken.

Brockenbuch, *n.*, -es, "er, Brocken book.

Brockenhausmädchen, *n.*, -s, —, maid of the Brocken Inn.

Brockenſtrauß, *m.*, -es, "e, nosegay of Brocken flowers.

Brockenſträußchen, *n.*, -s, —, little nosegay of Brocken flowers.

Brockenwirt, *m.*, -es, -e, mine host of the Brocken Inn.

Broſchü're, *f.*, -n, pamphlet.

Brot, *n.*, -es, -e, bread.

Brücke, *f.*, -n, bridge.

Bruder, *m.*, -s, ", brother.

brüllen, to roar.

brummen, to hum.

Brunnen, *m.*, -s, —, well.

Bruſt, *f.*, "e, breast, bosom.

Bruſtnadel, *f.*, -n, scarf-pin.

Bübchen, *n.*, -s, —, little fellow.

Buch, *n.*, -es, "er, book.

Buche, *f.*, -n, beech.

Bücherdefinition, *f.*, -en, book-definition.

Bücking, *m.*, -s, -e, a kind of herring, bloater.

buhlen, to be wanton, woo, caress.

Bündel, *n.*, -s, —, bundle.

Bundestag, *m.*, -es, -e, Federal Diet.

bunt, varicolored.

buntgekleidet, gayly (in motley colors) dressed.

buntſcheckig, motley, variegated.

Burg, *f.*, -en, castle, fortress.

Bürger, *m.*, -s, —, citizen.

Bürgerleute, *pl.*, citizens. [dent.

Burſch, *m.*, -en, -en, fellow, stu-

Burſchenſchafter, *m.*, -s, —, member of a students' society.

burſchikos', student-like, free and easy, jovial.

buſchig, bushy, shaggy.

Buſen, *m.*, -s, —, bosom.

Buſenband, *n.*, -es, "er, ribbon (worn on the breast), streamer.

C

chao'tiſch, chaotic.

Chara'de (*pron.* Scha-), *f.*, -n, charade.

Charak'ter, *m.*, -s, —, character.

Chauſſee' (*pron. as in French*), *f.*, -n, highway, turnpike.

Chiffer (*pron.* Sch-), *f.*, -n, cipher, character, figure.

China, *n.*, -s, China.

Chine'ſe, *m.*, -n, -n, Chinese.

chine′fiſch, Chinese.

Choral′, m., –8, ᵘe, anthem, hymn.

Chriſtentum, n.,–8, Christianity.

Chriſtlichkeit, f., Christianity.

Chriſtus, m., Christ.

Chriſtuskopf, m., –e8, ᵘe, head of Christ.

Chronik, f., –en, chronicle.

Cicero′ne, m., — or –8, –8 or –n, cicerone, guide.

Citat′ (pron. Tſi–), n., –e8, –e, quotation.

Citation′ (pron. Tſi–), f., –en, summons.

citieren (pron. tſi–), to cite, summon.

Cypreſ′ſe (pron. Tſi–), f., –n, cypress.

D

Da, there; conj., since.

dabei, thereat, at the same time.

dabei′=ſtehen, S., to stand alongside.

Dach, n., –e8, ᵘer, roof.

Dachtraufe, f., –n, rain spout.

dadurch), thereby.

dafür, for this, in return.

dage′gen, on the other hand.

daher, hence.

dahin, thither.

dahin′=hüpfen, to hop along.

dahin′=leben, to live on (uncon-cernedly).

damals, at that time.

Dame, f., –n, lady.

Damenfuß, m., –e8, ᵘe, lady's foot.

damit, therewith; in order that.

dämmern, to dawn; grow dusk; dämmernd, darkening, dusky, dim.

Dampf, m., –e8, ᵘe, steam.

dampfen, to steam.

dane′ben, alongside.

danken, to thank.

dann, then; — und wann, now and then.

daran, thereto, therein, upon the same, of it.

darauf, thereafter, upon it, at them, to this.

darin, therein.

dar=ſtellen, to portray, represent, depict.

Darſtellung, f., –en, portrayal.

darüber, about it, thereat, across it.

darunter, beneath this.

daſelbſt′, there.

dauernd, enduring, permanent.

davon, from this, from these, about it.

davor, before it, in front of it.

dazu, thereto, concerning it.

dazwi′ſchen, in between.

Decke, f., –n, ceiling, canopy.

deduzieren, to deduce.

definieren, to define.

Definition′, f., –en, definition.

deinig, thine, of thine.

deklamieren, to declaim.

Dekret′, n., –8, –e, decree.

Delinquen'tentracht, f., –en, convict's garb.

demago'gisch, demagogic.

demnach, according to this.

Demonstration', f., –en, demonstration.

demonstrieren, to demonstrate.

denken, dachte, gedacht, to think.

denn, conj., for; adv., indeed.

dennoch, nevertheless.

derglei'chen, such, the like.

derjenige, that one, the one.

derselbe, dieselbe, dasselbe, the same, he, she, it.

derwei'len, while.

deshalb, on this account.

desto, the (w. comparatives).

deutlich, distinct.

deutsch, German.

Deutschland, n., –s, Germany.

deutschruhig, of German calmness.

Dezen'nium, n., –s, –ien, decade.

Dialekt', m., –s, –e, dialect.

Diamant', m., –en, –en, diamond.

diaman'tenbesäet, studded with diamonds.

dicht, dense, close.

Dichter, m., –s, —, poet; =mensch, m., –en, –en, poet.

Dichtkunst, f., "e, art of poetry.

dick, thick, stout.

Dickicht, n., –s, –e, thicket.

dickmaurig, thick-walled.

Diebstahl, m., –s, "e, larceny, theft.

dienen, to serve.

dieser, this; the latter.

Ding, n., –es, –e, thing, object.

diploma'tisch, diplomatic.

diskursieren, to discourse, hold forth.

disputieren, to dispute.

Dissertation', f., –en, dissertation.

Distelkopf, m., –es, "e, thistle-top.

distinguieren, to discriminate, distinguish.

Dithyram'be, f., –n, dithyramb.

divers', diverse, sundry.

doch, nevertheless, however, after all, still, indeed.

Doktor, m., –s, –en, doctor.

Dom, m., –es, –e, cathedral.

Donner, m., –s, —, thunder.

doppelt, double.

Dorf, n., –es, "er, village.

Dorn, m., –s, –en; or Dorne, f., –n, thorn.

dort, dorten, there.

dortig, of that place, there.

Dozen'tenmiene, f., –n, air of a professor, professorial style.

dozieren, to lecture.

drängen, to throng, swell; be turbulent.

drauf, upon it; at it.

draußen, outside.

drehen, to turn; sich —, to revolve.

drei, three.

drein, into it, in unison with.

drein=schauen, to look on.

dreißigjährig, of thirty years.

dreist, bold, without fear.

dreiunddreißig, thirty-three.
drin, therein.
dringen, a, u, to penetrate, press.
dritte, der, the third.
dröhnend, resounding, with a thud.
drollig, droll, humorous.
drüben, across there.
Duell', n., -s, -e, duel.
duellieren (sich), to fight duels.
Duft, m., -es, ̈e, scent, perfume.
duften, to be fragrant, give forth perfume.
duftig, fragrant, odorous.
dumm, stupid.
dummklug, foolishly wise, would-be clever.
dumpf, dull.
dumpfig, dull, close, musty.
dumpfkatho'lisch, gloomy Catholic.
dunkel, dark, vague.
Dunkelheit, f., -en, darkness.
dünn, thin.
durch, through, on account of, for.
durchaus', throughout; — keine, absolutely no, no ... at all.
durchbrechen, S., to break through.
durchfrösteln, to send a cold shiver through.
durch=hauen, S., to cut through.
Durchmesser, m.,-s, —, diameter.
durch=schimmern, to shine through.
durchsichtig, transparent, clear.

durchstöbern, to rummage through.
durchwallen, to voyage through, wander.
durchwandern, to traverse, travel over.
durchzittern, to vibrate through.
dürfen, durfte, gedurft, to be permitted, dare.
Durst, m., -es, thirst.
düster, dark, gloomy, somber, dusky.
Dutzend, n., -s, -e, dozen.

E

eben, just.
Ebene, f., -n, plain.
ebenfalls, likewise.
Ebenmaß, n., -es, symmetry.
ebenso, just so, just as.
ebensogut, just as well as.
ebensoviel, just as many.
Echo, n., -s, -s, echo.
echt, genuine.
echtdeutsch, genuinely German.
Ecke, f., -n, corner.
eckig, angular.
edel, noble.
Effekt', m., -s, -e, effect.
ehe, before; eher, rather.
Ehefrau, f., -en, wife.
Ehrfurcht, f., awe, reverence.
ehrfurchtsvoll, reverent, deferential.
ehrlich, honest, honorable.
ehrsam, respectable, worthy.

Eichbaum, m., -s, "e, oak-tree.
Eiche, f., -n, oak.
Eichhörnchen, n.,-s, —, squirrel.
eidlich, on oath.
Eifer, m., -s, zeal, enthusiasm.
eifern, to inveigh (against, über),
 denounce.
eifrig, zealous, passionate.
eigen, own, peculiar, particular.
eigentlich, true, proper; really;
 of right.
Eigentümlichkeit, f., -en, pecul-
 iarity.
eilen, to hasten.
einan'der, each other.
ein=atmen, to breathe in.
Einbildung, f.,-en, imagination.
Eindruck, m., -s, "e, impression.
einfach, simple.
Einfachheit, f., simplicity.
Einfalt, f., simplicity.
Einfältigkeit, f., simplicity.
Einfassung, f., -en, enclosure.
ein=flößen, to breathe into, in-
 fuse, inspire with.
eingeboren, native.
eingefangen, captured, caught.
eingerichtet, provided, equipped.
Einheit, f., -en, unity.
ein=heizen, to make a fire.
einher'=jagen, to dash along.
einher'=laufen, S., to run about.
einher'=reiten, i, i, to ride along.
einher'=wandeln, to move along.
einher'=ziehen, S., to proceed,
 troop along, migrate.
einig, some.

einigemal, a few times.
ein=kehren, to enter, stop, put up.
ein=kleiden, to clothe.
ein=klemmen, to wedge in.
ein=laden, u, a, to invite.
einmal, once, at some time;
 nicht —, not even.
ein=packen, to pack, put in.
Einrichtung, f., -en, arrange-
 ment.
einsam, lonely.
ein=sammeln, to gather in.
ein=schlagen, S., to strike into,
 pursue, follow.
ein=schlummern, to fall asleep.
ein=schmeißen, i, i, to smash.
ein=schmelzen, S., to melt down.
ein=schmuggeln, to smuggle in.
ein=schnupfen, to inhale (through
 the nose), snuff.
ein=schreiben, S., to inscribe.
ein=sehen, S., to see, perceive.
einseitig, one-sided, partial, su-
 perficial.
Einspänner, m., -s, —, one
 horse team.
einst, once upon a time.
ein=stecken, to put in one's pocket.
ein=stimmen, to join in.
ein=teilen, to divide, classify.
Einteilung, f., -en, classification.
Eintritt, m., -s, -e, entrance.
Einverständnis, n., -ses, -se,
 concord, agreement, understanding.
ein=wechseln, to exchange.

Einwohner, *m.*, –s, —, inhabitant.

einzeln, single, detailed; das Einzelne, the individual thing, details.

einzig, single, only.

Eisen, *n.*, –s, —, iron.

Eisensporn, *m.*, –es, —sporen, iron spur.

eisern, iron.

Elefant', *m.*, –en, –en, elephant.

ele'gisch, elegiac.

elendiglich, miserably.

Elfenkönigin, *f.*, –nen, elf queen.

embrassieren, to embrace.

Empfang, *m.*, –s, ᵘe, receipt, reception; in — nehmen, to receive.

empfangen, i, a, to receive.

empfehlen, a, o, to recommend.

empfinden, a, u, to perceive, feel.

Empfindung, *f.*, –en, sensation, feeling.

empor', up, upwards.

empor'-johlen, to yodel forth.

empor'-schießen, *S.*, to shoot up.

empor'-schwingen (sich), a, u, to soar, rise, make one's way.

empor'-steigen, *S.*, to ascend.

empor'-zischen, to boil up.

Ende, *n.*, –s, –n, end.

endlich, finally.

Endurteil, *n.*, –s, –e, final judgment.

eng, narrow, close-fitting.

Engel, *m.*, –s, —, angel.

Englein, *n.*, –s, —, little angel.

englisch, English.

Enkel, *m.*, –s, —, grandson.

entfalten, to unfold, develop.

Entfaltung, *f.*, –en, unfolding, straightening out.

entfernt, distant, at a distance.

entfließen, o, o, to escape.

entführen, to abduct, carry off.

entge'gen, towards.

enthalten, *S.*, to contain.

entrinnen, a, o, to escape.

entscheiden, *S.*, to decide.

entschlossen, determined.

Entschuldigung, *f.*, –en, pardon.

Entsetzen, *n.*, –s, terror, horror.

entsetz'lich, terrible, horrible.

entstehen, *S.*, to arise, ensue.

entweder, either.

entwickeln, to develop.

entzaubern, to disenchant.

entzücken, to enrapture, captivate.

Entzückungsphrase, *f.*, –n, exclamation of rapture.

Epos, *n.*, —, Epen, epic.

erbauen, to erect.

Erbbegräbnis, *n.*, –ses, –se, family vault.

erbeben, to quake.

erbleichen, i, i, to pale.

erblicken, to see, perceive.

Erddunst, *m.*, –es, ᵘe, vapor of the earth.

Erde, *f.*, –n, earth.

erdenken, *S.*, to imagine, discover.

Erdſcholle, *f.*, –n, (earth-clod), bit of soil.

erfahren, u, a, to learn.

erfaſſen, to lay hold of, grasp.

erfinden, *S.*, to invent, discover.

Erfinder, *m.*, -8, —, inventor.

erfolgreich, successful.

erfragen, to inquire for.

erfreuen (ſich), to rejoice.

erfreulich, pleasant.

erfüllen, to fulfil.

ergänzen, to supplement.

ergießen, *S.* (ſich), to pour forth.

erglänzen, to shine, beam.

ergötzlich, amusing, delightful.

ergreifen, i, i, to seize.

ergrübeln, to excogitate.

erhaben, sublime.

erhalten, *S.*, to obtain; preserve.

erhaſchen, to snatch up.

erheben, *S.*, to elevate; ſich —, to rise.

erhellen, to illuminate.

erinnern (ſich), to remember, call up reminiscences.

Erinnerung, *f.*, –en, remembrance, memory.

erkennen, *S.*, to recognize.

Erklärung, *f.*, –en, explanation.

erklingen, *S.*, to sound, resound, be filled with music.

erlauben, to permit.

erleben, to experience.

erleichtern, to lighten.

erlogen, false, affected, simulated.

erloſchen, died out, extinct.

erlöſen, to save, rescue.

ermangeln, to lack, fail.

Ermangelung, *f.*, want, lack.

ermorden, to murder.

erneuen, to renew, revive.

ernſt, serious.

ernſtfromm, earnestly devout.

ernſthaft, serious, solemn.

erquicken, to refresh.

Erquickung, *f.*, –en, refreshment.

erraten, *S.*, to guess, divine.

erregen, to cause, produce.

erſchaffen, u, a, to create.

erſchallen, o, o, *and wk.*, to resound.

erſcheinen, *S.*, to appear, be published.

Erſcheinung, *f.*, –en, appearance, phenomenon, production.

Erſcheinungswelt, *f.*, –en, world of phenomena, outward world.

erſchlafft, enfeebled, enervated.

erſchließen, *S.* (ſich), to open.

erſchöpfen, to exhaust.

erſchrecken, a, o, to be frightened; *wk.*, to frighten.

erſchrecklich, terrifying.

erſt, first; only, only then.

Erſtaunen, *n.*, -8, astonishment; in — ſetzen, to astonish.

erſtaunlich, astonishing.

erſtaunt, astonished, amazed.

erſteigen, *S.*, to ascend.

erſtrecken (ſich), to extend to (auf).

ertragen, *S.*, to bear.

erwachen, to awake.

erwachſen, grown up.

erwählen, to choose, elect.

erwähnen, to mention; erwähnt, aforesaid.

erwärmen, to warm.

erwarten, to await, expect.

Erwartung, f., –en, expectation.

erwehren (sich), to refrain from.

erwerben, a, o, to acquire.

erwidern, to answer, reply, return.

Erz, n., –es, –e, ore.

erzählen, to relate.

Erzähler, m., –s, —, narrator.

Erzählung, f., –en, tale, narrative.

erzeigen, to show.

erzeugen, to beget; Erzeugte, offspring, daughter.

Erzstück, n., –es, –e, piece of ore.

Esel, m., –s, —, ass.

Eseltreiber, m., –s, —, donkey driver.

esote'risch, esoteric.

Espenlaub, n., –es, aspen leaf (foliage).

essen, aß, gegessen, to eat.

Essen, n., –s, —, meal, food, fare.

etablieren, to establish.

etrus'kisch, Etruscan.

etwa, perhaps, perchance.

etwas, something, somewhat.

euer, your.

Eule, f., –n, owl.

europä'isch, European.

ewig, perpetual, eternal, immortal.

Ewigkeit, f., –en, eternity.

Exemplar', n., –s, –e, copy, specimen.

exote'risch, exoteric.

exzerpieren, to make excerpts from.

F

fabelhaft, fabulous.

Fabelreich, n., –es, –e, realm of fable.

Fabrik'preis, m., –es, –e, manufacturer's price.

Fackelglanz, m., –es, glare of torches.

Fackeltanz, m., –es, "e, torch dance.

Faden, m., –s, ", thread.

Faksi'mile, n., –s, –s, facsimile.

Fakultät', f., –en, faculty.

Fall, m., –es, "e, case.

fallen, ie, a, to fall.

fällen, to fell; pronounce (Urteil).

falsch, false.

Fältchen, n., –s, —, little fold, wrinkle.

Falte, f., –n, fold.

falten, to fold.

Familiarität', f., –en, familiarity.

Fami'lie, f., –n, family.

fangen, i, a, to capture.

Farbe, f., –n, color.

farbig, colored.

Faser, f., –n, fibre.

fassen, to grasp.

faſt, almost.
Fauſtbild, _n._, –es, –er, Faust picture.
Faxe, _f._, –n, tomfoolery.
Feder, _f._, –n, feather.
Fee, _f._, –n, fairy.
fehlen, to be lacking.
Fehler, _m._, –s, —, defect.
feiern, to celebrate.
Feinheit, _f._, –en, delicate touch.
Feld, _n._, –es, –er, field.
Felſen, _m._, –s, —, rock.
Felſenbruſt, _f._, ⁻e, rocky bosom.
Felſenburg, _f._, –en, rock castle.
Felſenwand, _f._, ⁻e, wall of rock.
Felsſtück, _n._, –s, –e, rock.
Fenſter, _n._, –s, —, window.
Fenſterlein, _n._, –s, —, little window.
Fenſterſcheibe, _f._, –n, window-pane.
Ferienzeit, _f._, –en, vacation.
Ferne, _f._, –n, distance.
ferner, further, furthermore.
fertig, done, ready.
Feſſel, _f._, –n, fetter.
feſt, fixed, firm; close.
feſt-halten, _S._, to hold fast, fix, retain.
feſt-klammern (ſich), to cling to.
feſtlich, festive.
Feſtlichkeit, _f._, –en, festivity.
fett, fat.
Fetzen, _m._, –s, —, bit.
feuchten, to moisten.
Feuer, _n._, –s, —, fire, enthusiasm.

Feuerball, _m._, –s, ⁻e, fire ball.
Feuersbrunſt, _f._, ⁻e, conflagration.
Feuerſtelle, _f._, –n, fire-place, hearth, domicile.
Fieber, _n._, –s, —, fever, chill.
fiedeln, to fiddle.
Filzhut, _m._, –es, ⁻e, felt hat.
finden, a, u, to find.
fiſtulieren, to sing falsetto.
flach, flat; das flache Land, plain.
Fläche, _f._, –n, plain.
flachshaarig, flaxen-haired.
flackern, to flicker.
Flamme, _f._, –n, flame.
Flaſche, _f._, –n, bottle.
flattern, to flutter, wave.
Fleck, _m._, –s, –e, spot.
Fleiſch, _n._, –es, meat.
Fleiſchſuppe, _f._, –n, broth.
Fleiß, _m._, –es, diligence.
fleißig, diligently.
flicken, to mend, patch up.
Fliege, _f._, –n, fly.
fliegen, o, o, to fly.
fliehen, o, o, to flee.
fließen, o, o, to flow.
flimmern, to glisten.
Florenz', _n._, Florence.
florieren, to flourish.
Flöte, _f._, –n, flute.
flötenſüß, sweet as a flute.
fluchen, to curse.
Fluß, _m._, –es, ⁻e, river.
flüſtern, to whisper.
folgen, to follow.
folglich, consequently.

Form, f., -en, form, line; manner.

Forſtboden, m., -8, —, forest soil.

fort, away.

fort=drängen, to crowd away.

fort=reiſen, to depart.

Fortſetzung, f., -en, continuation.

fort=ſpringen, S., to bound off.

fortwährend, continually.

fort=wandeln, to proceed.

Frage, f., -n, question.

fragen, wk. (pret. also frug), to ask.

Fragment', n., -8, -e, fragment.

Frankfurt=am=Mainer, m., -8, —, man from Frankfurt on the Main.

Franziska'nerglocke, f., -n, bell of the Franciscan cloister.

franzö'ſiſch, French.

Frau, f., -en, woman, lady, Mrs.

Frauengeſtalt, f., -en, female figure.

Frauenzimmer, n., -8, —, woman.

Fräulein, n., -8, —, young lady.

frei, free, open.

Freiheit, f., -en, liberty.

Freiheitsheld, m., -en, -en, champion of liberty.

freilich, to be sure, indeed.

freiwillig, voluntary.

fremd, strange, of others; der Fremde, the stranger.

Fremde, f., foreign parts.

Fremdenbuch, n., -e8, "er, visitors' book. [joyous.

Freude, f., -n, joy; freudig,

Freudigkeit, f., joy, pleasure.

freudvoll, joyous, full of joy.

freuen (ſich), to rejoice.

Freund, m., -e8, -e, friend.

freundlich, friendly, kindly, pleasant.

freundſchaftlich, friendly.

frieren, o, o, to freeze; frierend, icy, cold.

Frieſe, m., -n, -n, Frisian.

friſch, fresh.

Friſeur', m., -8, -e, hair-dresser.

friſieren, to dress (the hair), curl.

froh, glad.

fröhlich, glad, happy.

Fröhlichkeit, f., joyousness.

fromm, pious, honest, pure, simple-hearted.

Frömmigkeit, f., -en, piety.

Frucht, f., "e, fruit.

früh, early.

Frühling, m., -8, -e, spring.

frühlingsgrün, (spring-green), green.

Frühlingsluft, f., "e, spring breeze.

Frühſtück, n., -8, -e, breakfast.

fühlbar, perceptible.

fühlen, to feel.

führen, to lead.

füllen, to fill.

fünfte, der, the fifth.

fünfundzwanzig, twenty-five.
fünfzehn, fifteen.
fünfzig, fifty.
funkeln, to sparkle, glitter.
für, for.
Furcht, f., fear.
furchtbar, fearful.
fürchten (sich), to be afraid.
Fürst, m., –en, –en, prince.
Fürstenknecht, m., –es, –e, prince's lackey, mercenary.
Fuß, m., –es, ⁈e, foot.
Füßchen, n., –s, —, little foot.
fußhoch, ankle-high, foot-deep.
Fußsteig, m., –es, –e, footpath.
Fußweg, m., –es, –e, footpath.
Fußzeug, n., –s, (foot-gear), boots.
Fütterungsstunde, f., –n, feeding time.

G

gaffen, to gape.
gähnen, to yawn.
galant', galant.
Gang, m., –es, ⁈e, passage, gait, walk.
ganz, entire; exact; very; das Ganze, the whole.
gänzlich, entirely.
gar, very; indeed; — kein, none at all; — nicht, not at all; — nichts, nothing at all.
Gardeleutnant, m., –s, –s, lieutenant of a regiment of the guards.

Garderobeaufwand, m., –s, (extravagant) expenditure for costumes.
Gardi'ne, f., –n, curtain.
gären, to ferment, seethe.
Garten, m., –s, ⁈, garden.
Gast, m., –es, ⁈e, guest.
Gasthof, m., –es, ⁈e, inn, hotel.
gastlich, hospitable.
Gau, m., –s, –e or –en, shire, district, Gau.
Gebäude, n., –es, —, building.
Gebell(e), n., –s, barking, bark.
geben, a, e, to give, produce; es gibt, there is (are).
Gebet, n., –es, –e, prayer.
gebieten, o, o, to order, command.
gebildet, cultured, educated.
Gebirge, n., –s, —, mountains.
gebirgig, mountainous.
Gebirgshöhe, f., –n, altitude of mountains.
geblümt, flowered, figured.
Gebrauch, m., –s, ⁈e, custom.
gebräuchlich, usual, customary.
Gedächtnis, n., –ses, –se, memory.
Gedächtnisbuch, n., –es, ⁈er, visitors' book.
gedämpft, subdued, hushed.
Gedanke, m., –ns, –n, thought.
gedeihen, ie, ie, to thrive.
Gedicht, n., –es, –e, poem.
gedrängt, charged, filled, impelled.
geduckt, bending down, crouching.
Geduld, f., patience.
geeignet, suitable.

Gefahr, *f.*, –en, danger.
gefährlich, dangerous.
gefallen, ie, a, to please.
Geflacker, *n.*, –s, flickering.
Gefolge, *n.*, –s, —, retinue.
Gefühl, *n.*, –s, –e, feeling, sentiment, sense.
gefühlvoll, full of feeling, soulful, sentimental.
gegen, towards, against, for.
Gegend, *f.*, –en, region.
Gegensatz, *m.*, –es, "e, opposite, contrast.
Gegenstand, *m.*, –s, "e, object, topic.
gegenü'ber, opposite.
Gegenwart, *f.*, presence.
geharnischt, mail-clad.
geheiligt, sacred.
geheim, secret, covert, privy.
Geheimnis, *n.*, –ses, –se, secret.
geheimnisvoll, mysterious.
gehen, ging, gegangen, to go, walk.
gehören, to belong.
gehörig, proper, fitting.
Geige, *f.*, –n, violin.
Geist, *m.*, –es, –er, spirit, mind, ghost.
Geisterberg, *m.*, –es, –e, spectre mountain.
Geisterschlacht, *f.*, –en, battle of spirits.
geistreich, witty, clever, bright.
geklopft, *part. adj.*, broken (*of ore*).
Gelächter, *n.*, –s, laughter.
gelangen, to reach, attain, arrive.

gelb, yellow.
gelbledern, of yellow leather.
gelblich, yellowish.
Geld, *n.*, –es, –er, money.
Gelegenheit, *f.*, –en, occasion.
gelehrt, learned.
Geliebte, *f.*, *inflected as adj.*, sweetheart, beloved, ladylove.
gelingen, a, u, (*also impers.*), to succeed.
gell, gellend, shrill.
gelobt, promised; das —e Land, the Promised Land (Palestine).
gelten, a, o, to be worth, be considered.
Gemach, *n.*, –es, "er, apartment.
Gemahlin, *f.*, –nen, wife, spouse.
Gemälde, *n.*, –s, —, painting.
Gemeinde, *f.*, –n, congregation.
Gemeinschaft, *f.*, –en, community; in —, in common.
Gemüt, *n.*, –s, –er, temperament, heart, soul.
gemütberuhigend, tranquilizing.
gemütlich, comfortable, cozy, snug, enjoyable, jovial, genial.
Gemütswelt, *f.*, –en, world of feeling, inner world.
genau, exact, particular, detailed.
Genauigkeit, *f.*, exactness.
General'intendanz', *f.*, –en, management.
genießen, o, o, to enjoy.
Genitiv, *m.*, –s, –e, genitive.
Genosse, *m.*, –n, –n, companion, fellow.

genug, enough.

Genügsamkeit, f., contentment, moderation.

Genuß, m., –es, ᵘe, enjoyment.

geöffnet, open.

Geograph′, m., –en, –en, geographer.

Geographie′, f., –n, geography.

geogra′phisch, geographical.

Geometrie′, f., geometry.

gerade, straight.

geraten, ie, a, to come to (an), hit upon.

Gera′tewohl, n., random.

geräuchert, smoked.

Geräusch, n., –es, –e, noise.

Gericht, n., –es, –e, court (of (law); dish.

gern, willingly; gern + verb, like to...

Geruch, m., –s, ᵘe, odor.

Gerücht, n., –es, –e, rumor, report.

Geschäft, n., –s, –e, business.

geschäftig, busy.

geschehen, a, e, to happen, take place, be done.

Geschenk, n., –es, –e, present.

Geschichtchen, n.,–s, —, little tale.

Geschichte, f., –n, history, story.

Geschichtsforscher, m., –s, —, historian.

Geschirr, n., –s, –e, harness.

Geschlecht, n., –es, –er, race, family.

Geschmack, m., –s, ᵘe, taste, flavor.

Geschwätz, n., –es, –e, idle talk.

Geselle, m., –n, –n, fellow.

gesellig, social.

Gesellschaft, f., –en, company.

Gesetzbuch, n., –s, ᵘer, law book, code.

Gesetzentwurf, m., –es, ᵘe, draft of a law.

Gesicht, n., –s, –er, face; zu — bekommen, to catch sight of.

Gesichtchen, n., –s, —, little face.

Gesin′ge, n., –s, constant singing, eternal singsong.

Gesinnung, f., –en, sentiment, disposition.

Gespenst, n., –es, –er, ghost.

Gespenstererzählung, f., –en, ghost story.

Gespensterfurcht, f., fear of ghosts.

Gespensterglaube, m., –ns, belief in ghosts.

Gespräch, n., –es, –e, conversation.

gespreizt, strutting.

Gestalt, f., –en, form, figure.

gestalten′ to shape, form.

gestehen, S., to confess.

Gestein, n., –s, –e, rocks.

gestern, yesterday.

gestimmt, tuned, attuned.

Gestrüpp, n., –s, –e, underbrush

Gesundheit, f., –en, health.

Gesund′heitsflanell′, m., –s, –e, hygienic flannel.

getäuscht, disappointed.

getreu, faithful.

Gevatterin, *f.*, –nen, gossip, co-sponsor.

Gewächs, *n.*, –es, –e, plant.

gewagt, daring, venturesome, dangerous.

gewahren, to perceive.

gewähren, to give, afford.

Gewalt, *f.*, power, might.

gewaltig, powerful, mighty, tremendous.

gewaltsam, violent.

Gewand, *n.*, –es, "er, garment, robe.

gewandt, adept, skilful.

gewappnet, escutcheoned.

Gewässer, *n.*, –s, —, water.

gewinnen, a, o, to obtain, acquire.

gewiß, certain.

Gewissen, *n.*, –s, —, conscience.

Gewohnheit, *f.*, –en, habit, custom.

gewöhnlich, usual, ordinary, regular.

Gewühl', *n.*, –s, –e, turmoil.

gezackt, jagged.

Gezänk, *n.*, –s, squabbling.

geziemen, to befit.

gießen, o, o, to pour, shed.

Gießkanne, *f.*, –n, watering can.

giftreich, rich in poison.

gigan'tisch, gigantic.

Gildenhaus, *n.*, –es, "er, guild-hall.

Gipfel, *m.*, –s, —, summit.

glänzen, to shine; glänzend, brilliant, oily.

Glas, *n.*, –es, "er, glass.

Glasmalerei', *f.*, –en, painting on glass, stained glass.

glatt, smooth, polished, sleek.

glätten, to smoothe.

Glaube(n), *m.*, –ns, faith.

glauben, to believe.

glaubhaft, trustworthy.

gleich, equal, like, same.

gleich (= sogleich), straightway, directly.

gleichen, i, i, to be like, resemble.

gleichgeboren, born equal.

gleichgestimmt, of like mind; ein G—er, a kindred soul.

Gleichgewicht, *n.*, –s, balance of power.

gleichgültig, immaterial; indifferent.

Gleichgültigkeit, *f.*, indifference.

Gleichmäßigkeit, *f.*, –en, uniformity.

gleichsam, just as if, as it were.

gleiten, i, i, to glide.

Glied, *n.*, –es, –er, limb; *pl.*, form, figure.

glimmen, o, o, to glimmer; kleines G—, faint glimmer.

glitscherig, slippery.

Glöckchen, *n.*, –s, —, little bell.

Glocke, *f.*, –n, bell.

Glockenblümchen, *n.*, –s, —, bell-flower.

Glockengeläute, *n.*, –s, sound of bells, chime.

Glockenſchlag, m., -es, ⁿe, stroke of a bell.

Glöcklein, n., -s, —, little bell.

Glotauge, n., -s, -n, goggle-eye, staring eye.

Glück, n., -es, happiness, luck.

glücklich, happy, fortunate.

glücklicherweiſe, fortunately.

glühen, to glow.

Gnadenſtelle, f., -n, place of mercy, sanctuary.

gnädig, gracious.

Gold, n., -es, gold.

Golddecke, f., -n, cloth of gold.

golden, golden; adv., with golden light.

goldig, golden.

Goslarſch, of Goslar.

Gott, m., -es, ⁿer, God.

Gotteshaus, n., -es, ⁿer, house of God.

gottgeboren, born of God.

Gottheit, f., -en, godhead.

Göttin, f., -nen, goddess.

Göttinger, adj., of Göttingen.

Göttingerin, f., -nen, inhabitant of Göttingen.

göttingiſch, of Göttingen.

gottläſterlich, blasphemous.

Gottloſigkeit, f., godlessness.

Grab, n., -es, ⁿer, grave.

Grabſtein, m., -es, -e, tomb-stone.

Grad, m., -es, -e, degree.

grade, see gerade.

Graf, m., -en, -en, count.

Granit'block, m., -es, ⁿe, block of granite.

Granit'felſen, m., -s,—, granite rock.

Gras, n., -es, ⁿer, grass.

gräßlich, horrible.

grau, gray.

grauen, to shudder; das G—, horror.

Grazie, f., -n, charm, grace.

Greifswalder, m., -s, —, man from Greifswald, student of the University of Greifswald.

Greis, m., -es, -e, old man.

Greuel, m., -s, —, horror.

griechiſch, Greek, Hellenic.

Groſchen, m., -s, —, groat, Groschen (coin worth about 2½ cents).

groß, great, large, grand.

Größe, f., -n, size.

Großmutter, f., ⁿ, grandmother.

Grübchen, n., -s, —, dimple.

Grube, f., -n, mine.

Grubenlicht, n., -es, -er, miners' lamp.

grün, green.

Grund, m., -es, ⁿe, ground; cause; im —, at bottom; zu Grunde gehen, to be ruined.

grundgelehrt, very learned, profound.

Gründlichkeit, f., thoroughness.

grünfunkelnd, green-sparkling.

grünlich, greenish.

Grünſpan, m., -s, verdigris.

Gruppe, f., -n, group.

Gruß, *m.*, –es, ˮe, greeting, salutation.

grüßen, to greet.

Guelfenorden, *m.*, –s, —, Guelphic Order.

Guilloti'ne (*pron. as in French, but with four syllables*), *f.*, –n, guillotine.

gut, good.   [pleasure.

Gutdünken, *n.*, –s, judgment,

gütig, kind.

H

Haar, *n.*, –es, –e, hair.

Haarbüschel, *m. and n.*, –s, —, tuft of hair.

haben, hatte, gehabt, to have.

Hahnenschrei, *m.*, –es, –e, crowing of the cock.

halb, half.

halberloschen, half obliterated.

halbjährig, semi-annual.

halbkreisartig, semi-circular.

halbverstedt, half concealed.

Hälfte, *f.*, –n, half.

Halle, *f.*, –n, hall.

Hallen'ser, *m.*, –s, —, native of Halle, student of the University of Halle.

Hallesch, of Halle.

Hals, *m.*, –es, ˮe, neck; über Hals und Kopf, head over heels, helter-skelter.

halsbrechend, break-neck; mit —er Gefahr, at the risk of breaking one's neck.

halten, ie, a, to hold, keep, observe; — für, to think, consider.

Hammer, *m.*, –s, ˮ, hammer.

Hand, *f.*, ˮe, hand.

Handbuch, *n.*, –s, ˮer, handbook.

Händchen, *n.*, –s, —, little hand.

handeln, to act.

Handlungsbeflissene, der, (*infl. as adj.*), commercial traveler.

Handwerksbursche, *m.*, –n, –n, journeyman.

hangen, hängen, i, a, to hang, cling, be attached.

Härchen, *n.*, –s, —, little hair.

Harlekin, *m.*, –s, –s, harlequin.

harmlos, innocent, simple.

Harmonie', *f.*, –en, harmony.

harmo'nisch, harmonious.

harren, to wait.

hart, hard, tough.

Harz, *m.*, –es, Hartz; ₌prinzessin, *f.*, –nen, Hartz princess.

Harzreisebuch, *n.*, –es, ˮer, guide book to the Hartz.

Harzreisende, der, (*infl. as adj.*), traveler in the Hartz.

Harzwald, *m.*, –es, ˮer, Hartz forest.

Hase, *m.*, –n, –n, hare.

häßlich, ugly.

Hast, *f.*, haste, speed.

hastig, hasty.

Hastigkeit, *f.*, haste, precipitation.

Hauch, *m.*, –es, –e, breath.

hauchen, to breathe.

hauen, hieb, gehauen, to hew, cut, strike.

Haupt, n., -es, ͞er, head.

Hauptgegenstand, m., -s, ͞e, chief topic.

Haupthahn, m., -s, ͞e, prize cock.

Häuptlein, n., -s, —, little head.

hauptsächlich, chiefly.

Hauptspaß, m., -es, ͞e, best (part of the) joke.

Hauptstück, n., -es, -e, chapter.

Haus, n., -es, ͞er, house, home.

häuserhoch, tall as a house.

Hausflur, m., -s, -e, corridor.

Hauskatze, f., -n, house-cat.

häuslich, domestic.

Hausmädchen, n., -s, —, chambermaid.

Haustüre, f., -n, house-door.

Hautübel, n., -s, —, skin disease.

heben, o, o, (sich), to rise.

hegen, to cherish, entertain, harbor, hold, be bound by.

Heidelbeerstrauch, m., -es, ͞e, huckleberry bush.

heidnisch, heathen.

Heiland, m., -s, -e, savior.

heilen, to heal.

heilig, sacred, holy.

heilsam, wholesome.

heimisch, native.

heimlich, intimate, familiar.

Heimlichkeit, f., -en, seclusion.

heim=suchen, to befall, betide.

heiß, hot.

heißen, ie, ei, to be called; be.

heiter, merry, serene.

Held, m., -en, -en, hero.

helfen, a, o, to help, assist.

hell, bright.

hellgrün, bright green.

helmartig, helmet-shaped.

Hemd, n., -es, -en, shirt.

Hemmung, f., -en, hindrance.

her, hither, ago, along; hin und —, to and fro.

herab', down, downward.

herab'=beugen, to bend down.

herab=fallen, S., to fall down.

herab'=gießen, S., to pour down.

herab'=hängen, S., to hang down; reach down.

herab'=schauen, to look down.

herab'=schießen, S., to shoot down.

herab'=stören, to blow down, scatter.

herab'=strömen, to pour down.

herab'=taumeln, to tumble down.

herab'=triefen, o, o, and wk., to trickle down.

herab'=werfen, S., to throw down.

heran'=springen, S., to jump along.

herauf', up.

herauf'=gehen, S., to go up.

herauf'=kommen, S., to come up.

herauf'=taumeln, to stumble up, reel up.

herauf'=winden, a, u, to haul up.

heraus'=bringen, S., to draw out.
heraus'=fließen, S., to stream forth.
heraus'=klopfen, to beat out.
heraus'=kommen, S., to get out; auf eins —, to amount to one and the same thing, be immaterial.
heraus'=philosophieren, to philosophize away.
heraus'=schauen, to look out.
heraus=schneiden, S., to cut out.
Herberge, f., –n, hostelry; guild house.
Herde, f., –n, herd.   [bell.
Herdenglöckchen, n., –s, —, herd
herein', in.
herein'=kommen, S., to come in.
herein'=treten, S., to step in, enter.
herein'=werfen, S., to throw in,
Hering, m., –s, –e, herring.
her=kommen, S., to come from, be taken from.
hernach, afterwards.
hero'isch, heroic.
Herr, m., –n, –en, gentleman, Mr., Sir.
herrlich, splendid, glorious, fine.
Herrlichkeit, f., –en, splendor, magnificence, glory.
herrschen, to rule, prevail.
her=rühren, to originate from, be due to.
her=sagen, to repeat, recite.
herum', around.
herum'=drehen, to spin around.

herum'=fliegen, S., to fly around.
herum'=klettern, to climb about.
herum'=schlagen (sich), S., to fight.
herum'=springen, S., to frisk about.
herum'=tänzeln, to dance around.
herum'=trippeln, to trip.
herun'ter=regnen, to rain, pour down.
hervor'=blinken, to peep out.
hervor'=blühen, to blossom forth.
hervor'=bringen, S., to produce.
hervor'=dringen, S., to well forth.
hervor'=gehen, S., to appear.
hervor'=glänzen, to shine forth.
hervor'=gucken, to peep out.
hervor'=klingen, S., to sound forth.
hervor'=lauschen, to peep forth.
hervor'=leuchten, to shine forth.
hervor'=sintern, to trickle, ooze out.
hervor'=sprießen, o, o, to sprout, shoot forth.
hervor'=springen, S., to spring forth.
hervor'=sprudeln, to gush forth.
hervor'=sprühen, to shoot forth.
hervor'=steigen, S., to climb out.
hervor'=tauchen, to emerge.
hervor'=treten, S., to step out, stand out, be prominent, project, emerge, appear, rise.
Herz, n., –ens, –en, heart.
her=zählen, to recount, enumerate.

herzen, to fondle.

Herzgeliebte, die, (*infl. as adj.*), heart's beloved.

Herzklopfen, *n.*, -s, heart beat.

herzlich, heartily.

Herzog, *m.*, -s, -e, duke.

herzu-eilen, to hasten to the spot.

hetzen, to hound on, set on; hunt.

heulen, to howl.

heute, to-day.

heutzutage, at the present day.

Hexa'meter, *m.*, -s, —, hexameter.

Hexe, *f.*, -n, witch.

He'xenaltar', *m.*, -s, -e, witch's altar.

hier, here.

hierauf, hereupon.

Himmel, *m.*, -s, —, heaven.

himmelgroß, great as heaven, heaven-wide.

himmelhoch, high as heaven, towering.

Himmelsbläue, *f.*, azure of heaven.

himmlisch, heavenly.

hin, thither, along; — und her, to and fro, hither and thither.

hinab', down.

hinab'-beugen, to bend down.

hinab'-eilen, to hasten down.

hinab'-gehen, *S.*, to go down.

hinab'-klettern, to climb down.

hinab'-laufen, *S.*, to run down; extend.

hinab'-leiten, to lead down.

hinab'-rauschen, to rush down.

hinab'-schauen, to look down.

hinab'-steigen, *S.*, to descend.

hinab'-ziehen, *S.*, to descend.

hinauf', up, upward.

hinauf'-klettern, to climb up.

hinauf'-sehen, *S.*, to look up.

hinauf'-sehnen (sich), to yearn (upwards) for.

hinauf'-steigen, *S.*, to ascend.

hinaus', out; zum . . . —, out from.

hinaus'-laufen, *S.*, to come to, end up with.

hinaus'-wandern, to walk out.

hin-bemerken, to offer a remark.

Hindernis, *n.*, -ses, -se, obstacle.

hin-eilen, to hasten thither.

hinein', into.

hinein'-fallen, *S.*, to fall into.

hinein'-flimmern, to flicker into.

hinein'-passen, to fit in.

hinein'-plumpsen, to plump into.

hinein'-schauen, to look into.

hinein'-schnitzeln, to carve into.

hinein'-schwatzen, to rant to.

hinein'-spinnen, *S.*, to weave into.

hinein'-vegetieren, to vegetate into.

hin-geben, *S.*, to give, present, give up; portray, represent.

hinge'gen, on the other hand.

hin-lächeln, to say smiling.

hinlänglich, sufficient.

hinnen, hence.

Hinrichtungsscene, f., –n, execution scene.

hin=rieseln, to trickle along.

hin=schreiten, S., to proceed, walk along.

hin=sehen, S., to look thither.

hin=setzen (sich), to sit down, seat oneself.

Hinsicht, f., –en, regard, respect, point of view; in —, as regards.

hin=stellen, to set down, place.

Hinsterben, n., –s, dying, death.

hinsterbend, dying, faint, weak.

hinten, at the back, in the rear.

hinter, behind, beyond.

Hinterleder, n., –s, —, (hind leather), breech leather.

hinterm = hinter dem.

hin=trippeln, to trip along.

hinü'ber=springen, S., to leap across.

hinü'ber=tragen, S., to carry across.

hinun'ter, down.

hinun'ter=gehen, S., to go down.

hinun'ter=schauen, to look down.

hinun'ter=steigen, S., to descend.

hinun'ter=stürzen, to fall down, be precipitated; sich —, to plunge down.

hin=werfen, S., to cast, diffuse.

hin=ziehen, S., to extend.

hinzu'=fügen, to add.

hinzu'=notieren, to add.

hinzu'=setzen, to add.

Hirngespinst, n., –es, –e, phantom (of the brain), chimera.

Hirsch, m., –es, –e, deer.

Hirt, m., –en, –en, herdsman.

Hirtenknabe, m., –n, –n, shepherd-boy.

Histo'riker, m., –s, —, historian.

histo'risch, historical.

hoch, high; höchst, most.

hochberühmt, illustrious.

hochgebenedeit, most blessed, blessed.

Hochgefühl, n., –s, –e, high-flown sentiment.

hochgelahrt, highly learned.

hochrot, flushed.

Hochzeit, f., –en, wedding.

Hof, m., –es, ᵘe, court.

hoffen, to hope.

Hoffnung, f., –en, hope.

höflich, courtly, polite.

Höflichkeit, f., –en, politeness, civility, compliment.

Hofrat, m., –s, ᵘe, councillor of the court, Hofrat.

Hofschauspieler, m., –s, —, court-player.

Höhe, f., –n, height; in die —, up.

höhnen, to scorn, mock.

hold, fair, lovely.

holdselig, benign, charming, sweet.

holen, to fetch, take; draw (Atem).

holpern, to stumble, jolt.

holprig, uneven, hobbling, rough.

ḫölzern, wooden.
Holzſchnitt, *m.*, –š, –e, wood-cut.
honorieren, to pay.
hörbar, audible.
horch! hark!
hordenweiš, in hordes.
hören, to hear; attend a course of lectures on.
Horizont', *m.*,–š, –e, horizon.
Horn, *n.*, –eš, "er, horn.
Hoſe, *f.*, –n, pair of trousers, breeches.
Hotel', *n.*, –š, –š, hotel.
Houri, *f.*, –š, houri.
hübſch, pretty, nice.
Hügel, *m.*, –š, —, hill.
huldigen, to do homage.
huldreich, gracious.
humori'ſtiſch, ironical, humorous, ludicrous.
humpeln, to hobble.
Hund, *m.*, –eš, –e, dog.
hundert, hundred.
hundertmal, a hundred times.
Hundštag, *m.*, –eš, –e, dog-day.
hungrig, hungry.
hüpfen, to hop.
Hütte, *f.*, –n, hut.
Hypotheš'chen, *n.*, –š, —, little hypothesis.

J

Jdee', *f.*, –n, idea.
Jde'engang, *m.*,–eš, "e, train of ideas.
idyl'liſch, idyllic.

illuminieren, to illuminate, color.
Jlluſion', *f.*, –en, illusion.
illu'ſter, illustrious, eminent.
im = in dem.
immatrikulieren, to matriculate.
immer, always, ever.
immerfort, forever.
immerhin, after all.
immerwährend, continual, everlasting.
imponie'rend, imposing.
impoſant', imposing.
in, in, into.
indem', in that, through the fact that, in as much as.
indeš', indeſ'ſen, however.
Jndivi'duum, *n.*, –š, –duen, individual.
ineinan'der, into each other.
inner, inward.
innig, deep, profound, intimate.
inš = in daš.
Jnſchrift, *f.*, –en, inscription.
Jntendanz', *f.*, –en, management.
intereſſant', interesting.
intereſſieren, to interest.
Jronie', *f.*, irony.
irren, to err, wander aimlessly.
Jrrtum, *m.*,–š, "er, error.
Jta'lien, *n.*, –š, Italy.

J

ja, yes, yea.
Jäckchen, *n.*, –š, —, little jacket.

Jade, f., -n, jacket.
jagen, chase, drive, sweep along, fly.
Jäger, m., -8, —, hunter.
Jahr, n., -e8, -e, year.
Jahrhun'dert, n., -8, -e, century.
jahrhun'dertelang, for centuries.
Jahrmarkt, m., -8, "e, fair.
jammern, to lament, grieve, moan.
Janitscha'renoper, f., Janissary opera.
jauchzen, to shout.
je, the (with comparatives).
jeder, jede, jedes, each, every, every one.
jedesmal, every time.
jedoch', however.
jemand, some one.
jener, that, yon; the former.
jetzig, of the present day.
jetzo, now.
jetzt, now.
Joch, n., -e8, -e, yoke.
johlen, to shout, yell.
jubeln, to shout or sing jubilantly.
Jude, m., -n, -n, Jew.
Jugend, f., youth.
Juli, m., -8, July.
jung, young, youthful.
Junge, m., -n, -n, boy.
Jüngling, m., -8, -e, youtn.
Jurisprudenz', f., jurisprudence.

juri'stisch, juristic, pertaining to the department of law.
just, just.
Justiz'rat, -8, "e, councillor of justice; der geheime —, privy councillor of justice.

K

Kabinett', n., -8, -e, cabinet.
Käfer, m., -8, —, beetle, chafer.
Kaffee, m., -8, coffee.
kahl, bald, bare.
Kahlkopf, m., -e8, "e, bald head.
Kaiser, m., -8, —, emperor.
Kaisererinnerung, f., -en, imperial association (memory).
Kaiserkrone, f., -n, imperial crown.
kaiserlich, imperial, royal.
Kaiserstuhl, m., -8, "e, imperial throne.
Kalb, n., -e8, "er, calf.
Kalbsbraten, m., -8, —, roast of veal.
kalt, cold.
Kälte, f., cold.
Kamel', n., -8, -e, camel.
Kamin'fegeloch, n., -e8, "er, ('chimney-sweeping-hole') hole of a chimney.
Kamisol', n., -8, -e, jacket.
Kammer, f., -n, room.
Kammermusicus, m., —, -ci, chamber-musician, musician of the royal household.
kämpfen, to struggle.

Kana'rienvogel, *m.*, –s, ⁿ, canary.

kärglich, charily, niggardly.

karmoiſin'rot (*pron.* oi *as in French*), crimson.

Kartof'fel, *f.*, –n, potato.

Karyati'de, *f.*, –n, caryatid.

Karzer, *m.*, –s, —, lock-up (of the university).

Käſe, *m.*, –s, —, cheese.

Kaska'de, *f.*, –n, cascade.

Kaſtagnet'te, *f.*, –n, castanet.

Kaſte, *f.*, –n, caste, class.

Kaſten, *m.*, –s, —, box, chest.

Kaſuiſt', *m.*, –en, –en, casuist.

Katze, *f.*, –n, cat.

Kaufmann, *m.*, –s, –leute, merchant.

kaum, scarcely.

Kavalier', *m.*, –s, –e, cavalier.

keck, bold.

Kegel, *m.*, –s, —, cone.

keifend, scolding, peevish, clamorous.

kein, no, none.

kennen, kannte, gekannt, to know, be acquainted with.

Kenntnis, *f.*, –ſe, knowledge.

Kind, *n.*, –es, –er, child.

Kindchen, *n.*, –s, —, little child.

Kindheit, *f.*, childhood.

kindlich, child-like.

Kinn, *n.*, –s, –e, chin.

Kirche, *f.*, –n, church.   [bell.

Kirchenglocke, *f.*, –n, church-

Kirchenvatertext, *m.*, –es, –e, church-father text.

Kirchhof, *m.*, –es, ⁿe, churchyard.

klagen, to complain.

Klang, *m.*, –es, ⁿe, sound.

klappern, to chatter.

klar, clear, pure.

Klaſſe, *f.*, –n, class.

klaſſifizieren, to classify.

klatſchen, to crack.

Klauſtaler, of Klaustal.

Klavier', *n.*, –s, –e, piano.

Kleeblatt, *n.*, –s, ⁿer, cloverleaf, trio.

Kleid, *n.*, –es, –er, dress; *pl.*, clothes.

kleiden, to clothe.

Kleiderſchrank, *m.*, –es, ⁿe, wardrobe.

Kleidungsſtück, *n.*, –es, –e, article of clothing.

klein, small.

klettern, to climb, clamber.

klingeln, to ring.

klingen, a, u, to sound.

Klippe, *f.*, –n, cliff.

klirren, to ring.

klopfen, to knock, beat, tap.

Kloſterſchule, *f.*, –n, cloister-school.

klug, prudent, wise.

Knabe, *m.*, –n, –n, boy.

Knabenauge, *n.*, –s, –n, boyish eye.

Knall, *m.*, –s, –e, sound, report.

Knappe, *m.*, –n, –n, page, squire.

Knappentroß, *m.*, -es, -e, throng of pages.

knäuelartig, like a (tangled) skein.

knebelbärtig, mustached.

Knecht, *m.*, -es, -e, servant; slave.

kneifen, i, i, to pinch.

kneten, to knead, fashion.

knieen, to kneel.

Knopf, *m.*, -es, ⁻e, button.

Knospe, *f.*, -n, bud.

knüpfen, to tie, join; sich — an, to be linked with.

Knüppelweg, *m.*, -es, -e, corduroy road.

knurrig, growling.

Kohl, *m.*, -s, kale, cabbage.

Kohle, *f.*, -n, coal.

Kolle'ge, *m.*, -n, -n, colleague.

kollegia'lisch, like a colleague.

Kolorit', *n.*, -s, -e, coloring, hue, tint.

koloffal', colossal, immense.

komforta'bel, comfortable.

komisch, comic, amusing.

kommen, a, o, to come.

Komment, *m.*, -s, -s, 'Comment.'

Kompen'dium, *n.*, -s, -ien, compend, digest.

Kompila'tor, *m.*, -s, -to'ren, compiler.

kompliziert', complicated.

konditioniert', in condition.

Kongreß', *m.*, -es, -e, congress.

König, *m.*, -s, -e, king.

Königin, *f.*, -nen, queen.

königlich, royal.

Königshaupt, *n.*, -es, ⁻er, royal head.

können, konnte, gekonnt, to be able, can.

konsequent', consistent.

konsiliieren, to suspend; konsiliiert werden, to receive the *consilium abeundi* (advice to withdraw), be suspended, be rusticated.

konstruieren, to construe.

Kontor'jüngling, *m.*, -s, -e, office youth, counting-house clerk.

konträr', contrary.

kontrastieren, to contrast.

Konvenienz'stimmung, *f.*, -en, conventional frame of mind.

Kopf, *m.*, -es, ⁻e, head.

Kopfabschneiderei, *f.*, -en, decapitation.

Köpfchen, *n.*, -s, —, little head.

Ko'ran, *m.*, -s, Koran.

Korps (*pron.* Kor), *n.*, —, —, corps.

Korpusjurisausgabe, *f.*, -n, edition of the corpus juris, i.e. of the body of the (Roman) law.

korrespondieren, to correspond.

Korridor, *m.*, -s, -e, corridor.

Korruption', *f.*, corruption, mutilation.

kostbar, costly, precious.

Kostüm', *n.*, -s, -e, costume.

Kot, *m.*, –8, dirt.
kotig, dirty, muddy.
krachen, to crash, crash down.
Kraft, *f.*, "e, strength, power, force.
Kralle, *f.*, –n, claw.
Krämer, *m.*, –8, —, shop-keeper.
krampfstillend, soothing.
krank, sick.
krankhaft, morbid.
Kräuterduft, *m.*, –es, "e, fragrance of herbs.
Kräutlein, *n.*, –8, —, little plant.
Krebsschaden, *m.*, –8, ", cancer, canker.
Kreide, *f.*, chalk.
kreideweiß, white as chalk.
Kreis, *m.*, –es, –e, circle.
kreischen, to scream.
Kreuz, *n.*, –es, –e, cross.
kreuzehrlich, thoroughly honest.
kreuzigen, to crucify.
kriegerisch, warlike, martial.
Kriegsrätin, *f.*, –nen, wife of a councillor of war.
kristallen, of crystal.
Kristallleuchter, *m.*, –8, —, crystal chandelier.
Kritik', *f.*, –en, critique.
Krone, *f.*, –n, crown.
Kropfleute, *pl.*, people with goiter.
Krume, *f.*, –n, crumb.
krumm, crooked.
Kruzifix', *n.*, –es, –e, crucifix.

Kugel, *f.*, –n, ball.
Kuh, *f.*, "e, cow.
Kühle, *f.*, coolness.
Kühlein, *n.*, –8, —, little cow.
kühlen, to cool.
kühn, bold, valiant.
Kühnheit, *f.*, –en, boldness, valor, courage.
Kultur', *f.*, –en, culture.
kümmerlich, disconsolate, woe-begone, thin.
kümmern (sich), to worry, bother, care.
kund=geben, *S.*, to make known.
künftig, future; in the future.
Kunstkniff, *m.*, –8, –e, trick, artifice.
künstlich, artificial.
Kunststück, *n.*, –es, –e, trick, accomplishment.
Kupfernase, *f.*, –n, copper-colored nose.
Kupfertafel, *f.*, –n, copper-plate; diagram.
kurieren, to cure.
kurz, short, low (Stirn).
kürzlich, recently.
Kuß, *m.*, –es, "e, kiss.
küssen, to kiss.

L

Labyrinth', *n.*, –8, –e, laby-rinth.
labyrin'thisch, labyrinthic, mazy, bewildering.
lächeln, to smile.

lachen, to laugh.

Lade, f., -n, chest, box.

Ladenſchwengel, m., -ß, —, counter-jumper.

lallen, to babble, murmur.

Lämmerſchwänzchen, n., -ß, —, lamb's tail.

Lampe, f., -n, lamp.

Land, n., -eß, ᵘer, land.

Landeßvater, m., -ß, ᵘ, sovereign.

Landkarte, f., -n, map.

Landſchaft, f., -en, landscape.

Landßmann, m., -ß, -leute, fellow-countryman.

Landßmännin, f., -nen, woman born in the same country with another person, country-woman.

Landſtraße, f., -n, highway.

Landwehr, f., -en, militia.

lang, adj., long.

langbärtig, long-bearded.

lange, adv., long; by far.

langen, to reach, reach out.

langerſehnt, long yearned for.

langfleiſchig ('long-fleshy'), elongated.

länglich viereckig, oblong.

langſam, slow.

Langſamkeit, f., slowness.

längſt, long ago.

langweilig, tedious.

Lärm, m., -ß, noise.

Lärmen, m., -ß, noise.

laſſen, ie, a, to let, allow, cause.

Laſter, n., -ß, —, vice.

Latein, n., -ß, Latin.

Latern'chen, n., -ß, —, little lantern.

Later'ne, f., -n, lantern, street-lamp.

Lattenwerk, n., -ß, lattice-work.

lau, lukewarm, mild.

Laubwerk, n., -ß, foliage.

lauern, to lurk, spy.

Lauf, m., -eß, ᵘe, course.

laufen, ie, au, to run.

Laune, f., -n, humor, whimsicality, fancy.

lauſchen, to listen.

Lauſcher, m., -ß, —, listener, eavesdropper.

Laut, m., -eß, -e, sound, tone.

laut, loud, hilarious.

läuten, to ring, tinkle.

lauter, nothing but, sheer.

läutern, to refine.

leben, to live; lebe(t) wohl, farewell.

Leben, n., -ß, —, life.

leben'dig, alive, living.

Lebensatemchen, n., -ß, —, breath of life, spark of life.

Lebensbreite, f., breadth of life.

Lebensgröße, f., life-size.

Lebensmut, m., -eß, energy, ambition.

Lebenstiefe, f., -n, depth of life.

lebhaft, lively, vivid.

leblos, lifeless, inanimate.

Leckerkramverfertiger, m., -ß, —, makers of dainties, confectioner.

ledern, of leather.

leer, empty.
leeren, to empty.
legen, to lay; ſich —, to lie down.
Lehnſtuhl, m., -ß, ⁿe, armchair.
Lehrbuch, n., -eß, ⁿer, text-book.
Lehrſaal, m., -ß, -ſäle, lecture-room.
Leib, m., -eß, -er, body, person, figure; — deß Herrn, Host.
Leibrock, m., -ß, ⁿe, coat.
Leiche, f., -n, corpse.
leicht, light, easy, faint.
leichthin, casually.
Leid, n., -eß, woe, affliction.
leiden, litt, gelitten, to suffer.
Leiden, n., -ß, —, suffering.
Leidenſchaft, f., -en, passion.
leider, alas, unfortunately.
leidvoll, sad, sorrowful.
Leinen, n., -ß, linen.
leiſe, soft, gentle, slight.
leiten, to guide.
Leiter, f., -n, ladder.
Leiterſproſſe, f., -n, ladder round.
lernen, to learn.
leſen, a, e, to read.
letzt, last; der letztere, the latter.
leuchten, to give light, shine.
Leute, pl., people.
Libel'lenauge, n., -ß, -n, dragon-fly eye.
Licht, n., -eß, -er, light.
lichten (ſich), to light up; become illumined.

Lichttropfen, m., -ß, —, drop of light.
lieb, dear, kind, good; Liebeß, kindness.
Liebe, f., love.
lieben, to love.
Liebende, der, (infl. as adj.), lover.
liebenswürdig, amiable, charming.
Liebenswürdigkeit, f., -en, amiability.   [poet.
Liebesdichter, m., -ß, —, erotic
Liebespaar, n., -ß, -e, pair of lovers.   [pangs of love.
Liebesſchmerz, m., -eß, -en,
Liebestraum, m., -eß, ⁿe, dream of love.
Liebhaber, m., -ß, —, lover.
lieblich, lovely, tender, sweet.
Lieblichkeit, f., loveliness, grace, charm.
Lieblingsberg, m., -eß, -e, favorite mountain.
Lieb'lingsinſtrument', n., -ß, -e, favorite instrument.
Lieblofigkeit, f., lovelessness, heartlessness.
Liebreiz, m., -eß, -e, charm.
Lied, n., -eß, -er, song.
liegen, a, e, to lie.
Lilie, f., -n, lily.
Lilienfinger, m., -ß, —, lily finger.
Lilienohr, n., -ß, -en, lily ear.
Linie, f., -n, line.
link, left.

Lippe, *f.*, -n, lip.
lispeln, to lisp, whisper.
Litteratur', *f.*, -en, literature.
loben, to praise.
löblich, laudable.
Loch, *n.*, -es, "er, hole.
Locke, *f.*, -n, lock.
Lockenköpfchen, *n.*, -s, —, little head of curls.
lockig, curly.
lodern, to flame.
logieren (*pron.* g *as in French*), to lodge.
Logis' (*pron. as in French*), *n.*, —, —, room, lodgings.
logisch, logical; logische Taten, feats in logic.
Lohn, *m.*, -es, "e, reward.
Lore = Leonore.
Los, *n.*, -es, -e, prize (in a lottery).
los, loose, wanton, gay.
los=blasen, *S.*, to blow away at, let loose, send forth.
Lösegeld, *n.*, -es, -er, ransom.
Luft, *f.*, "e, air, breeze.
luftig, airy.
lügen, o, o, to lie, tell a lie.
Lumpenkerl, *m.*, -s, -e, scoundrel, worthless fellow.
Lumpenpack, *n.*, -s, rabble.
lumpig, mean, beggarly.
Lust, *f.*, pleasure, joy, gaiety, revelry; desire.
lustig, merry.
Lyraklang, *m.*, -es, "e, strain of the lyre.

M

machen, to make, put.
Macht, *f.*, "e, power, might.
Mädchen, *n.*, -s, —, girl.
Mädchenauge, *n.*, -s, -n, maiden's eye, girlish eye.
Mädchensinn, *m.*, -s, -e, maiden heart.
Mädchenzunge, *f.*, -n, maiden's tongue, girlish tongue.
Magd, *f.*, "e, maid-servant.
Magen, *m.*, -s, —, stomach.
mager, lean, thin.
Magnet'nadel, *f.*, -n, magnetic needle.
Mähne, *f.*, -n, mane.
Mai, *m.*, -s, May.
Mainacht, *f.*, "e, night in May.
majestä'tisch, majestic.
Makkaro'ni, macaroni.
Makler, *m.*, -s, —, broker.
Mal, *n.*, -s, -e, time; mal, once, some day; nicht —, not even.
malerisch, picturesque.
Malheur, *n.*, -s, -e (French = Unglück), accident, mischief.
Malice (*pron.* Malie'ße), *f.*, -n, malice; — haben auf, to have a grudge against.
man, people, they, one.
manch (-er, -e, -es), many.
mancherlei, of various kinds.
Mandarin', *m.*, -en, -en, mandarin.
Mangel, *m.*, -s, ", lack.

mangelhaft, incomplete, imperfect.

manier'lich, refined, pretty.

Mann, *m.*, –es, "er, man.

Manna, *f.*, manna.

mannigfaltig, manifold, varied.

Manschet'te, *f.*, –n, cuff.

Mantel, *m.*, –s, ", mantle, cloak.

Manufaktur'waren=Gesicht, *n.*, –es, –er, dry-goods face, 'shoddy' face.

Märchen, *n.*, –s, —, fairy-tale.

Märchenbild, *n.*, –es, –er, fairy-tale picture.

Märchenfabel, *f.*, –n, fairy tale.

märchenhaft, pertaining to the realm of fable.

Märchenlust, *f.*, fairy-tale delights.

Mark, *n.*, –s, marrow.

Markt, *m.*, –s, "e, market, market-place.

Marmorbild, *n.*, –es, –er, marble statue.

marode, played out, done for.

marschieren, to march.

Marterfels, *m.*, –en, –en, rock of torture, martyr's rock.

Maschi'nenbewegung, *f.*, –en, motion of machinery.

Mäßigkeit, *f.*, –en, moderation, temperance.

materiell', material.

mathema'tisch, mathematical.

Matro'senlärmen, *m.*, –s, noise, shouts of the sailors.

matt, faint, dim, weak.

Mauer, *f.*, –n, wall.

Maul, *n.*, –s, "er, mouth (primarily of animals).

meckern, to bleat.

Mecklenburger, *m.*, –s, —, man from Mecklenburg.

Medaillon' (*pron. as in French*), *n.*, –s, –s, medallion, locket.

medice'isch, of Medici.

Meer, *n.*, –es, –e, sea.

Meeresbrandung, *f.*, –en, sea-breakers.

Meerungetüm, *n.*, –es, –e, sea-monster.

mehr, more, any more.

mehrere, several, a number of.

mehrmals, several times.

Meile, *f.*, –n, mile.

mein, my.

meinen, to mean, think, reflect, say; es ehrlich — mit, to be kindly disposed towards.

Meinung, *f.*, –en, opinion.

meist, most; =ens, mostly.

Meister, *m.*, –s, —, master.

meisterhaft, masterful.

Melodie', *f.*, –en, melody.

Memoi'ren, *f. pl.*, memoirs.

Menge, *f.*, –n, quantity.

Mensch, *m.*, –en, –en, man.

Menschenfuß, *m.*, –es, "e, human foot.

Menschenherz, *n.*, –ens, –en, human heart.

Menschenstrom, *m.*, –es, "e. human stream.

menſchlich, human.

merken, to mark, notice.

merkwürbig, remarkable, noteworthy.

Merkwürbigkeit, f., –en, curiosity, object of interest.

Meſſe, f., –n, fair.

Metall', n., –ß, –e, metal.

Metall'becken, n., –ß, —, metal basin.

Miene, f., –n, air, mien.

Milch, f., milk.

Milchmäbchen, n., –ß, —, milkmaid.

milb, mild.

milbern, to soften, tone down.

Minaret', n., –ß, –ß, minaret.

minber, less.

Miniatur', f., –en, miniature.

Mini'ſter, m., –ß, —, minister.

miſchen, to mix, mingle.

Miſchung, f., –en, mixture, combination.

Mißgebürtchen, n., –ß, —, (little) abortion.

Mißgeſchick, n., –ß, –e, ill fortune.

mißgeſtaltet, misshapen.

mißlich, critical, precarious.

mißmütig, ill-humored, displeased.

Miſtgabel, f., –n, ('manure fork'), pitchfork.

mit, with.

mit=beten, to pray (with others).

mit=bringen, irreg., to bring along.

Mitglieb, n., –ß, –er, member.

mit=kommen, S., to come along.

Mitleib, n., –ß, compassion.

mit=nehmen, S., to take along.

mit=ſingen, S., to join in singing.

Mittag, m., –ß, –e, noon; — halten, to dine.

Mittageſſen, n., –ß, —, dinner.

Mittagßtiſch, m., –eß, –e, dinner.

Mitte, f., –n, middle, centre.

Mittel, n., –ß, —, means.

mitten, in the midst (of).

mittenburch, through the centre.

Mitternacht, f., midnight.

Möbel, n., –ß, —, furniture.

Modell', n., –ß, –e, model.

mobern', modern.

mögen, mochte, gemocht, may, be able, like to.

möglich, possible.

Möglichkeit, f., –en, possibility.

Mohr, m., –en, –en, moor.

Monat, m., –ß, –e, month.

Mönchßſchrift, f., –en, monkish writing.

Monb, m., –eß, –e, moon.

Monbſchein, m., –ß, moonlight.

Mooßart, f., –en, variety of moss.

Mooßbank, f., "e, bank of moss.

Mooßroſe, f., –n, moss-rose.

Mopß, m., –eß, –e, pug-dog.

morben, to murder.

mörberlich, murderous.

Morgen, *m.*, –s, —, morning;
morgen, to-morrow.
Morgenluft, *f.*, "e, morning
breeze.
Morgentau, *m.*, –es, morning
dew.
Morgenwind, *m.*, –es, –e, morning breeze.
müde, tired.
Mühe, *f.*, –n, trouble, difficulty.
Muhme, *f.*, –n, aunt.
mühsam, laborious.
Mund, *m.*, –es, mouth, lips.
mundfaul, slow, drawling.
Mündlein, *n.*, –s, —, little
mouth, lips.
munter, merry, cheery, blithe.
Münze, *f.*, –n, mint.
murmeln, to murmur.
mürrisch, peevish, sullen.
Musik', *f.*, music.
müssen, mußte, gemußt, must,
have to.
Mut, *m.*, –es, spirit, mood; zu
Mute sein, to feel; zu Mute
werden, to begin to feel; mit
lustigem Mute, cheerfully, mer-
rily.
mutbeseelt, inspired with courage.
Mutter, *f.*, ", mother.
Mutwillen, *m.*, –s, playfulness,
playful humor.
Mütze, *f.*, –n, cap.
mystifizieren, to mystify, play a
joke on.
mystisch, mystical.

N

nach, after, according to, to
judge by, to, at.
Nachbar, *m.*, –s, –n, neighbor.
Nachbarskind, *n.*, –es, –er, neighbor's child.
nach=beten, to repeat (a prayer).
nachdem', *conj.*, after.
nach=empfinden, a, u, to perceive
after one, enter into the spirit
of.
nach=folgen, to follow.
Nachfolger, *m.*, –s, —, successor.
nachher, afterwards.
nachlässig, careless.
nach=lesen, *S.*, to read, look up.
nach=reißen, *S.*, to crack (a joke)
after (in imitation of) some
one else.
Nacht, *f.*, "e, night; des Nachts,
at night.
Nachtigall, *f.*, –en, nightingale.
Nachtigallenlaut, *m.*, –es, –e,
song of nightingales.
nächtlich, nocturnal, dark, by
night.
Nachtmantel, *m.*, –s, ", night
robe.
Nachtmütze, *f.*, –n, nightcap.
Nachtwandler, *m.*, –s, —, som-
nambulist.
Nachtwandlerzustand, *m.*, –es,
"e, somnambulistic state.
Nachtzeit, *f.*, –en, night-time.
Nacken, *m.*, –s, —, neck.

nackt, naked, bare.

Nadel, f., –n, needle.

Nadelholz, n., –es, "er, conifers.

nah, near. [vicinity.

Nähe, f., nearness, proximity;

nähen, to sew.

nähern (sich), to approach.

näher=treten, S., to step forward, approach.

Nähnadel, f., –n, needle.

Nahrung, f., nourishment.

Naivetät', f., naiveté, artlessness.

Name, m., –ns, –n, name.

namentlich, particularly; that is to say.

nämlich, that is to say; the fact is; you must know.

Narr, m., –en, –en, fool.

närrisch, stupid, foolish, absurd.

naschen, to eat (drink) on the sly, pilfer, sip.

Nase, f., –n, nose.

naß, wet.

National'heldengedicht, n., –es, –e, national epic.

National'tragödie, f., –n, national tragedy.

Natur', f., –en, nature.

Natur'anblick, m., –s, –e, view of nature.

Natur'erscheinung, f., –en, natural phenomenon.

Natur'geschichte, f., natural history.

Natur'laut, m., –s, –e, sound of nature, primitive sound.

natür'lich, natural; of course.

Natur'schönheit, f., –en, beauty of nature.

Natur'wissenschaft, f., –en, natural science.

Nebel, m., –s, —, fog, mist.

Nebelgeist, m., –es, –er, nebulous spirit.

Nebelgestalt, f., –en, nebulous form.

Nebelglanz, m., –es, hazy sheen.

Nebelkappe, f., –n, cap of mist.

Nebelmasse, f., –n, mass of vapor.

Nebelmeer, n., –es, –e, sea of mist.

neben, beside.

nebeneinan'der, side by side.

Nebengebäude, n., –s, —, outbuilding.

neckend, roguish, coquettish.

negativ', negative.

nehmen, nahm, genommen, to take.

neigen (sich), to bend, sink.

nennen, nannte, genannt, to name, call, mention.

Nest, n., –es, –er, nest; insignificant little town.

Nestchen, n., –s, —, little nest.

nett, nice, neat, trim.

neu, new; compar., neuer, recent.

neugeboren, new-born.

neugierig, curious.

Neuigkeit, f., –en, piece of news.

neuschwarz, fresh black.

nicht, not.

Nichte, *f.*, -n, niece.
nichts, nothing.
nichttoll, not mad.
nicken, to nod.
nie, never; =mals, never.
nieder, low, humble.
nieder=reißen, *S.*, to tear down.
nieder=schauen, to look down.
nieder=sinken, a, u, to sink down.
niedlich, nice, neat.
niedrig, low.
niemand, nobody.
nimmermehr, nevermore.
nirgends, nowhere.
nisten, to nest.
noch, still; nor; =mals, again.
nördlich, to the north.
Nordsee, *f.*, North Sea.
Nordseite, *f.*, north side.
Not, *f.*, "e, need; zur —, at a pinch; not tun, to be necessary.
Notiz', *f.*, -en, note, reference.
Noti'zenstolz, *m.*, -es, ('citation-pride'), pedantic pride.
noto'risch, notorious.
notwendig, necessary, inevitable.
nüchtern, empty, dreary, bare, simple, matter of fact.
nun, now.
nur, only.
Nürnberger, of Nuremberg.
nützlich, useful, practical.
Nützlichkeit, *f.*, utility.

O

ob, whether.

Obdach, *n.*, -s, shelter.
oben, above.
obendrein', in addition, besides.
ober, upper.
Oberharz, *m.*, -es, Upper Hartz.
obgleich', although.
objektiv', objective.
obschon', obzwar', although.
oder, or.
Ofen, *m.*, -s, ", stove.
offen, open; =bar, evident.
offenba'ren, to reveal.
öffentlich, open, public.
öffnen, to open.
Öffnung, *f.*, -en, opening.
oft, often.
öfter, repeated, frequent.
Oheim, *m.*, -s, -e, uncle.
ohne, without.
Ohr, *n.*, -s, -en, ear.
onomatopö'isch, onomatopoetic.
Oper, *f.*, -n, opera.
Opferaltar, *m.*, -s, -e, sacrificial altar.
Orden, *m.*, -s, —, order.
ordentlich, regular, respectable, proper, decent.
Ordnung, *f.*, -en, order.
Orgel, *f.*, -n, organ.
Orient, *m.*, -s, orient.
orientie'ren (sich), to get one's bearings, familiarize oneself (with).
Ort, *m.*, -es, *pl.* -e, *and* Örter, place.
Osten, *m.*, -s, east.
Ostero'der, of Osterode.

öſtlich, eastern.

öſtreichiſch (öſterreichiſch), Austrian.

Oſtſeite, f., east side.

P

Paar, n., -es, -e, pair; ein paar, a few.

Palaſt', m., -s, ᵘe, palace.

Pandek'tenſtall, m., -es, ᵘe, Pandect stable.

Pandek'tentitel, m., -s, —, Pandect title.

Pantof'fel, m., -s, pl. — or -n, slipper.

Papier', n., -s, -e, paper.

Papier'chen, n., -s, —, slip of paper.

Papier'geld, n., -es, -er, paper money.

Paragraph', m., -en, -en, paragraph.

Parterre' (pron. as in French), n., -s, -s, ground floor.

Parterre'fenſter, n., -s, —, ground floor window.

Partie', f., -(e)n, region, landscape, view.

Parze, f., -n, one of the (three) Parcae (Fates), Fatal Sister.

paſſen, to suit, be applicable, be apropos.

paſſieren, to happen.

pathe'tiſch, pathetic, full of feeling.

patrio'tiſch, patriotic.

Pauke, f., -n, drum.

pauken, to drum.

Pauſe, f., -n, pause.

pechdunkel, pitch-dark.

Peitſche, f., -n, whip.

Pergament'rolle, f.; -n, roll of parchment.

Perle, f., -n, pearl.

Perſon', f., -en, person, character.

perſonifizieren, to personify.

Perſpektiv', n., -s, -e, field-glass.

Peterſi'lienſuppe, f., -n, parsley soup.

Petriſchlüſſel, m., -s, —, St. Peter's key.

Petſchaft, n., -s, -e, seal.

Pfad, m., -es, -e, path.

Pfeifchen, n., -s, —, little pipe.

Pfeife, f., -n, pipe.

pfeifen, i, i, to pipe, whistle.

Pfeifenkopf, m., -es, ᵘe, pipe-bowl.

Pfeifenquaſt, m., -s, ᵘe, pipe-tassel.

Pfeiler, m., -s, —, pillar, column.

Pferd, n., -es, -e, horse.

Pferdefuß, m., -es, ᵘe, horse's foot.

Pflanze, f., -n, plant.

Pflaſter, n., -s, —, pavement.

pflegen, to be accustomed.

Pflicht, f., -en, duty.

pflücken, to pluck.

Pforte, f., -n, gate.

Phantaſie', f., -en, imagination.

phanta'ſtiſch, fantastic.

Phili′ſter, *m.*, –s, —, Philistine.

Phili′ſternaſe, *f.*, –n, Philistine nose.

Phili′ſtertroß, *m.*, –es, –e, pack of Philistines.

philiſtrö′ſe, like a Philistine.

Philiſtröſität′, *f.*, Philistinism.

philoſophie′ren, to philosophise.

piepen, piepſen, to peep, chirp, twitter.

pikant′, piquant.

pikieren, to offend.

Piſto′le, *f.*, –n, pistol.

plätſchern, to murmur, babble.

Platz, *m.*, –es, ″e, place.

plötzlich, suddenly.

pochen, to tap, knock.

Poeſie′, *f.*, –n, poesy, poetry.

poe′tiſch, poetic.

Politik′, *f.*, politics, political insight, policy.

poli′tiſch, political.

poli′tiſch=kühn, bold as to politics; Politiſch=Kühnes, political daring.

poltern, to stumble, bluster, swagger.

Portion′, *f.*, –en, portion, quantity.

Porzellan′figür‵chen, *n.*, –s, —, little porcelain figure.

poſitiv′, positive.

poſſier′lich, ludicrous.

Pracht, *f.*, splendor.

prächtig, splendid.

Prachtſaal, *m.*, –s, –ſäle, splendid hall.

Prägſtock, *m.*, –es, ″e, coining press, die.

predigen, to preach.

Preis, *m.*, –es, praise.

preiſen, ie, ie, to praise.

Preuße, *m.*, –n, –n, Prussian.

Prieſter, *m.*, –s, —, priest.

Prinz, *m.*, –en, –en, prince.

Prinzeſ′ſin, *f.*, –nen, princess.

Prinzip′, *n.*, –s, –ien, principle.

Privat′dozent‵, *m.*, –en, –en, lecturer, privatdocent.

problema′tiſch, hypothetical.

Profax, *m.*, –en, –en, pro-rector.

Profeſ′ſor, *m.*, –s, –en, professor.

Promotions′kutſche, *f.*, –n, graduation carriage.

Prozent′, *n.*, –es, –e, percent.

Prügel, *m.*, –s, —, club; *pl.*, flogging.

Publikum, *n.*, –s, public.

Pudel, *m.*, –s, —, poodle; = Pedell′, beadle.

pudeldeutſch, ('poodle-German') of poodle-like devotion.

Punſchbowle (*pron.* =bohle), *f.*, –n, punch-bowl.

Punſchglas, *n.*, –es, ″er, punch glass.

pur, pure.

Purifikation′, *f.*, 'purification.'

Purpurroſe, *f.*, –n, dark red (crimson) rose.

Pyrami′de, *f.*, –n, pyramid.

Q

Quadrat′meilen=Gesicht, *n.,* –s, –er, square-mile face.

quälen, to torment.

qualifiziert′, qualified, petty.

qualmig, smoky, reeky.

qualvoll, grievous, tormenting.

Quarantä′ne (*pron.* ka–), *f.,* –n, quarantine.

Quelle, *f.,* –n, spring.

Quellengemurmel, *n.,* –s, murmuring of springs.

Quellengeriesel, *n.,* –s, bubbling of springs.

quergelegt, laid across.

R

Radius, *m.,* —, –ien, radius.

ragen, to tower, rise.

Rahmen, *m.,* –s, —, frame, picture-frame.

randlos, without brim.

ranken, to creep, trail.

Ranzen, *m.,* –s, —, knapsack.

rasch, quick.

rastlos, without rest.

raten, ie, a, to counsel, advise.

Rathaus, *n.,* –es, ″er, town hall.

rätselhaft, mysterious, enigmatic.

Ratskeller, *m.,* –s, —, basement (cellar) of the town hall, Ratskeller.

rauchen, to smoke.

räucherig, smoky.

rauschen, to rush, rustle.

Rechnung, *f.,* –en, account, bill.

recht, right, very; einem — geben, to acknowledge that one is right, agree with one.

Recht, *n.,* –s, –e, right, law, justice; mit —, justly.

Rechtsgelehrte, *m.,* –n, –n, man learned in the law.

Rechts′system′, *n.,* –s, –e, system of law.

recken, to extend.

Rede, *f.,* –n, speech, word, conversation.

Redensart, *f.,* –en, saying, expression.

regardieren, to have regard for.

Regel, *f.,* –n, rule, direction.

regen, to stir.

Regenschleier, *m.,* –s, —, veil of rain.

regieren, to rule, govern.

regsam, agile, quick, nimble.

regungslos, motionless.

reiben, ie, ie, to rub.

Reich, *n.,* –es, –e, realm, empire.

reich, rich.

reichen, to reach, extend.

reif, ripe.

Reihe, *f.,* –n, row.

reimen, to rime.

rein, clean, neat, clear.

Reise, *f.,* –n, journey, trip.

Reisebrief, *m.,* –es, –e, letter of a traveler.

reifen, to journey, travel.

Reifende, m., (*infl. as adj.*), traveler.

Reifig, n., –8, brushwood, twigs.

reißen, i, i, to tear; Witze —, to crack jokes.

Reiz, m., –eš, –e, charm.

reizen, to charm.

refreieren (*pron.* refre–ie′ren) (fich), to refresh oneself.

Relegations′rat, m., –8, ″e, councilor of relegation (rustication).

renommieren, to boast, brag.

Respekt′, m., –8, respect.

Rest, m., –eš, –e, remnant, remains, remainder.

restaurieren (fich), to refresh oneself.

Resultat′, n., –8, –e, result.

retten (fich), to escape.

Revolutions′dilettant′, m., –en, –en, dilettante revolutionist.

Revolutions′zeit, f., –en, period of the revolution.

rezitieren, to recite.

Richtung, f., –en, direction.

riechen, o, o, to smell.

Riefe, m., –n, –n, giant.

riefeln, to percolate, run.

Riefenauge, n., –8, –n, giant eye.

Riefendom, m., –8, –e, gigantic cathedral.

Riefenkelch, m., –8, –e, giant calix.

Riefenpanorama, n., –8, –8, giant panorama.

Riefenschmerz, m., –eš, –en, gigantic anguish.

Riefenweib, n., –eš, –er, giant woman.

riefig, gigantic.

Rindfleisch, n., –eš, beef.

Rindvieh, n., –8, cattle.

Ring, m., –eš, –e, ring.

ringsum, round about.

Ritter, m., –8, —, knight.

ritterlich, knightly.

Rock, m., –eš, ″e, coat, skirt.

Röhrchen, n., –8, —, little reed, cane; spanisches —, bamboo cane.

Rohrgeflüster, n., –8, murmuring of reeds.

Rolle, f., –n, part, rôle.

rollen, to roll.

Roman′, m., –8, –e, novel.

roman′tisch, romantic.

Römer, m., –8, —, Roman.

römisch, Roman.

Röselein, n., –8, —, little rose.

Rosenduft, m., –eš, ″e, scent of roses.

Rosenhauch, m., –eš, –e, rosy hue.

Rosenschein, m., –8, roseate gleam.

Rosenstelle, f., –n, bower of roses.

Roß, n., –eš, –e, steed, charger.

rosten, to rust.

rot, red.

rotbäckig, red-cheeked.

Rotbeerstrauch, m., –eš, ″e, raspberry bush.

rotbekreuzt, with red crosses.

rotblühend, blooming red.

rotglühend, glowing red.

Rotrod, m., -8, "e, red-coat.

Rubin', m., -8, pl. -e and -en, ruby.

Rücken, m., -8, —, back.

Rückseite, f., -n, rear.

rufen, ie, u, to call, call out.

Ruhe, f., quiet, rest, peace.

ruhen, to rest.

Ruhestätte, f., -n, resting place.

ruhig, quiet, peaceful, calm.

Ruhm, m., -es, glory.

rühmen, to boast, boast of.

rühren, to touch, move.

Rührung, f., emotion.

Rumpelkammer, f., -n, lumber-room.

rund, round.

Runde, f., -n, round; in der —, around.

rütteln, to shake.

S

Saal, m., -es, pl. Säle, hall, room.

Saaltüre, f., -n, door of a hall (= room).

Sache, f., -n, thing, affair.

Sachse, m., -n, -n, Saxon.

sachte, gently.

safran'gelb, saffron yellow.

Sage, f., -n, report, legend.

sagen, to say.

Sahne, f., cream.

Salat', m., -8, -e, salad.

salzlos, without salt, insipid.

Sammetpolster, n., -8, —, velvet cushion.

samt, together with.

Sand, m., -es, sand.

sanft, gentle, tender.

Sangesfülle, f., wealth of song.

satt, satiated; — werden, to have enough.

Satz, m., -es, "e, sentence, proposition.

Sau, f., -en, sow.

sauer, sour, bitter, hard, difficult; es sich — werden lassen, to take life hard.

saufen, soff, gesoffen, to drink (of animals).

säugen, to suckle.

sausen, to rush, roar, whiz.

Scepter, n., -8, —, sceptre.

Schacht, m., -8, pl. -e, "e, -en, shaft.

Schaf, n., -es, -e, sheep.

Schäfchen, n., -8, —, little sheep.

Schäfer, m., -8, —, shepherd.

Schale, f., -n, dish, bowl.

Schalk, m., -8, -e, rogue, rascal.

schalkhaft, roguish.

schallen, to sound.

scharf, sharp.

scharfgezackt, sharp-toothed.

Schatten, m., -8, —, shade, shadow.

schauen, to look, see.

schauerlich, gruesome.

schauern, to shiver, rustle.

schaukeln, to rock, roll.

schäumen, to foam.

Schaumgewand, n., –es, ⁿer, garment of foam.

Schauspiel, n., –s, –e, drama.

Schau'spielerinnenskandal', m., –s, –e, actresses' scandal.

Schau'spielerskandal', m., –s, –e, actors' scandal.

scheiden, ie, ie, to separate, discriminate, distinguish.

Schein, m., –es, –e, sheen, gleam, appearance.

scheinbar, apparent.

scheinen, ie, ie, to shine, seem.

Scheinwesen, n., –s, semblance, pretense.

schelmisch, roguish.

Schemel, m., –s, —, foot-stool.

schenken, to present.

Schere, f., –n, shears.

Schicksal, n., –s, –e, fate.

schieben, o, o, to shove.

schießen, o, o, to shoot.

Schiff, n., –es, –e, ship; nave (= from Latin navis, ship).

schiffen, to sail.

Schilderei', f., –en, painting.

Schimmel, m., –s, —, white horse.

Schimmer, m., –s, —, shimmer, gleam.

schimmern, to gleam, glisten.

Schindluderchen, n., –s, —, ('little carrion'), 'poor dog.'

Schippe, f., –n, shovel.

Schlachtroß, n., –es, –e, battle steed.

Schlaf, m., –es, sleep.

schlafen, ie, a, to sleep.

Schlafgemach, n., –s, ⁿer, bed-chamber.

schläfrig, sleepy.

Schlafzimmer, n., –s, —, bed-room.

Schlag, m., –(e)s, ⁿe, beat, stroke.

schlagen, u, a, to strike.

schlank, slender.

schlappen, to hobble, drag.

schlau, sly, cunning.

schlecht, bad, poor.

schleichen, i, i, to sneak, steal away.

Schleier, m., –s, —, veil.

schlendern, to saunter.

Schleppe, f., –n, train.

schließen, o, o, to close, conclude.

schließlich, finally.

schlimmbewegt, hard tossed, tempest tossed.

schlingen, a, u, to fling, throw.

Schloß, n., –es, ⁿer, castle.

schlottern, to shuffle.

schlummern, to slumber.

schmachten, to languish, starve.

schmackhaft, dainty, palatable.

schmal, narrow, thin.

schmecken, to taste.

Schmeichler, m., –s, —, flatterer.

schmeißen, i, i (sich), to come to blows.

schmelzen, o, o, to melt, blend.

Schmerz, m., –es, –en, pain, suffering.

Schmerzgefühl, n., -s, -e, feeling of pain.

schmiedebunkel, dark with smithies.

schmieden, to chain, forge; concoct, get up.

schmücken, to adorn.

schmunzeln, to smirk.

schmutzig, dirty.

schnappen, to gasp, snap.

schnarchen, to snore.

schnarren, to rattle, whir.

Schnee, m., -s, snow.

schneiden, schnitt, geschnitten, to cut; ein Gesicht —, to make a face; pl., to make grimaces.

Schneider, m., -s, —, tailor.

Schneidergesell, m., -en, -en, journeyman tailor.

Schneiderherberge, f., -n, tailors' guild house.

Schneiderlein, n., -s, —, little tailor.

schnell, quick, fast.

Schnitzelei', f., -en, carving.

schnitzen, to carve.

Schnupfen, m., -s, —, cold.

schnüren, to buckle, pack.

schnurrbärtig, moustached.

Schnurre, m., -n, -n (student's slang), night watchman, university policeman.

schnurren, to buzz, whiz, hum.

schon, already.

schön, pretty, handsome, fine; die Schöne, the fair one.

Schönheit, f., -en, beauty.

Schönheitsgöttin, f., -nen, goddess of beauty.

schöpfen, to draw (water, etc.).

Schoß, m., -es, ᵘe, lap, bosom.

Schrank, m., -es, ᵘe, closet, press, wardrobe, cupboard.

Schranke, f., -n, barrier, bar.

schreiben, ie, ie, to write.

schreien, ie, ie, to scream, shout.

schreiten, i, i, to step, proceed.

Schrift, f., -en, book, writing, pamphlet.

schriftlich, in writing, in 'black and white.'

Schriftsteller, m., -s, —, author.

schrillen, to jabber.

schroff, abrupt, angular, gruff, harsh.

Schublade, f., -n, drawer.

Schuld, f., -en, debt, guilt; schuld sein, to be the cause, be to blame.

schuldbeladen, guilt-laden.

schuldlos, guiltless.

Schule, f., -n, school.

Schulknabe, m., -n, -n, schoolboy, pupil.

Schullehrer, m., -s, —, schoolteacher.

Schulstolz, m., -es, scholastic pride, pedantic conceit.

Schulter, f., -n, shoulder.

Schuppe, f., -n, scale.

Schürze, f., -n, apron.

Schurzfell, n., -s, -e, leather apron.

Schuß, m., -es, ᵘe, shot.

Schüssel, _f._, –n, dish.

schütteln, to shake.

Schützenhof, _m._, –es, ᵘe, grounds of a rifle club; shooting-match.

Schwabe, _m._, –n, –n, Suabian.

schwächen, to weaken.

schwadronieren, to swagger, brag, 'talk big.'

schwanken, to totter, reel.

Schwanz, _m._, –es, ᵘe, tail.

Schwarm, _m._, –s, ᵘe, swarm.

schwärmerisch, extravagantly enthusiastic, sentimental.

schwarz, black, swarthy.

schwärzlich, blackish, black.

schwarzseiden, of black silk.

schwatzen, to chat, chatter.

schweben, to float, hover.

schweigen, ie, ie, to be silent.

schweigsam, taciturn.

Schweiß, _m._, –es, perspiration.

Schweizer, _m._, –s, —, Swiss.

schweizerisch, Swiss.

schwelgen, to revel, indulge in riotous living.

schwellen, o, o, to swell; schwellend, undulating.

schwer, heavy, difficult.

schwerfällig, ponderous.

Schwert, _n._, –es, –er, sword.

Schwester, _f._, –n, sister.

Schwesterchen, _n._, –s, —, little sister.

schwimmen, a, o, to swim.

Schwindel, _m._, –s, dizziness, giddiness.

schwindlig, dizzy.

schwingen, a, u, to swing.

sechs, six.

sechste, der, the sixth.

See, _f._, –n, sea.

Seele, _f._, –n, soul.

Seelenangst, _f._, ᵘe, mortal terror.

Seelenerguß, _m._, –es, ᵘe, 'soul' effusion.

Seelennot, _f._, ᵘe, distress of soul, mortal distress.

Segen, _m._, –s, —, blessing.

segnen, to bless.

sehen, a, e, to see.

Sehnsucht, _f._, longing, yearning, desire.

sehnsuchtbebend, trembling (tremulous) with longing.

Sehnsuchtglut, _f._, ardent longing.

sehnsüchtig, longing, yearning.

Sehnsuchtseufzer, _m._, –s, —, sigh of yearning.

Sehnsuchtslaut, _m._, –es, –e, note of yearning.

sehnsuchtsvoll, full of yearning.

sehr, very, much.

Seide, _f._, –n, silk.

seiden, silk, silken.

Seidenzeug, _n._, –es, –e, silk stuff.

Seil, _n._, –es, –e, rope.

sein, war, gewesen, to be.

Sein, _n._, –s, being.

sein, his, its.

seit, _prep. and conj._, since, for.

Seite, *f.*, –n, side.

Seitenbrett, *n.*, –s, –er, side plank.

Seitenloch, *n.*, –es, "er, side opening, hole in the wall.

Seitenweg, *m.*, –es, –e, byway.

selber, selbst, self (myself), even.

selbstgefällig, self-complacent.

selbstsüchtig, selfish.

Selbstzufriedenheit, *f.*, self-complacency.

selig, blessed, happy, sainted, departed, late.

Seligkeit, *f.*, –en, beatitude, bliss.

selten, rare; seldom.

seltsam, strange.

Seme'sterwelle, *f.*, –n, semestral wave.

Senat', *m.*, –s, –e, senate, council.

sentimental', sentimental.

Sentimentalität', *f.*, sentimentality.

setzen, to set, put; cross; posit, suppose (Fall); sich —, to seat oneself.

seufzen, to sigh.

Seufzer, *m.*, –s, —, sigh.

Shawl, *m.*, –s, –s, shawl.

sich, *reflex. pron.*, himself, *etc.*; each other.

sicher, safe, sure, certain.

Sicherheit, *f.*, confidence, self-assurance, self-possession.

sichtbar, visible.

sieben, seven.

Siebenmeilenstiefel, *m.*, –s, —, seven league boot.

Silberblick, *m.*, –s, –e, gleam of silver.

silbergrau, silver-gray.

silberhaarig, silver-haired.

silberhell, bright as silver.

Silberhütte, *f.*, –n, smelting-house for silver.

silbern, of silver.

Silberquelle, *f.*, –n, silver spring.

singen, a, u, to sing.

Singvogel, *m.*, –s, ", song-bird.

Sinn, *m.*, –es, –e, mind, sense, disposition.

Sinnbild, *n.*, –es, –er, emblem, symbol.

sinnig, thoughtful, contemplative, pensive, charming.

Sitte, *f.*, –n, habit, manner, custom.

sitzen, saß, gesessen, to sit.

Slave, *m.*, –n, –n, Slav.

smarag'den, *adj.*, emerald.

so, so, then, however; — ein,

sobald', as soon as.   [such a.

sogar', even.

sogenannt, so-called.

Sohn, *m.*, –es, "e, son.

solan'ge, as long as.

solch, such.

solcherlei, such.

sollen, shall, ought, is to, is said to.

Sommer, *m.*, –s, —, summer.

Sommerabend, *m.*, –s, –e, summer evening.

Sommerabendhauch, *m.*, –es, –e, summer evening breath.

sonderlich, especially.

sondern, but.

Sonne, *f.*, –n, sun.

Sonnenaufgang, *m.*, –s, ᵘe, sunrise.

Sonnenlicht, *n.*, –s, –er, sunlight, sunbeam.

Sonnenschein, *m.*, –s, sunshine.

Sonnenstrahl, *m.*, –s, –en, sunbeam.

Sonnenuntergang, *m.*, –s, ᵘe, sunset.

Sonnenuntergangsstelle, *f.*, –n, sunset passage.

Sonnenwirt, *m.*, –s, –e, mine host of the "Sun."

sonnig, sunny.

Sonntagswetter, *n.*, –s, Sunday weather, fine weather.

sonst, otherwise, formerly.

sonstig, other.

Sorge, *f.*, –n, care, worry.

sorgen, to care, provide for.

sorgenkrank, careworn.

Sorgfalt, *f.*, care.

sowie, as well as.

sowohl ... als, both ... and.

Spalt, *m.*, –es, –e, cleft.

spanisch, Spanish.

sparsam, sparse, sparing.

spät, late.

späterhin, later on.

Spatz, *m.*, –en, –en, sparrow.

spazieren, to walk.

Speck, *m.*, –s, bacon.

Speichel, *m.*, –s, spittle.

speisen, to eat, dine.

Speisetisch, *m.*, –es, –e, dining table.

spekulieren, to speculate, ruminate, reflect.

Spezial'karte, *f.*, –n, local map, topographical map.

speziell', special, particular.

Spiegel, *m.*, –s, —, mirror.

Spielball, *m.*, –es, ᵘe, ball, plaything.

spielen, to play; spielend, playful.

Spießbürger, *m.*, –s, —, Philistine.

spinnen, a, o, to spin.

Spinnrad, *n.*, –es, ᵘer, spinning-wheel.

Spinnweb, *n.*, –es, –e, cobweb.

spitzbübisch, rascally.

Spitze, *f.*, –n, summit.

Sporn, *m.*, –s, *pl.* Sporen, spur.

sprechen, a, o, to speak, say.

sprengen, to burst, burst open, split.

Springbrunnen, *m.*, –s, —, fountain.

springen, a, u, to spring, jump.

Sprosse, *f.*, –n, round, rung.

Sprung, *m.*, –es, ᵘe, leap.

Spuk, *m.*, –s, –e, spook.

spukend, ghostly, spectral.

Spukgeschichte, *f.*, –n, ghost story.

Spur, *f.*, –en, trace, track.

spurlos, without a trace.

ſtaatspfiffig, like a shrewd statesman.

Stadt, f., ᵘe, city.

Städtchen, n., -s, —, little town.

Stadtmotto, n., -s, -s, motto of a city.

ſtahlblau, steel-blue.

Stamm, m., -es, ᵘe, stock, tribe.

ſtammen, to descend.

Stand, m., -es, ᵘe, estate, rank, position; im ſtande ſein, to be able.

Standbild, n., -es, -er, statue.

Stange, f., -n, tall beer-glass, 'schooner.'

Stanze, f., -n, stanza.

ſtark, strong.

ſtärken, to strengthen, give vigor to.

ſtarr, rigid.

ſtatt, instead of.

ſtatt=finden, S., to take place.

ſtattlich, stately.

Staubfaden, m., -s, ᵘ, stamen.

Staubfädenverſchiedenheit, f., -en, difference as to stamens.

ſtaunen, to marvel.

ſtecken, to stick, put.

Stecknadel, f., -n, pin.

ſtehen; ſtand, geſtanden, to stand; ſtehen bleiben, to stand still.

ſtehlen, a, o, to steal.

ſteif, stiff.

ſteigen, ie, ie, to ascend, mount, climb; descend.

Steiger, m., -s, —, foreman, inspector.

ſteil, steep.

Stein, m., -es, -e, stone, bould⸗⸗.

ſteinalt, very old, decrepit.

Steingruppe, f., -n, group of stones.

Steinpforte, f., -n, stone gateway.

Steinſpalt, m., -s, -e, cleft in the rock, crevice.

Steintiſch, m., -es, -e, stone table.

Stelle, f., -n, place, spot, passage.

ſtellen, to place; ſich — auf, to mount.

Stellung, f., -en, position.

Stephanskirche, f., St. Stephen's Church.

ſterben, a, o, to die.

Stern, m., -es, -e, star.

Sternenſchein, m., -s, starlight.

Sternwarte, f., -n, observatory.

Stich, m., -es, -e, stitch.

Stiefel, m., -s, —, boot.

Stiftchen, n., -s, —, little pin, peg.

ſtiften, to found, create, cause.

ſtill, quiet, silent.

ſtillſtehend, standing still, stationary.

Stimme, f., -n, voice.

ſtimmen, to tune, attune; dispose, frame.

Stirn(e), f., -en, forehead, brow.

Stock, m., -es, ᵘe, stick, cane.

Stockfiſch, m., -es, -e, stock-fish, codfish.

Stollen, *m.*, –s, —, *and* Stolle, *f.*, –n, gallery.

stolz, proud.

Stolz, *m.*, –es, pride.

stören, to disturb.

stoßen, ie, o, to hit, knock; chance.

Strafe, *f.*, –n, penalty.

Strahl, *m.*, –s, –en, ray, beam.

strahlen, to beam; strahlend, radiant.

Strahlenfaden, *m.*, –s, ^{n}, (= Staubfaden), stamen.

Strahlenflut, *f.*, –en, flood of light.

Strahlenpracht, *f.*, shining splendor.

Straße, *f.*, –n, street.

sträuben (sich), to bristle up, stand on end.

Straußfeder, *f.*, –n, ostrich feather.

streben, to strive.

Strecke, *f.*, –n, short distance.

streichen, i, i, to stroke.

Streifen, *m.*, –s, —, stripe.

Streit, *m.*, –es, –e, quarrel, altercation, dispute.

Streitwagen, *m.*, –s, —, war chariot.

streng, strict, severe, stern, austere.

Strohhalm, *m.*, –s, –e, straw (blade).

Strohlager, *n.*, –s, —, straw bed.

Strom, *m.*, –es, ^{n}e, stream, river.

strömen, to stream, pour.

Strumpf, *m.*, –es, ^{n}e, stocking.

Stube, *f.*, –n, room.

Stubentür, *f.*, –en, door of a room.

Stück, *n.*, –es, –e, piece.

Student', *m.*, –en, –en, student.

Studen'tengeneration', *f.*, –en, generation of students.

Studen'tenname, *m.*, –ns, –n, student's name.

studieren, to study.

Studium, *n.*, –s, –ien, study.

Stuhl, *m.*, –s, ^{n}e, chair, seat, throne.

stumm, dumb, silent.

Stunde, *f.*, –n, hour, league.

stundenlang, for hours at a time.

Sturm, *m.*, –es, ^{n}e, storm.

stürmisch, stormy.

stürzen, to fall, pour, gush, rush.

stützen, to support, prop.

subjektiv', subjective.

suchen, to seek.

summ, hum!

summen, to hum, buzz.

Sumpf, *m.*, –es, ^{n}e, swamp.

Sumpfstelle, *f.*, –n, swampy place.

sündenmüde, weary of sin.

süß, sweet.

Syllogis'mus, *m.*, —, –en, syllogism.

symbo'lisch, symbolic.

System', *n.*, –s, –e, system.

systema'tisch, systematic.

System'chen, *n.*, –s, —, little system.

T

Tabak, m., -s, -e, tobacco.

Tabakrauchen, n., -s, tobacco smoking.

tadeln, to censure.

tafeln, to dine, banquet.

Tag, m., -es, -e, day.

Tageslicht, n., -es, daylight.

täglich, daily.

Tal, n., -es, "er, valley.

Taler, m., -s, —, (coin worth about 72 cents), dollar, Taler.

Tanne, f., -n, fir.

Tannenbaum, m., -es, "e, fir-tree.

tannendüster, of gloomy firs.

Tannengrün, n., -s, green of fir-trees.

Tannenwald, m., -es, "er, fir forest.

tantenhaft, aunt-like.

tanzen, to dance.

Tänzer, m., -s, —, dancer.

Tanztour, f., -en, dance, figure, pirouette.

Tapet', n., -s, -e, tapis, carpet; aufs —kommen, to become the subject of conversation.

Tasche, f., -n, pocket.

Taschenbuch, n., -es, "er, hand-book.

Tat, f., -en, deed, feat.

Tatkraft, f., energy.

Taubenbraten, m., -s, —, roast pigeon.

täuschen, to disappoint.

täuschend, deceiving, deceptive, causing perfect illusion.

Täuschung, f., -en, deception, illusion.

tausend, thousand. [old.

tausendjährig, a thousand years

Teil, m., -s, -e, part.

teilen, to divide.

teils, partly.

Teller, m., -s, —, plate.

teuer, dear, esteemed, precious.

Teufel, m., -s, —, devil.

Teufelskanzel, f., -n, devil's pulpit.

Teuto'ne, m., -n, -n, Teuton.

Text, m., -es, -e, text.

Thea'ter, n., -s, —, theater.

Thea'terbesucher, m., -s, —, theater-goer.

Thea'terbüffett', n., -s, -s, theater buffet.

The'dansant (French, 'dancing tea'), an informal dancing party, at which tea is served.

Thee, m., -s, tea.

Theegesellschaft, f., -en, tea party.

Theetisch, m., -es, -e, tea-table.

Theodor, m., -s, Theodore.

Thron, m., -es, -e, throne.

Thüringer, m., -s, —, Thuringian.

tief, deep, profound.

Tiefe, f., -n, depth.

Tiefsinn, m., -s, melancholy, pensiveness.

tieffinnig, deep, thoughtful.

Tier, *n.*, –es, –e, animal, beast.

Tierbildung, *f.*, –en, shape of beasts.

Tiſch, *m.*, –es, –e, table; nach —, after dinner.

Tita′nin, *f.*, –nen, (female) Titan.

Titelchen, *n.*, –s, —, tittle.

Titelſucht, *f.*, mania for titles.

toben, to rage, rave.

Tochter, *f.*, ̈, daughter.

Tod, *m.*, –es, death.

Todesangſt, *f.*, ̈e, deathly fear.

Todesſtille, *f.*, stillness of death.

Todeswunde, *f.*, –n, death (mortal) wound.

tolerant′, tolerant.

toll, mad, madding, madcap, erratic.

Tollhauslärm, *m.*, –es, noise as of a mad-house, bedlam.

Ton, *m.*, –es, –e, clay; *m.*, –es, ̈e, tone, sound, noise.

Tonart, *f.*, –en, (tone-variety), key, strain, tune.

tönen, to resound.

Tonne, *f.*, –n, bucket.

Tonnenſeil, *n.*, –s, –e, bucket rope.

Tonpfeife, *f.*, –n, clay pipe.

Topf, *m.*, –es, ̈e, pot.

Topographie′, *f.*, –en, topography.

Tor, *n.*, –es, –e, gate.

toſen, to be in an uproar.

tot, dead.

töten, to kill.

Totenhemd, *n.*, –es, –e(n), shroud.

tot=lachen (ſich), to die for laughter.

tot=ſchießen, *S.*, to shoot dead.

tot=ſchlagen, *S.*, to strike dead, kill.

tot=weinen (ſich), to die of weeping.

Tracht, *f.*, –en, garb, costume.

traditionell′, traditional.

tragen, u, a, to bear, carry, wear.

Trägerin, *f.*, –nen, bearer, carrier.

Tran, *m.*, –es, –e, whale-oil; im — ſein, to be tipsy.

Träne, *f.*, –n, tear. [of tears.

Tränenbach, *m.*, –es, ̈e, stream

Trank, *m.*, –es, ̈e, drink, beverage.

tranſcendental′grau, 'transcendentally' gray, gray beyond belief.

trauern, to mourn, grieve.

traulich, cozy, familiar, genial.

Traum, *m.*, –es, ̈e, dream.

träumen, to dream.

träumeriſch, dreamy.

traumhaft, dreamy, vague.

traurig, sad.

treffen, a, o, to strike, hit; meet.

Treiben, *n.*, –s, doings, carrying-on, turmoil; activity.

Treppe, *f.*, –n, stairway, steps.

treten, a, e, to step, come.

treu, true, faithful.

Treue, *f.*, fidelity.

treuherzig, simple-hearted, un-
sophisticated.

trillern, to trill, hum.

trinfen, a, u, to drink.

troden, dry.

Trompe'te, f., –n, trumpet.

trompe'ten, to trumpet.

Trompe'terftüdchen, n., –s, —,
piece played on a trumpet,
trumpet blasts.

Tropfen, m., –s, —, drop.

Troß, m., –es, –e, train, throng.

Troftlofigfeit, f., hopelessness,
forlornness.

Tröftung, f., –en, consolation.

trübe, sad.

Trümmer, pl., debris, ruins.

trunfen, drunk.

Tugend, f., –en, virtue.

tun, tat, getan, to do.

Tür, f., –en, door.

Türfe, m., –n, –n, Turk.

türfifch, Turkish.

Turm, m., –s, "e, tower.

turmartig, tower-like.

Turmhälfte, f., –n, half of a
tower.

Turmplatte, f., –n, (tower-slab),
platform or top of tower.

Turmwarte, f., –n, observatory
tower.

U

über, over, beyond, along, about,
concerning.

überall', everywhere.

überbies', besides, moreover.

übereinan'der, one above the
other.

überflüffig, superfluous.

Übergang, m., –s, "e, transi-
tion.

über=gehen, S., to pass over.

überhaupt', as a matter of fact,
in fact, in general.

über=laufen, S., to run over.

übernach'ten, to spend the night.

überfä'en, to strew.

überfchau'en, to survey.

überfchau'ern, to blow over
freshly (with a fresh breeze).

überfchwem'men, to inundate.

Überfetzung, f., –en, translation.

überto'ben, tr., to drown (with
noise).

überwin'den, a, u, to overcome,
surmount.

überzie'hen, S., to cover, envelop.

übrig, remaining, left; die
übrigen, the rest of us; —
bleiben, to be left over.

Ufer, n., –s, —, bank.

Uhr, f., –en, watch, clock; o'clock.

Uhrtafche, f., –n, watch-pocket.

um, prep., about; um . . . willen,
for the sake of, on account of;
um fo, all the; conj., in order to,
for, for the purpose of.

umarmen, to embrace.

um=bilden, to transform.

umbuften, to spread fragrance
around.

umfrieden, to enclose, seclude, shelter.

um=gehen, _S._, to associate.

umher'=irren, to wander about.

umher'=steigen, _S._, to climb about.

umhin'; nicht — können, not to be able to refrain from.

umhüllen, to envelop, enshroud.

umhüpfen, to hop around.

umklammern, to embrace, entwine.

umranken, to entwine, grow around.

umrauschen, to rustle around, surge around.

Umriß, _m._, -es, -e, outline, contour.

umschließen, _S._, to enclose, surround, wrap.

umschlingen, _S._, to encircle, embrace.

umsonst', in vain, for nothing.

Umweg, _m._, -es, -e, detour.

unaufhalt'sam, impetuous.

unbedeckt', uncovered.

un'bedeutend, insignificant.

unbedingt', unconditional, unqualified, unreserved.

Un'befangenheit, _f._, ease of manner.

Un'behaglichkeit, _f._, -en, discomfort.

un'bekannt, unknown, unacquainted.

un'belauscht, unobserved.

unberu'fen, unbidden

unbeschreib'bar, indescribable.

un'bewußt, unconscious.

unend'lich, infinite, boundless.

un'entworren, not disentangled, unanalyzed, confused.

unerbitt'lich, inexorable.

un'erfreulich, unpleasant.

unerhört', unheard of.

unermeß'lich, boundless.

un'erschaffen, uncreated, increate.

unerschöpf'lich, inexhaustible.

unerschütt'lich, immovable.

un'gebunden, unbound.

un'gefähr, approximately.

un'gehenkt, not hanged.

un'geheuer, huge.

Un'gemach, _n._, -s, -e, discomfort, vexation, mishap.

un'gewöhnlich, unusual, strange.

un'gläubig, incredulous.

un'glückselig, unhappy, luckless.

Unhalt'barkeit, _f._, untenability.

un'heimlich, uncanny, eerie.

un'höflich, impolite, uncivil.

Universal'genie', _n._, -s, -s, universal genius.

Universität', _f._, -en, university.

Universitäts'gespräch, _n._, -s, -e, university talk.

Universitäts'pedell', _m._, -s, -e, university beadle.

Universitäts'pyrami'de, _f._, -n, university pyramid.

Universitäts'stadt, _f._, ⁿe, university town.

un'mäßig, immoderate.

Un'mittelbarkeit, _f._, direct contact with nature, immediacy.

Unmut, _m._, –s, dislike.

un'ordentlich, extraordinary, irregular, disorderly.

un'reif, unripe, immature.

un'sanft, not gentle, rough.

un'schicklich, improper.

un'schuldig, innocent.

unser, our.

unsereins, the like of us.

un'sicher, uncertain.

un'sichtbar, invisible.

Un'sinn, _m._, –s, nonsense.

unsterb'lich, immortal.

Unsterb'lichkeit, _f._, immortality

Unsterb'lichkeitsgedanke, _m._, –ns, –n, idea of immortality.

unten, below.

unter, below, under, among.

unterdes', unterdes'sen, meanwhile.

untereinan'der, among each other.

unter=gehen, _S._, to go down, perish.

unterhalten, _S._, to entertain.

Unterhal'tung, _f._, –en, conversation.

Un'terharz, _m._, –es, Lower Hartz.

un'terirdisch, subterranean.

Unterkinn, _n._, –s, –e, double chin.

unterlassen, _S._, to leave undone.

unterscheiden, _S._, to distinguish.

Unterschei'dung, _f._, –en, distinction.

Un'terschied, _m._, –es, –e, distinction, difference.

unterst, lowest.

Untersu'chung, _f._, –en, investigation.

Un'tertanstreue, _f._, loyalty (of a subject).

Un'vernünftigkeit, _f._, irrationality.

un'verstanden, not comprehended. [dent.

un'vorsichtig, careless, impru-

un'weit, _w. gen._, not far from.

unwidersteh'lich, irresistible.

un'willig, displeased.

unwillkür'lich, involuntary.

unzäh'lig, innumerable.

uralt, ancient, long gone by.

Urenkel, _m._, –s, —, great-grandchild.

Ursprung, _m._, –es, "e, origin.

u.s.w. = und so weiter, and so forth.

𝔙

Banda'le, _m._, –n, –n, Vandal.

Base, _f._, –n, vase.

Bater, _m._, –s, ", father.

Baterland, _n._, –es, fatherland.

Baterstadt, _f._, "e, native town.

Beilchen, _n._, –s, —, violet.

veilchenblau, violet-blue.

Beilchenstrauß, _m._, –es, "e, bunch of violets.

Vene'dig, *n.*, -s, Venice.

verab'reden, to agree upon, make an appointment.

verachten, to despise.

verändern, to change.

veran'lassen, to occasion, cause.

verbergen, a, o, to hide, conceal.

verbieten, o, o, to forbid.

verbinden, *S.*, to join, connect, unite.

verblichen, faded, dim, lusterless.

verbluten, to bleed to death.

verbreiten, to spread.

verdenken, *S.*, to think ill of, think the worse of.

verderben, a, o, to spoil.

verdienen, to deserve.

verdrängen, to crowd out, supersede.

verdrießlich, cross, annoyed.

verehren, to esteem, revere.

Verehrung, *f.*, reverence, esteem.

vereinigen, to unite.

Vereinigung, *f.*, -en, union.

verfallen, *S.*, to decay.

Verfasser, *m.*, -s, —, author.

verfehlen, to miss.

verflechten, o, o, to entangle, engage.

verfließen, *S.*, to pass, elapse.

verge'bens, in vain.

vergehen, *S.*, to pass away, forsake, leave.

vergessen, a, e, to forget.

vergleichend, comparative.

Vergleichung, *f.*, -en, comparison.

Vergnügen, *n.*, -s, —, pleasure.

vergnügt, pleased, cheerful, merry, in good humor.

vergoldet, gilded.

vergraben, u, a, to bury.

Verhältnis, *n.*, -ses, -se, relation, condition.

Verhandlung, *f.*, -en, negotiation.

Verherrlichung, *f.*, -en, glorification.

verhüllen, to cover, conceal.

verhungern, to die of starvation.

verirren (sich), to go astray, lose one's way.

verkaufen, to sell.

Verkörperung, *f.*, -en, embodiment.

verkümmern, to languish, waste away.

verlangen, to call for, demand, desire.

verlassen, *S.*, to leave.

verlegen, to change the position of, shift.

verleiden, to make distasteful, spoil.

verletzen, to wound, hurt.

verliebt, in love.

verlieren, o, o, to lose.

verlocken, to entice.

verloren, lost, vanished.

vermögen, *irreg.*, to be able.

Vernunft, *f.*, reason.

vernünftig, reasonable, sensible.

Vernunftschluß, *m.*, -es, "e, process of reasoning.

verpflanzen, to transplant.

Verpflichtung, f., -en, obligation.

verraten, S., to betray, reveal.

verrucht, infamous.

verrückt, crazy, mad.

Vers, m., -es, -e, verse.

versagen, to deny.

versammeln, to gather, assemble.

Versammlung, f., -en, gathering, assembly.

versäumen, to miss, neglect.

verschaffen, to provide.

verschämt, bashful.

verscheuchen, to frighten off, dispel.

verschieden, different, diverse.

verschiedenartig, differing in kind.

verschimmelt, mouldy.

verschleiert, veiled.

verschlingen, S., to clasp, interlace, devour.

verschlossen, hidden, sealed.

verschollen, vanished, antiquated, old-fashioned.

verschreiben, S., to write for, send for.

verschweigen, S., to withhold (by silence).

verschwinden, a, u, to disappear.

versehen, S., to provide, fill, do, perform; sich — (w. gen.), to be aware of, expect.

Versehen, n., -s, —, mistake.

versetzen, to transplant.

versichern, to assure, testify.

versinken, a, u, to sink into, sink.

versperren, to block, hinder.

Verstand, m., -es, understanding, reason.

verständig, intelligent, sensible.

Versteck, n., -s, -e, hiding-place.

verstecken, to hide.

verstehen, S., to understand; es versteht sich (von selbst), it is a matter of course.

versteinert, petrified.

verstohlen, secret, sly.

verstorben, dead, deceased.

versunken, lost, buried (in).

vertauschen, to exchange.

vertiefen (sich), to become absorbed.

vertragen, S., to endure, bear, stand.

vertrauen, to confide.

verun'glücken, to perish (through an accident); verunglückt, misplaced, abortive.

verwachsen, S., to grow together, entwine, interweave.

verwalten, to manage.

verwandeln, to transform; sich —, to be transformed.

verweben, o, o, and weak, to weave together.

verwehren, to deny, refuse, prevent.

verwickeln, to envelop.

verwirrt, confused.

verworren, confused.

verwundern (sich), to be astonished, wonder, marvel.

Verwunderung, f., astonishment.

verwünschen, to curse, enchant;
— zu, to condemn (by en-
chantment) to.

verzaubert, enchanted.

verzehren, to consume, eat.

verzeihen, ie, ie, to pardon.

Verzerrung, f., –en, distortion.

verzieren, to decorate.

Vetter, m., –s, –n, cousin.

Vieh, n., –s, cattle.

Viehseuche, f., –n, cattle plague.

Viehstand, m., –s, live stock.

viel, much; pl., many; adv., very.

vielfach, numerous.

vielleicht', perhaps.

vielmehr', rather.

vielteuer, very dear, beloved.

vier, four.

viereckig, four cornered.

vierte, der, the fourth.

Vierteljahrhun'dert, n., –s, –e,
quarter of a century.

Viertelstun'de, f., –n, quarter of
an hour.

vierzehn, fourteen.

Vogel, m., –s, ᵘ, bird.

Vögelgesang, m., –s, ᵘe, song of
birds.

Vöglein (Vögelein), n., –s, —,
little bird.

Volk, n., –es, ᵘer, people.

Völkchen, n., –s, —, little people.

Völkerwanderung, f., –en, migration of nations, migrations.

Volkslied, n., –es, –er, folk-song.

volkstümlich, popular, national.

voll, full.

vollauf', in full, unstintedly.

voller, full of.

Vollmond, m., –es, –e, full
moon.

Vollreife, f., full maturity.

vollständig, complete.

von, of, from, about, concerning.

voneinan'der; sich — tun, to
part, open.

vor, before, in front of, outside
of, at; ago.

voran', ahead, in advance.

vor'aus, in advance.

vorbei'=fließen, S., to flow by.

vorbei'=gehen, S., to pass by.

vorbei'=reiten, i, i, to ride by.

vorbei'=rennen, rannte, gerannt,
to run by.

vorgebeugt, bending forward.

vorher, before.

vor'herrschend, predominant.

vorig, previous.

vor=kommen, S., to seem, appear, impress (one).

vor=lesen, S., to read aloud (to
others).

vor'letzt, last but one.

Vor'mittag, m., –s, –e, forenoon.

vorn, front; von —, from the
beginning.

vor'nehm, of consequence, important, distinguished.

vor=nehmen (sich), S., to make up
one's mind, resolve.

Vornehmheit, f., distinction (of
manners).

Vorſchein, m., -s; zum — kom=
men, to appear.
Vorſchlag, m., -s, "e, proposal.
vor=ſchweben, to hover about,
haunt.
vor=ſetzen, to place before.
Vortreff'lichkeit, f., -en, excellence.
vorü'ber=gehen, S., to pass by.
vorü'ber=jagen, to gallop by.
vorü'ber=rollen, to roll by.
vorü'ber=ſteigen, S., to climb
past.
vorü'ber=ziehen, S., to pass by.
vor=zeichnen, to mark out, pre-
scribe, draw, design.
Vorzug, m., -es, "e, excellence,
advantage.
vorzüg'lich, excellent.
vor'zugsweiſe, preferably.

W

wach, awake.
wachſam, watchful, alert.
wachſen, u, a, to grow.
Wacht, f., -en, watch.
Wachtſtube, f., -n, guard-room.
wackeln, to wobble.
wacker, upright, honest.
Wade, f., -n, calf (of the leg).
Waffenglanz, m., -es, gleam of
arms.
Wage, f., -n, balance, scales.
Wagen, m., -s, —, carriage,
wagon.
wagen, to dare.

Wahlſtätte, f., -n, battle-field,
arena.
wahnſinnig, mad, frantic.
wahr, true. [ing.
während, conj., while; prep., dur-
wahrhaft, true.
Wahrheit, f., -en, truth.
wahrlich, truly.
wahrſchein'lich, probably.
Waiſenkind, n., -es, -er, orphan.
Wald, m., -es, "er, forest, wood.
waldbedeckt, wooded.
Walddickicht, n., -s, -e, forest
thicket.
Walddorn, m., -s, -e and -en,
forest thorn.
Waldhütte, f., -n, forest hut.
Waldkirche, f., -n, forest church.
Waldung, f., -en, forest, grove.
Waldvogel, m., -s, ", forest
bird.
walten, to reign, rule.
Walze, f., -n, cylinder.
wampig, bloated.
Wand, f., "e, wall.
wandeln, to walk, move; geſpreizt
—, to strut along.
Wanderer, m., -s, —, wanderer.
wandern, to wander, travel.
Wanduhr, f., -en, clock.
Wange, f., -n, cheek.
wappnen, to arm, armor.
Ware, f., -n, ware, goods.
warm, warm. Wärme, f., warmth.
warnen, to warn.
Warte, f., -n, observatory.
Wäſcherin, f., -nen, laundress.

Waſſer, *n.*, -8, —, water, stream.

Waſſeraufgießen, *n.*, -8, watering.

Waſſerfall, *m.*, -8, "e, waterfall.

Waſſerfee, *f.*, -n, water fairy, nymph.

Waſſerglas, *n.*, -es, "er, glass of water.

wäſſ(e)rig, watery.

Wechſel (*pron.* Wекſel), *m.*, -8, —, change.

wechſeln, to change.

wechſelſeitig, mutual, reciprocal.

wechſelweiſe, by turns, alternately.

weckеn, to awaken, arouse.

weder, neither.

Weender, *adj.*, of Weende.

Weg, *m.*, -e8, -e, way, road.

weg, away, gone.

wegen, on account of.   [traveler.

Weggenoſſe, *m.*, -n, -n, fellow-

wegkundig, 'road-wise,' familiar with the roads.

weg=reiſen, to depart, leave.

weg=ſchnappen, to snap up.

Wegweiſer, *m.*, -8, —, guide.

wehen, to wave, blow.

Wehmut, *f.*, sadness, melancholy, grief.

wehmütig, sad.

Weib, *n.*, -e8, -er, woman, wife.

weich, soft.

Weide, *f.*, -n, pasture.

weil, because.

weilen, to tarry, sojourn.

Wein, *m.*, -e8, -e, wine.

weinen, to weep.

Weinglas, *n.*, -e8, "er, wineglass.

Weiſe, *f.*, -n, way, manner; tune, air, melody.

Weisheit, *f.*, wisdom.

weiß, white.

Weißbier, *n.*, -8, -e, ale.

weißwallend, surging white.

weit, wide, extensive, far; — und breit, far and wide.

weitberühmt, far-famed.

weiter=gehen, *S.*, to proceed.

weiter=ſpringen, *S.*, to hasten on.

weitläuftig (weitläufig), extensive, expansive, rambling.

weitſchallend, far resounding, far-reaching.

welch (-er, -e, -e8), who, which, what.

welk, drooping.

welken, to fade, wither.

Welle, *f.*, -n, wave.

Welt, *f.*, -en, world.

weltberühmt, world-famous.

Weltgeſchichte, *f.*, universal history.

Weltkugel, *f.*, -n, globe, orb.

Wendung, *f.*, -en, turn, whirl.

wenig, little, small.

Wenigkeit, *f.*, -en, littleness; meine —, your humble servant.

wenn, if, when.

wer, who, he who, whoever.

werden, ward (wurde), geworden, to become.

werfen, a, o, to throw, drop; farrow.

Werk, n., -es, -e, work.

Werkeltagsstimmung, f., -en, everyday (commonplace) mood.

Wesen, n., -s, —, creature.

Weste, f., -n, vest.

Westen, m., -s, west.

Westseite, f., west side.

Wetter, n., -s, —, weather.

Wichtelmännchen, n., -s, —, elfin-folk, goblin, gnome.

wichtig, important.

wickeln, to wrap, wind.

Widerdruck, m., -es, -e, answering pressure.

widerhal'len, to resound.

Widerle'gung, f., -en, refutation.

Wi'derschein, m., -s, -e, reflection, image reflected (by).

widersprechen, S., to contradict.

wider=tönen, to re-echo.

wie, as, like; as if; how, what.

wieder, again.

wieder=finden, S., to find again.

Wiedergruß, m., -es, "e, return greeting.

wieder=kommen, S., to return.

wiehern, to neigh.

Wiese, f., -n, meadow.

Wiesenblümchen, n., -s, —, meadow flower.

Wiesental, n., -es, "er, meadow-vale.

wild, wild.

Wilddieb, m., -es, -e, poacher.

wildfremd, utterly strange, exotic.

Wildheit, f., -en, wildness.

wildschroff, wild and rugged.

Willen, m., -s, —, will.

wimmern, to moan, whimper.

Wimper, f., -n, (eye)lash.

Wind, m., -es, -e, wind.

windig, airy, light as the wind.

Windstoß, m., -es, "e, gust of wind.

Windung, f., -en, winding.

Wink, m., -es, -e, hint.

Winkel, m., -s, —, angle.

Winter, m., -s, —, winter.

winterlich, wintry.

Wintersturm, m., -es, "e, winter storm.

wirken, to work, effect, produce an effect.

wirklich, real, actual.

Wirt, m., -s, -e, host.

wirtschaften, to carry on.

Wirtshaus, n., -es, "er, tavern, inn, hostelry.

Wirtshaussonne, f., -n, ('tavern sun') the "Sun."

Wirtsstube, f., -n, public room, dining room (of an inn).

wißbegierig, eager for information.

wissen, wußte, gewußt, to know.

Wissenschaft, f., -en, science.

wissenschaftlich, scientific.

Witz, m., -es, -e, wit; joke.

witzig, witty.

wo, where; when.

wobei', in which, among which.

woburch', whereby. [wave, billow.

wogen, to wave. Woge, f., –n,

wohin', whither.

wohl, well, probably, presumably, indeed.

wohlbekannt, well-known.

wohlbepackt, well laden.

wohlbestallt, duly appointed.

wohlgeharnischt, well mailed.

wohlgelaunt, good-humored.

wohlgenährt, well-fed.

wohlvertraut, familiar.

wohlwollend, benevolent.

wohnen, to live, dwell.

Wohnung, f., –en, dwelling.

Wolke, f., –n, cloud.

Wolkenhaus, n., –es, "er, house among the clouds.

wolkenlos, cloudless, serene.

Wolkenroß, n., –es, –e, cloud steed.

wolkig, cloudy.

wollen, wollte, gewollt, will, wish, intend.

womit', with which, wherewith.

Wonne, f., bliss.

woran', by which.

worauf', whereupon, upon which.

woraus', out of which.

worin', wherein, in which.

Wort, n., –es, pl. –e and "er, word.

worun'ter, among which.

wovon', of which.

Wunde, f., –n, wound.

Wunder, n., –s, —, wonder, miracle.

wunderbar, wonderful, strange.

Wunderblume, f., –n, fairy (magic) flower.

Wundergeschichte, f., –n, tale of wonder.

wunderlich, curious, rare, wonderful, strange.

wundern (sich), to be amazed.

wundersam, strange.

wunderschmerzlich, wondrous sad. [beauty.

wunderschön, of wondrous '

Wunsch, m., –es, "e, wish.

wünschen, to wish, desire.

Wurm, m., –es, "er, worm.

Wurst, f., "e, sausage.

Wurzel, f., –n, root.

wüst, desolate, dreary; mad.

3

z.B. = zum Beispiel, for example.

zagend, faint-hearted.

Zahl, f., –en, number, figure.

zählen, to count.

zahm, tame, cultivated.

zähmen, to tame, tone down.

Zahn, m., –es, "e, tooth.

zanken (sich), to quarrel.

zart, tender.

zärtlich, tender, affectionate.

Zärtlichkeit, f., –en, tenderness.

Zauber, m., –s, magic, charm, spell.

Zauberformel, *f.*, –n, magic
formula, charm.

Zaubergeschichte, *f.*, –n, tale of
magic.

Zauberin, *f.*, –nen, sorceress,
witch.

Zauberschlaf, *m.*, –es, magic
sleep.

Zauberschloß, *n.*, –es, "er, enchanted castle.

Zaun, *m.*, –es, "e, hedge.

zeichnen, to draw, outline, define,
jot down, sketch.

zeigen, to show; sich —, to appear.

Zeisig, *m.*, –s, –e, siskin.

Zeit, *f.*, –en, time.

Zeitalter, *n.*, –s, —, age.

zeitig, in time.

Zeitpunkt, *m.*, –s, –e, moment.

zerbrechen, *S.*, to break asunder.

zerfetzen, to tear.

zerfließen, *S.*, to melt, dissolve.

zerreißen, *S.*, to tear apart, part,
burst.

zerrinnen, a, o, to melt away, be
dissolved.

zerschmettern, to crush.

zerspringen, *S.*, to burst.

zerstören, to destroy.

zerstreuen, to scatter.

Zerstreuung, *f.*, –en, absent-
mindedness.

Zeug, *n.*, –s, –e, stuff, material.

Ziegelbach, *n.*, –es, "er, tile roof.

ziegelrot, brick-red.

Ziegenböckchen, *n.*, –s, —, he
goat, 'billy-goat.'

ziehen, zog, gezogen, to proceed,
pass, flit, come, enter; draw.

Ziel, *n.*, –es, –e, goal.

ziemlich, tolerably.

zierlich, neat, dainty.

Zimmer, *n.*, –s, —, room.

Zimmerchen, *n.*, –s, —, little
room.

Zimmergenosse, *m.*, –n, –n, room-
mate.

Zinne, *f.*, –n, battlement.

Zither, *f.*, –n, zither.

Zitherklang, *m.*, –es, "e, sound
of the zither.

zitro'nenreich, rich in lemons.

zittern, to tremble.

Zögling, *m.*, –s, –e, pupil, ward,
charge.

zornig, angry.

zu, at, to, for.

zu=bereiten, to prepare.

zu=bringen, *irreg.*, to spend.

zucken, to twitch, quiver; shrug.

zuerst', at first, first.

zufällig, accidental.

zu=flüstern, to whisper to.

Zug, *m.*, –es, "e, line, lineament,
feature, trait.

zugleich', at the same time.

zu=halten, *S.*, to shut, stop up.

zum = zu dem.

zumal', especially.

zu=nageln, to nail up, fence in.

Zunge, *f.*, –n, tongue.

zur = zu der.

zu=rauschen, to murmur towards,
rush to.

zürnend, angry.

zurück′, back.

zurück′=denken, S., to think back.

zurück′=erhalten, S., to receive in return.

zurück′=kehren, to return.

zurück′=kommen, S., to come back.

zurück′=lassen, S., to leave behind.

zurück′=legen, to traverse.

zurück′=sehnen (sich), to yearn.

zurück′=stürzen, to rush back.

zurück′=versetzen, to bring back.

zurück′=ziehen (sich), S., to withdraw, recede.

zusam′men, together.

Zusam′menhang, m., –es, relation, connection.

zusam′men=kneifen, S., to pinch, pucker (together).

zusam′men=kommen, S., to meet.

zusam′men=kräufeln, to curl together, shrivel up.

zusam′men=rinnen, a, o, to run together, blend.

zusam′men=schrumpfen, to shrink.

zusam′men=setzen, to mix, compose.

zusam′men=stellen, to group together.

zusam′men=treffen, S., to meet.

zusam′men=wachsen, S., to grow together (into one).

zu=schlagen, S., to strike at.

zu=schreiben, S., to attribute.

zu=sehen, S., to look on (at), witness.

zu=sprechen, S., to attack, partake of.

Zu′stimmung, f., –en, assent.

zu=tragen (sich), S., to happen.

zuwei′len, at times.

zu=werfen, S., to throw at.

zu=ziehen, S., to bring down upon.

zwanzig, twenty.

zwar, to be sure, in truth, indeed; und —, and that.

Zweck, m., –es, –e, purpose.

Zweckmäßigkeit, f., adaptation to an end.

zwei, two.

zweideutig, ambiguous, vague, dim.

Zweig, m., –es, –e, twig, branch.

Zwerg, m., –es, –e, dwarf.

Zwergenlied, n., –es, –er, dwarf's song.

zwerghaft, dwarf-like.

Zwerglein, n., –s, —, little dwarf.

Zwinger, m., –s, —, donjon, keep.

Zwingherrnburg, f., –en, tyrant's stronghold.

zwischen, between.

zwischendrein, in between.

zwitschern, to twitter.

zwölf, twelve.

zwölfte, der, the twelfth.

ADVERTISEMENTS

Heath's Modern Language Series.

GERMAN GRAMMARS AND READERS.

Nix's Erstes deutsches Schulbuch. For primary classes. Illus. 202 pp. 35 cts.

Joynes-Meissner German Grammar. Half leather. $1.15.

Joynes's Shorter German Grammar. Part I of the above. 80 cts.

Alternative Exercises. Two sets. Can be used, for the sake of change, instead of those in the *Joynes-Meissner* itself. 54 pages. 15 cts.

Joynes and Wesselhoeft's German Grammar. $1.15.

Fraser and Van der Smissen's German Grammar. $1.10.

Harris's German Lessons. Elementary Grammar and Exercises for a short course, or as introductory to advanced grammar. Cloth. 60 cts.

Sheldon's Short German Grammar. For those who want to begin reading as soon as possible, and have had training in some other languages. Cloth. 60c.

Ball's German Grammar. 90 cts.

Ball's German Drill Book. Companion to any grammar. 80 cts.

Spanhoofd's Lehrbuch der deutschen Sprache. Grammar, conversation, and exercises, with vocabularies. $1.00.

Foster's Geschichten und Märchen. For young children. 25 cts.

Guerber's Märchen und Erzählungen, I. With vocabulary and questions in German on the text. Cloth. 162 pages. 60 cts.

Guerber's Märchen und Erzählungen, II. With Vocabulary. Follows the above or serves as independent reader. Cloth. 202 pages. 65 cts.

Joynes's Shorter German Reader. 60 cts.

Deutsch's Colloquial German Reader. 90 cts.

Spanhoofd's Deutsches Lesebuch. 75 cts.

Boisen's German Prose Reader. 90 cts.

Huss's German Reader. 70 cts.

Gore's German Science Reader. 75 cts.

Harris's German Composition. 50 cts.

Wesselhoeft's Exercises. Conversation and composition. 50 cts.

Wesselhoeft's German Composition. 40 cts.

Hatfield's Materials for German Composition. Based on *Immensee* and on *Höher als die Kirche*. Paper. 33 pages. Each, 12 cts.

Horning's Materials for German Composition. Based on *Der Schwiegersohn*. 32 pages. 12 cts. Part II only. 16 pages. 5 cts.

Stüven's Praktische Anfangsgründe. Cloth. 203 pages. 70 cts.

Krüger and Smith's Conversation Book. 40 pages. 25 cts.

Meissner's German Conversation. 65 cts.

Deutsches Liederbuch. With music. 164 pages. 75 cts.

Heath's German Dictionary. Retail price, $1.50.

Heath's Modern Language Series.

ELEMENTARY GERMAN TEXTS.

Grimm's Märchen and Schiller's Der Taucher (van der Smissen). With vocabulary. *Märchen* in Roman Type. 45 cts.

Andersen's Märchen (Super). With vocabulary. 50 cts.

Andersen's Bilderbuch ohne Bilder (Bernhardt). Vocabulary. 30 cts.

Campe's Robinson der Jüngere (Ibershoff). Vocabulary. 40 cts.

Leander's Träumereien (van der Smissen). Vocabulary. 40 cts.

Volkmann's Kleine Geschichten (Bernhardt). Vocabulary. 30 cts.

Easy Selections for Sight Translation (Deering). 15 cts.

Storm's Geschichten aus der Tonne (Vogel). Vocabulary. 40 cts.

Storm's In St. Jürgen (Wright). Vocabulary. 30 cts.

Storm's Immensee (Bernhardt). Vocabulary. 30 cts.

Storm's Pole Poppenspäler (Bernhardt). Vocabulary. 40 cts.

Heyse's Niels mit der offenen Hand (Joynes). Vocab. and exercises. 30 cts.

Heyse's L'Arrabbiata (Bernhardt). With vocabulary. 25 cts.

Von Hillern's Höher als die Kirche (Clary). Vocab. and exercises. 30 cts.

Hauff's Der Zwerg Nase. No notes. 15 cts.

Hauff's Das kalte Herz (van der Smissen). Vocab. Roman type. 40 cts.

Ali Baba and the Forty Thieves. No notes. 20 cts.

Schiller's Der Taucher (van der Smissen). Vocabulary. 12 cts.

Schiller's Der Neffe als Onkel (Beresford-Webb). Notes and vocab. 30 cts.

Goethe's Das Märchen (Eggert). Vocabulary. 30 cts.

Baumbach's Waldnovellen (Bernhardt). Six stories. Vocabulary. 35 cts.

Spyri's Rosenresli (Boll). Vocabulary. 25 cts.

Spyri's Moni der Geissbub. With vocabulary by H. A. Guerber. 25 cts.

Zschokke's Der zerbrochene Krug (Joynes). Vocab. and exercises. 25 cts.

Baumbach's Nicotiana (Bernhardt). Vocabulary. 30 cts.

Elz's Er ist nicht eifersüchtig. With vocabulary by Prof. B. Wells. 20 cts.

Carmen Sylva's Aus meinem Königreich (Bernhardt). Vocabulary. 35 cts.

Gerstäcker's Germelshausen (Lewis). Notes and vocabulary. 30 cts.

Wichert's Als Verlobte empfehlen sich (Flom). Vocabulary. 25 cts.

Benedix's Nein (Spanhoofd). Vocabulary and exercises. 25 cts.

Benedix's Der Prozess (Wells). Vocabulary. 20 cts.

Lambert's Alltägliches. Vocabulary and exercises. 75 cts.

Der Weg zum Glück (Bernhardt). Vocabulary. 40 cts.

Mosher's Willkommen in Deutschland. Vocabulary and exercises. 75 cts.

Blüthgen's Das Peterle von Nürnberg (Bernhardt). Vocabulary. 35 cts.

Münchhausen: Reisen und Abenteuer (Schmidt). Vocabulary. 30 cts.

Heath's Modern Language Series.

INTERMEDIATE GERMAN TEXTS. (Partial List.)

Baumbach's Das Habichtsfräulein (Bernhardt). Vocabulary. 40 cts.

Heyse's Hochzeit auf Capri (Bernhardt). Vocabulary. 30 cts.

Hoffmann's Gymnasium zu Stolpenburg (Buehner). Vocabulary. 35 cts

Grillparzer's Der arme Spielmann (Howard). Vocabulary. 35 cts.

Seidel: Aus Goldenen Tagen (Bernhardt). Vocabulary. 35 cts.

Seidel's Leberecht Hühnchen (Spanhoofd). Vocabulary. 30 cts.

Auf der Sonnenseite (Bernhardt). Vocabulary. 35 cts.

Frommel's Mit Ränzel und Wanderstab (Bernhardt). Vocabulary. 35 cts.

Frommel's Eingeschneit (Bernhardt). Vocabulary. 30 cts.

Keller's Kleider machen Leute (Lambert). Vocabulary. 35 cts.

Liliencron's Anno 1870 (Bernhardt). Vocabulary. 40 cts.

Baumbach's Die Nonna (Bernhardt). Vocabulary. 30 cts.

Riehl's Der Fluch der Schönheit (Thomas). Vocabulary. 30 cts.

Riehl's Das Spielmannskind; Der stumme Ratsherr (Eaton). Vocabulary and exercises. 35 cts.

Ebner-Eschenbach's Die Freiherren von Gemperlein (Hohlfeld). 30 cts.

Freytag's Die Journalisten (Toy). 30 cts. With vocabulary. 40 cts.

Wilbrandt's Das Urteil des Paris (Wirt). 30 cts.

Schiller's Das Lied von der Glocke (Chamberlin). Vocabulary. 20 cts.

Schiller's Jungfrau von Orleans (Wells). Illus. 60 cts. Vocab., 70 cts.

Schiller's Maria Stuart (Rhoades). Illustrated. 60 cts. Vocab., 70 cts.

Schiller's Wilhelm Tell (Deering). Illustrated. 50 cts. Vocab., 70 cts.

Schiller's Ballads (Johnson). 60 cts.

Baumbach's Der Schwiegersohn (Bernhardt). 30 cts. Vocabulary, 40 cts.

Arnold's Fritz auf Ferien (Spanhoofd). Vocabulary. 25 cts.

Heyse's Das Mädchen von Treppi (Joynes). Vocab. and exercises. 30 cts.

Stille Wasser (Bernhardt). Three tales. Vocabulary. 35 cts.

Sudermann's Teja (Ford). Vocabulary. 25 cts.

Arnold's Aprilwetter (Fossler). Vocabulary. 35 cts.

Gerstäcker's Irrfahrten (Sturm). Vocabulary. 45 cts.

Benedix's Plautus und Terenz; Der Sonntagsjäger (Wells). 25 cts.

Moser's Köpnickerstrasse 120 (Wells). 30 cts.

Moser's Der Bibliothekar (Wells). Vocabulary. 40 cts.

Drei kleine Lustspiele. *Günstige Vorzeichen, Der Prozess, Einer muss heiraten.* Edited with notes by Prof. B. W. Wells. 30 cts.

Helbig's Komödie auf der Hochschule (Wells). 30 cts.

Stern's Die Wiedertäufer (Sturm). Vocabulary. 30 cts.

Heath's Modern Language Series.

INTERMEDIATE GERMAN TEXTS. (Partial List.)

Schiller's Geschichte des dreissigjährigen Krieges. Book III. With notes by Professor C. W. Prettyman, Dickinson College. 35 cts.

Schiller's Der Geisterseher (Joynes). Vocabulary. 30 cts.

Arndt, Deutsche Patrioten (Colwell). Vocabulary. 30 cts.

Selections for Sight Translation (Mondan). 15 cts.

Selections for Advanced Sight Translation (Chamberlin). 15 cts.

Aus Herz und Welt. Two stories, with notes by Dr. Wm. Bernhardt. 25 cts.

Novelletten-Bibliothek. Vol. I, five stories. Vol. II, six stories. Selected and edited with notes by Dr. Wilhelm Bernhardt. Each, 35 cts.

Unter dem Christbaum (Bernhardt). Notes. 35 cts.

Hoffmann's Historische Erzählungen (Beresford-Webb). Notes. 25 cts.

Benedix's Die Hochzeitsreise (Schiefferdecker). 25 cts.

Stökl's Alle Fünf (Bernhardt). Vocabulary. 30 cts.

Till Eulenspiegel (Betz). Vocabulary. 30 cts.

Wildenbruch's Neid (Prettyman). Vocabulary. 35 cts.

Wildenbruch's Das Edle Blut (Schmidt). Vocabulary. 25 cts.

Wildenbruch's Der Letzte (Schmidt). Vocabulary. 30 cts.

Wildenbruch's Harold (Eggert). 35 cts.

Stifter's Das Haidedorf (Heller). 20 cts.

Chamisso's Peter Schlemihl (Primer). 25 cts.

Eichendorff's Aus dem Leben eines Taugenichts (Osthaus). Vocab. 45 cts.

Heine's Die Harzreise (Vos). Vocabulary. 45 cts.

Jensen's Die braune Erica (Joynes). Vocabulary. 35 cts.

Lyrics and Ballads (Hatfield). 75 cts.

Meyer's Gustav Adolfs Page (Heller). 25 cts.

Sudermann's Johannes (Schmidt). 35 cts.

Sudermann's Heimat (Schmidt). 35 cts.

Sudermann's Der Katzensteg (Wells). Abridged. 40 cts.

Dahn's Sigwalt und Sigridh (Schmidt). 25 cts.

Keller's Romeo und Julia auf dem Dorfe (Adams). 30 cts.

Hauff's Lichtenstein (Vogel). Abridged. 75 cts.

Böhlau Ratsmädelgeschichten (Haevernick). Vocabulary. 40 cts.

Keller's Fähnlein der sieben Aufrechten (Howard). Vocabulary. 40 cts.

Riehl's Burg Neideck (Jonas). Vocabulary and exercises. 35 cts.

Lohmeyer's Geissbub von Engelberg (Bernhardt). Vocabulary. 40 cts.

Zschokke's Das Abenteuer der Neujahrsnacht (Handschin). Vocab. 35 cts.

Zschokke's Das Wirtshaus zu Cransac (Joynes). Vocabulary. 30 cts.

Heath's Modern Language Series.

ADVANCED GERMAN TEXTS.

Scheffel's Trompeter von Säkkingen (Wenckebach). Abridged. 50 cts.

Scheffel's Ekkehard (Wenckebach). Abridged. 55 cts.

Mörike's Mozart auf der Reise nach Prag (Howard). 35 cts.

Freytag's Soll und Haben (Files). Abridged. 55 cts.

Freytag's Aus dem Staat Friedrichs des Grossen (Hagar). 25 cts.

Freytag's Aus dem Jahrhundert des grossen Krieges (Rhoades). 35 cts.

Freytag's Rittmeister von Alt-Rosen (Hatfield). 50 cts.

Fulda's Der Talisman (Prettyman). 35 cts.

Körner's Zriny (Holzwarth). 35 cts.

Lessing's Minna von Barnhelm (Primer). 60 cts. With vocabulary, 65 cts.

Lessing's Nathan der Weise (Primer). 80 cts.

Lessing's Emilia Galotti (Winkler). 60 cts.

Schiller's Wallenstein's Tod (Eggert). 60 cts.

Goethe's Sesenheim (Huss). From *Dichtung und Wahrheit*. 30 cts.

Goethe's Meisterwerke (Bernhardt). $1.25.

Goethe's Dichtung und Wahrheit. (I-IV). Buchheim. 90 cts.

Goethe's Hermann und Dorothea (Hewett). 75 cts.

Goethe's Hermann und Dorothea (Adams). Vocabulary. 65 cts.

Goethe's Iphigenie (Rhoades). 60 cts.

Goethe's Egmont (Hatfield). 60 cts.

Goethe's Torquato Tasso (Thomas). 75 cts.

Goethe's Faust (Thomas). Part I, $1.15   Part II, $1.50.

Goethe's Poems. Selected and edited by Prof. Harris, Adelbert College. 90 cts.

Grillparzer's Der Traum, ein Leben (Meyer). 40 cts.

Ludwig's Zwischen Himmel und Erde (Meyer). 55 cts.

Heine's Poems. Selected and edited by Prof. White. 75 cts.

Tombo's Deutsche Reden. 90 cts.

Walther's Meereskunde. (Scientific German). 55 cts.

Thomas's German Anthology. $2.25.

Hodges' Scientific German. 75 cts.

Kayser's Die Elektronentheorie (Wright). 20 cts.

Lassar-Cohn's Die Chemie im täglichen Leben (Brooks). 45 cts.

Wagner's Entwicklungslehre (Wright). 30 cts.

Helmholtz's Populäre Vorträge (Shumway). 55 cts.

Wenckebach's Deutsche Literaturgeschichte. Vol. I (to 1100 A.D.) 50 cts.

Wenckebach's Meisterwerke des Mittelalters. $1.26.

Dahn's Ein Kampf um Rom (Wenckebach). Abridged. 55 cts.

Heath's Modern Language Series.

FRENCH GRAMMARS AND READERS.

Bruce's Grammaire Française. $1.15.

Clarke's Subjunctive Mood. An inductive treatise, with exercises. 50 cts.

Edgren's Compendious French Grammar. $1.15. Part I. 35 cts.

Fontaine's Livre de Lecture et de Conversation. 90 cts.

Fraser and Squair's French Grammar. $1.15.

Fraser and Squair's Abridged French Grammar. $1.10.

Fraser and Squair's Elementary French Grammar. 90 cts.

Grandgent's Essentials of French Grammar. $1.00.

Grandgent's Short French Grammar. 75 cts.

Roux's Lessons in Grammar and Composition, based on *Colomba*. 18 cts.

Hennequin's French Modal Auxiliaries. With exercises. 50 cts.

Houghton's French by Reading. $1.15.

Mansion's First Year French. For young beginners. 50 cts.

Méthode Hénin. 50 cts.

Bruce's Lectures Faciles. 60 cts.

Bruce's Dicteés Françaises. 30 cts.

Fontaine's Lectures Courantes. $1.00.

Giese's French Anecdotes. oo cts.

Hotchkiss' Le Primer Livre de Français. Boards. 35 cts.

Bowen's First Scientific Reader. 90 cts.

Davies' Elementary Scientific French Reader. 40 cts.

Lyon and Larpent's Primary French Translation Book. 60 cts.

Snow and Lebon's Easy French. 60 cts.

Super's Preparatory French Reader. 70 cts.

Bouvet's Exercises in Syntax and Composition. 75 cts.

Storr's Hints on French Syntax. With exercises. 30 cts.

Brigham's French Composition. 12 cts.

Comfort's Exercises in French Prose Composition. 30 cts.

Grandgent's French Composition. 50 cts.

Grandgent's Materials for French Composition. Each, 12 cts.

Kimball's Materials for French Composition. Each, 12 cts.

Mansion's Exercises in Composition. 160 pages. 60 cts.

Marcou's French Review Exercises. 25 cts.

Prisoners of the Temple (Guerber). For French Composition. 25 cts.

Story of Cupid and Psyche (Guerber). For French Composition. 18 cts.

Heath's French Dictionary. Retail price, $1.50.